Brighton

WHAT'S NEW | WHAT'S ON | WHAT'S BEST

www.timeout.com/brighton

Contents

Brighton by Area

Essentials

Time Out Digital Ltd
4th Floor
125 Shaftesbury Avenue
London WC2H 8AD
Tel: + 44 (0)20 7813 3000
Email: guides@timeout.com
www.timeout.com

Published by Time Out Digital Ltd, a wholly owned subsidiary of Time Out Group Ltd.
Time Out and the Time Out logo are trademarks of Time Out Group Ltd.

© **Time Out Group Ltd 2015**
Previous edition 2011

Editorial Director Sarah Guy
Group Finance Controller Margaret Wright

© **Time Out Group Ltd**
Founder Tony Elliott
Chief Executive Officer Tim Arthur
Managing Director Europe Noel Penzer
Publisher Alex Batho

10 9 8 7 6 5 4 3 2 1

This edition first published in Great Britain in 2015 by Ebury Publishing
20 Vauxhall Bridge Road, London SW1V 2SA

Ebury Publishing is part of the Penguin Random House group of companies whose addresses
can be found at global.penguinrandomhouse.com

Distributed in the US and Latin America by Publishers Group West (1-510-809-3700)

For further distribution details, see www.timeout.com

ISBN: 978-1-90504-296-8

A CIP catalogue record for this book is available from the British Library.

Printed and bound in China by Leo Paper Products Ltd.

Brighton Shortlist

The **Time Out Brighton Shortlist** is one of a series of annual guides that draws on Time Out's background as a magazine publisher to keep you current with everything that's going on in town. As well as Brighton's key sights and the best of its eating, drinking and leisure options, it picks out the most exciting venues to have opened in the last year and gives a full calendar of annual events. It also includes features on the important news, trends and openings, all compiled by locally based editors and writers. Whether you're visiting for the first time in your life or the first time this year, you'll find the *Time Out Brighton Shortlist* contains all you need to know, in a portable and easy-to-use format.

The guide divides Brighton & Hove into seven areas, each containing listings for Sights & Museums, Eating & Drinking, Shopping, Nightlife and Arts & Leisure, and maps pinpointing their locations. At the front of the book are chapters rounding up these scenes city-wide, and giving a shortlist of our overall picks. We also include itineraries for days out, plus essentials such as transport information and hotels.

Our listings give phone numbers as dialled both from Brighton and elsewhere in the UK. From abroad, use your country's exit code followed by 44 (the country code for the UK), 1273 for Brighton and the number given.

We have noted price categories by using one to four pound signs (**£-££££**), representing budget, moderate, expensive and luxury. As a rough guide for restaurants,

£ represents meals under £10 a head, ££ meals under £30, £££ meals under £50 and ££££ meals over £50. Guidelines for hotels are given in the chapter.

Major credit cards are accepted unless otherwise stated. All our listings are double-checked, but places do sometimes close or change their hours or prices, so it's a good idea to call a venue before visiting. While every effort has been made to ensure accuracy, the publishers cannot accept responsibility for any errors that this guide may contain.

Venues are marked on the maps using symbols numbered according to their order within the chapter and colour-coded as follows:

❶ Sights & Museums
❶ Eating & Drinking
❶ Shopping
❶ Nightlife
❶ Arts & Leisure

EDITORIAL
Editor Bella Todd
Copy Editor Ros Sales
Proofreader John Shandy Watson

DESIGN & PICTURE DESK
Senior Designer Kei Ishimaru
Designer Darryl Bell
Group Commercial Senior Designer
Jason Tansley
Picture Editor Jael Marschner
Deputy Picture Editor Ben Rowe
Picture Researcher Lizzy Owen

ADVERTISING
Account Managers Deborah Maclaren,
Helen Debenham at the Media Sales
House

MARKETING
Senior Publishing Brand Manager
Luthfa Begum
Head of Circulation Dan Collins

PRODUCTION
Production Controller
Katie Mulhern-Bhudia

About **Time Out**

Founded in 1968 by Tony Elliott, Time Out has expanded from humble London
beginnings (the original London Time Out magazine was a single fold-out sheet of
A5 paper) into the leading resource for those wanting to know what's happening in
the world's greatest cities. As well as our influential listings weeklies in London
and New York, we publish nearly 30 other listings magazines in cities as varied as
Beijing and Tel Aviv. The magazines established Time Out's trademark style: sharp
writing, informed reviewing and bang up-to-date inside knowledge of every scene.

Time Out made the natural leap into travel guides in the 1980s with the City Guide
series, which now extends to over 50 destinations around the world. Written and
researched by expert local writers and generously illustrated with original photography,
the full-size guides cover a larger area than our Shortlist guides (which are aimed at
the short-break travel market). Many of these cities, and others, are now also covered
on our website, www.timeout.com.

Throughout this rapid growth, the company has remained proudly independent.
This independence extends to the editorial content of all our publications. No
establishment has been featured because it has advertised, and no payment
has influenced any of our reviews.

Don't Miss

Brighton Pier

Sights & Museums

The city of Brighton & Hove exists for one reason alone: the sea. From 16th-century fishing village to 18th-century sea-bathing resort to modern micro-metropolis, Brighton has always been shaped by the sea. Just witness the way it draws day-trippers straight down Queens Road and West Street from the station to the beach – where the gaudy, candy floss-scented Brighton Pier (p90) and starling-haunted skeleton of the West Pier (p58) crouch on the city's shoulders, fighting over its soul. In summer 2015, this quintessential Brighton view will be altered forever with the erection of the 530-foot observation tower, the i360 (p55), in front of the West Pier.

The seafront stretches four miles from Brighton Marina to Hove Lagoon, with distinctive pockets that may be ghostly or gaudy, quaint or clubby. And beyond the city, the Undercliff Pass (p165) from Brighton Marina to Rottingdean allows you to experience more of the coastline up close.

A changing city

When the Prince of Wales (the future King George IV) came down for his first 'season' in 1783, Brighton's destiny as a tourist destination was sealed. Satirical novelist William Thackeray once wrote: 'It is the fashion to run down George IV, but what myriads of Londoners ought to thank him for inventing Brighton!' Before the arrival of the Prince and his entourage, there was little here of note.

A cursory wander through the city doesn't unearth much architecture dating from prior to the 1600s – though parts of St Nicholas Church (p102) date back to Norman times.

St Bartholomew's Church

SHORTLIST

Striking buildings
- Engineerium (p149)
- Royal Pavilion (p73)
- St Bartholomew's Church (p135)

Best parks
- The Level (p132)
- Preston Park (p135)
- St Ann's Well Gardens (p149)

For local history
- Brighton Fishing Museum (p90)
- Hove Museum (p149)
- Old Police Cells Museum (p90)

For nostalgic fun
- Mechanical Memories Museum (p90)
- Volk's Electric Railway (p112)

Picnic places
- Hove Lawns (p148)
- Royal Pavilion Gardens (p73)
- Wildflower Meadow at Preston Park (p135)

Overlooked attractions
- Hove Park Miniature Railway (p149)
- Kensington Street graffiti (p11)
- Madeira Drive lift (p10)

Best for families
- Booth Museum (p102)
- Brighton Museum (p73)
- Brighton Pier (p90)
- Sea Life Centre (p111)

Secret gardens
- Preston Manor walled garden (p132)
- Rookery Rock Garden (p135)
- Sunken garden, Kemp Town (p10)

Best views
- Dyke Road Park (p102)
- West Pier at sunset (p58)
- Devil's Dyke (p170)

That's mainly because, unlike Chichester or Lewes, Brighton was never a county seat or strategically important base. Yet the upper-class fashion for visiting Brighton from the mid-18th century onwards led to a grandiose building spree that defines Brighton's character today: Georgian buildings mix with whitewashed Regency and early Victorian townhouses – many in the largely residential areas of Seven Dials, Montpelier and Clifton Hill. Also distinctive are the yellow Regency buildings of Brunswick in Hove. Hove developed at the same time as Brighton, and the two (controversially) merged in 1997.

The maze of 16th century twittens known as the Lanes is the heart of historic Brighton, dating back to its days as a fishing village. The North Laine, directly below the train station, is now famous for its alternative shops, but was once the city's slum. The enormous St Bartholomew's Church (p135), its proportions fabled to match those of Noah's Ark, arrived in 1874 – and provides a historic anchor for the city's youngest district, the New England Quarter. This lies to the south of the Preston area, and includes London Road – a key retail destination in the 1930s, and the focus of exciting recent regeneration.

The latest development project, due to start in September 2015, centres on Circus Street at the foot of Kemp Town. This district, to the east of central Brighton, emerged in the early 19th century, and began to develop as a hub for the town's growing gay community from the 1920s onwards. It flanks Brighton Marina (p163), the largest marina in Europe.

Architectural quirks

The Victorians also built the Kings Road Arches (p55), once used by fishermen to store their boats, and including the newly renovated stretch know as the West Pier Arches, and the grand, iron-wrought Madeira Arches. Now home to galleries, clubs and cafés, these sets of arches beneath the promenades provide an atmospheric confluence of old and new. Music venue and nightclub Concorde 2 operates the Madeira Drive lift, an ornate, Grade II-listed lift linking Marine Parade with Madeira Drive.

The lift is something of an open secret, like the Sunken Garden at the corner of Bristol Gardens and Bristol Place in Kemp Town. Further from the public eye, but no less alluring, are several secret tunnels running to the sea. The ivy-lined brick passageway from the private garden in Sussex Square is said to have been the inspiration for the rabbit hole in *Alice In Wonderland* (Lewis Carroll was a regular visitor). More recently, it featured in *20,000 Days on Earth*, a docu-drama about rock musician Nick Cave, now resident in Sussex Square.

Museums & attractions

Brighton's historical, architectural and cultural centrepiece is, of course, the Royal Pavilion (p73). The Prince Regent's party palace was built in three stages between 1787 and 1822, and repeatedly polls as the city's top attraction. The Royal Pavilion Estate also encompasses Brighton Museum & Art Gallery (p73) and the Brighton Dome complex (p86), including the Concert Hall, Corn Exchange and Studio Theatre. The buildings share architectural features and connecting

West Pier Arches

DON'T MISS

Brighton Museum & Art Gallery

passageways, and together form the city's official Cultural Quarter. Funding has recently been secured to reconnect these historic buildings, with work due to start in 2016.

Across town, the gloomy Edwardian rooms of Preston Manor (p132) are a favourite with paranormal investigators. Other museums in the city are dedicated to natural history (the Booth Museum; p102), crime (the Old Police Cells Museum; p90), games (the Museum of Mechanical Memories, p90, and Brighton Toy Museum; p72) and the history of the seafront (Brighton Fishing Museum; p90).

You can also visit the world's oldest operating aquarium, the Victorian-pillared Sealife Centre (p111), and the charming Volks Electric Railway (p112). Hove has its own museum (p149), in addition to the West Blatchington Windmill (p149; it pops up in a watercolour by Constable) and the Engineerium (p149). The latter is housed in a Victorian-Gothic pumping station, and set to reopen in 2016 as the World of Engineering. Part museum of mechanical antiquities, part family theme park, it should

prove a big draw for both toddlers and steampunk fans.

Graffiti & outdoor art

From breathtaking graffiti murals to council-commissioned sculptures, the streets of Brighton are like one big, free gallery. The most famous street artist to use the city as a canvas is Banksy, and tourist trails often start at his *Kissing Coppers*, on the wall of the Prince Albert (p86). The original was actually sold (after being transferred on to canvas using specialist chemicals) in 2008. The pashing policemen you see today, encased in protective Perspex, are a fascimile. They're now surrounded by a huge mural by Sinna One and Req, featuring portraits of 25 dead musical icons.

Other street-art hotspots include Kensington Street (which has hosted portraits of Run DMC, Aung San Suu Kyi, and the Smurfs), the New England Quarter, and the area of Black Rock, near the Marina. Look out for telephone junction boxes sprayed to resemble retro music tapes by Cassette Lord.

Sculptures form a more permanent part of the Brighton landscape, often

CHURCHILL SQUARE
BRIGHTON'S SHOPPING CENTRE

BECAUSE YOU LOVE SHOPPING

Churchill Square Shopping Centre is Brighton's premier shopping destination. Situated in the heart of Brighton, it has over 85 leading high street stores all under one roof. Spoilt for choice, you will find all of the latest fashion offers with stores such as **Hollister**, **Urban Outfitters** and **Zara**. Alternatively, if you are looking for something for the home, then you will find inspiration in **Debenhams**, **Habitat** and **BHS**. Other big names include **Apple**, **H&M**, **Miss Selfridge** and **River Island** and much much more. The spacious, innovative design of the centre makes it a perfect destination for a day out, whether shopping, browsing or meeting friends. With regular events and promotions, you will always find a reason to visit Churchill Square.

Open 7 days a week with Late Night Shopping til 8pm on Thursdays. The Car Park is open 24 hours with over 1600 parking spaces available.

SEE WHAT'S GOING ON AT THE CENTRE churchillsquare.com

BRIGHTON'S PREMIER SHOPPING CENTRE

FOLLOW US ON FACEBOOK AND TWITTER: twitter.com/churchillsquare

CHURCHILLSQUARE.COM

sunglass hut · USC · Foot Locker · Levi's · jane norman

habitat® · hmv · RIVER ISLAND · ZARA · DEBENHAMS · next

nonchalantly incorporated into the life of the city. Hamish Black's *Afloat*, a bronze doughnut on the groyne next to Brighton Pier, is a popular meeting point. Charlie Hooker's *Twins*, outside Churchill Square, provides a handy ledge for tired shoppers. (To the latters' surprise, the work includes sensors that trigger sound in synch with the rising and falling sun). Charles Hadcock's *Passacaglia*, on the beach opposite Middle Street, is a curved cast-iron abstract work, and often mistaken for the rusting remains of a shipwreck. Most famous is Romany Mark Bruce's *AIDS Memorial Sculpture* (p109), in Kemp Town. The two intertwined figures form a shadow in the shape of the red HIV/AIDS ribbon. But Brighton's most enigmatic artwork is both sculpture and street art: the words 'I HAVE GREAT DESIRE MY DESIRE IS GREAT' have been anonymously etched into the wall of Madeira Drive Promenade in slowly rusting steel.

Park life

Brighton beach holds such sway in the popular imagination that the city's excellent parks often go overlooked. The largest is Preston Park (p135), home to Preston Manor, the velodrome, a large rose garden and (just across the road) the Rookery Rock Garden – Britain's largest public rock garden. The peaceful vibe changes dramatically every August when Preston Park hosts Brighton Pride.

Reopened in 2013, the Level (p132) near London Road now features a state-of-the-art playpark and skate park, interactive water fountains and a petanque area. Hidden away in the back streets between Hanover and Kemp Town, Queen's Park is a hilly, landscaped park, with a large playground, wildlife garden and duckpond.

In Hove, Hove Park is home to a miniature train (p149). The leafy and shady St Ann's Well Gardens (p149), whose spring (now a trickle) was once the centrepiece of an 18th-century health spa, is perhaps the city's most beautiful park. Within striking distance of the beach, Hove Lawns is an expanse of grass that runs parallel to Hove's elegant esplanade and pastel beach huts.

Rookery Rock Garden

Silo

Eating & Drinking

Brighton, traditionally, doesn't do buzz restaurants. Though home to more than 500 restaurants and cafés, it's always had a laid-back culinary scene where the ones shouting loudest about their dining experiences were the seagulls stealing your chips. But recently the pace has changed, the quality has sharpened, and national critics are starting to take note. The Brighton and Hove Food and Drink Festival (www.brightonfoodfestival.com), which showcases local produce, cooking and hospitality, is now an international success and a year-round presence. You'll now hear the mantra of 'local, seasonal, ethical' everywhere from chip shops to neighbourhood pubs.

Brighton is finally being taken seriously as a dining destination. It is stealing London's top chefs (at Sam's of Brighton; p119) and exporting its successes (64 Degrees; p93). It is also attracting groundbreaking ventures such as the UK's first no-waste restaurant, Silo (p79). As a consequence, last-minute table grabs are rarely an option these days at Brighton's best restaurants, and waiting lists for some hot new venues run to several months.

All this fresh activity is causing old favourites to pull their socks up. The original Gingerman (p62) in Norfolk Square, which opened in 2000 and spawned three other 'Ginger' offerings in and around the city, has just had its first refurb. Meanwhile, two of the Ginger group's former head chefs have united at the helm of a bold new dining concept – with three creative set menus, running side by side and evolving every week – at the Set (p67).

DON'T MISS

Seaside specials

Of course, sometimes all you want from the seaside is ice-cream and fish and chips. On this level, Brighton disappoints unless you turn, counterintuitively, away from the seafront. Bankers (p58) on Western Road is under five minutes' walk from the beach. Bardsley's (p135) is further, but great for a family meal. New on the scene is Wolfies of Hove (p158), which, uniquely in the city, has a dedicated gluten-free fryer. For memorable cones, Scoop & Crumb (p97) and Boho Gelato (p93) are a short walk from Brighton Pier. And large new parlour JoJo's Gelato (p63) is a brightly coloured children's fantasy.

Coffee culture

Brighton's coffee-house culture is also booming – to the point where we wouldn't be surprised to turn over a pebble on the beach and find another small independent roastery setting up its grinding equipment and sackcloth

Craft Beer Company

seats beneath. The expansion of Small Batch (see box p155) to six cafés (and one 'training lab') across the city only seems to have increased thirst for the bean. Horsham Coffee Roaster has just opened its first café here, Bond St Coffee (p74). The Marwood Café (p96), a coffee-house with an almost cultish reputation, now has a sibling in Presuming Ed (p141), housed in a former bank complete with many original fittings on London Road. It's not all about coffee, though. Check out Talk of Tea (p67) and Bluebird Tea (p80) to discover why tea leaves may be the new coffee beans in Brighton.

Home brews

The rise of the coffeehouse hasn't dented Brighton's pub and bar culture. There is a solid boozer on most backstreets in Brighton, while new arrivals such as the Joker (p138) and the Tempest Inn (p97) are offering something more distinctive (in the latter case, a man-made cave system replete with flickering lanterns and prehistoric-style animal drawings). Other drinking dens are specialising: in rum, whisky, tequila and, increasingly, craft beer. The North Laine Brewery (p79), Craft Beer Company (p105) and the most recent addition, the Brighton Beer Dispensary (p59) all serve local craft brews. The city now has its first gin distillery too. Outlets selling Brighton Gin, made with fresh orange and milk thistle, include Basketmakers (p74), Black Dove (p112) and ethical supermarket Hisbe (p145).

Vegetable patch

As befits a city in which an entire neighbourhood (Hanover) is nicknamed Muesli Mountain, Brighton is veggie heaven. Worthy enterprises such as the Brighton & Hove Food Partnership (www.bhfood.org.uk) and Infinity Foods (p83) enjoy real success. Indeed, a couple of the city's most acclaimed restaurants – Food for Friends (p94) and Terre à Terre (p97) – are vegetarian. Vegetarians are also well catered for by the fast, fresh, rotating menus at casual canteen-cafés Iydea (p63) and Foodilic (p96).

Vegans now have a more soulful alternative to Heather Mills' VBites (p89) in the form of the Italian-run Almond Tree Café (p102) in Seven

Dials. The owner of former veggie and gluten-free favourite the Jolly Green Café is now serving his very tasty 'friendly folk food' at the very tiny Helm Ston Café (p137), just outside North Laine.

Burger mania

In the early noughties, David Van Day, of Dollar and Bucks Fizz pop fame, ran a burger van in Brighton. Perhaps he was on to something. As if in rebellion from its reputation as a veggie and vegan paradise, the city has recently embarked on a full-blown love affair with the burger. The coolest kids in Brighton aren't forming bands – they're opening burger kitchens. There, they construct carefully sourced, wildly themed burgers with a basic disregard for the average human jaw-span. The trailblazer was the Troll's Pantry, now based at the Hobgoblin (p137). Burger Kult is building a similar, slightly saucier, reputation at the Mash Tun (p78), and Brighton Burger (p93) has just

taken over the kitchen at Hanover pub the Islington.

There are now several dedicated burger restaurants too, including the hip and edgy Meatliquor (p140) and upmarket Coggings & Co (p105). And long-established North Laine diner Rock Ola (p79) now runs 'burger bar' evenings. Going for a burger need no longer be something you do after doing something else: it's often the main event. But the trend may be coming full circle. The most effortlessly cool new offering is tiny takeaway Burger Brothers (p74). The duo who run it manage to combine gourmet quality with the original burger appeal: eating something charred and juicy on the go.

David Van Day's role, by the way, hasn't been entirely forgotten. Seafront burger bar Lucky Beach (p96) has dedicated a cheesy little number to him.

Seafood & eat it

Brighton's lack of truly great seafood restaurants has often surprised visitors. For years, the Regency (p66)

Burger Brothers

was the standard recommendation. But there are now several hot tickets on the seafood front, including flagship restaurants in the two biggest seafront hotels: the Salt Room (p67) at Hilton Brighton Metropole, and GB1 (62) at the Grand.

Meanwhile, champagne and oyster bar Riddle & Finns has opened a second premises (p66), on the site of the former Due South on the seafront. It offers a more formal and private setting to the original in the Lanes, as well as informal beach tables. Word is finally spreading about the Little Fish Market (p156), a 20-seat restaurant just off Western Road. The fresh, unfussy cooking here brings diners a real taste of the sea. And Brighton now has a neighbourhood pub dedicated to shellfish: the Urchin (p158) in Hove serves sharing dishes in beautiful copper pans, with side orders of craft beer.

Secret suppers

Some of the most exciting cooking in Brighton right now is taking place outside the restrictive boundaries of the traditional restaurant. Pop-up

kitchens and supper clubs are all the rage, offering one-off dining experiences in unexpected locations where you might not necessarily know your tablemates, or what's about to turn up on your plate.

Previously, this has been a hard scene for visitors to tap in to: you need to have your ear to the ground. But a new website now does that for you. Launched in 2014, Tabl.com hooks up inquisitive foodies with professional chefs who want to play, experiment and test new ventures. Through this free service, you might find Ethiopian and Eritrean street food pros Abycina road-testing a restaurant format, or the sous chef from the Coal Shed (p94) running a pop-up, or Michelin bib-winning chef Ed Heller (formerly of the Brunswick) developing his Duck Soup Project, an Asian grazing menu with 'no menu and no rules'. Silo (p79), 64 Degrees (p93) and Ollie Couillaud, now of Sam's of Brighton (p119), have all run events through Tabl.com. The website is Brighton born and bred, but you'll soon be hearing about it elsewhere, too – it has now launched in London.

GB1

Open Market

Shopping

B road generalisations about Brighton's shopping districts run something like this. North Laine: retro clothing, vintage oddities, hippy paraphernalia, records. The Lanes: jewellery, upmarket boutiques, tiny commercial galleries. Hove: mature fashion, bespoke furniture, really expensive cheese. Kemp Town: antiques, dog accessories, sex toys. Western Road: all the other stuff needed, by normal people, for normal life. For a wood-burning stove, you might also pop to Seven Dials. For a pound-shop card, you might brave London Road.

Not only are these generalisations outdated, but they discourage the one thing that characterises all great shopping sessions in Brighton: exploration. London Road is now an up-and-coming centre for alternative shopping. In its environs you'll find the Open Market, browser's haven South Coast Costumes (p145) and the home of 'roadkill couture', EatonNott (p144). Western Road is dotted with surprising new businesses, such as design-your-own perfume shop Eden (p70) and independent design studio and gift shop Dowse (p159). Hove continues to subdivide into distinct little shopping villages.

North Laine's Bond Street, Gardner Street and Trafalgar Street are increasingly home to the sort of smart and stylish women's boutiques more usually associated with the Lanes, to the south. Visitors tend to confuse these two laidback but fiercely independent shopping areas.

Entirely new retail areas are also emerging. The renovated West Pier Arches (p55), around the i360, now house a cluster of arty shops including top design store the

Snooper's Paradise

Lollipop Shoppe (p70). There is a strip of surprising independent shops along Upper North Street, parallel to Western Road. The Circus Street development, starting in September 2015, will create a new shopping zone at the foot of Kemp Town.

Successful local Etsy and Ebay traders are establishing bricks-and-mortar bases wherever they can get cheap rent – look for retro fashion label Dig For Victory (p122), Mrs Canticacq's Emporium (p161) and new knitting shop and craft hub YAK (p85). Following the successful iGigi (p159) model, many shops are now doubling as cafés. The new Compass Point Eatery (p114) in Kemp Town, Salvage Café (p157) in Hove, and Vine Street Vintage Brighton Market (p85) in North Laine all combine food with vintage finds.

An entrenched hippy spirit means you'll often find shops squatting inside other shops, rewarding the inquisitive with random surprises. Twenty local designers sell clothing and accessories at Snoopers Attic, above Snooper's Paradise (p85).

Taking this collaborative attitude to space a stage further is new North Laine addition It Is What It Is (102 Gloucester Road, www.popup brighton.com). At this permanent pop-up gallery and retail space, the seller changes every week and pays no rent. The intention is to help young entrepreneurs trying to kickstart a daring new venture.

Unusual businesses, after all, are what Brighton does best. Irregular Choice (p83), a quirky shoe company founded in Brighton in 1999, now has stores in Paris, London and Hong Kong, and pop-star fans including Nicki Minaj and Taylor Swift. And where else could you buy a cast of your own body part? Jamie McCartney's Brighton Body Casting (p162) now has a showroom in Hove, close to the relocated studio. The most common requests? 'Boobs, bums and baby bumps.'

Chain talk

Upmarket chains are finding a natural home on East Street, a semi-pedestrianised road that narrows towards the seafront, and accommodates a large taxi rank and square of restaurants at the North Street end. Here you'll find the likes of Hobbs, French Connection, Reiss, All Saints and a new Hugo Boss, as well as L'Occitane and Molton Brown.

The mainstream high-street shops are ranged along North Street and Western Road, which meet at Churchill Square Shopping Centre (Russell Place, BN1 2TD, www.churchillsquare.com). Despite the seagulls and emos engaged in a turf war on its forecourt, this three-storey mall has something for most shoppers. A large Topshop recently joined more than 80 retailers, including two big department stores (BHS and Debenhams), a large Zara and Urban Outfitters, and Apple and Lego stores. The top floor is a food court, while the piazza hosts a farmers' market every Wednesday.

Market value

There are several good markets in Brighton. As ever, it's North Laine that leads the way. The most significant is the Brighton Farm Market at Diplocks Yard on North Road (9.30am-4.30pm Sat), drawing farmers and producers from across Sussex to sell barrows of fresh vegetables, alongside cakes, cheese, fish, meat, bread and flowers. On Sundays (11am-6pm) the same site hosts the Yard Vintage & Makers Market, with handmade jewellery and vintage clothing.

The Brighton Street Market takes place every Saturday (9am-5pm) along Upper Gardner Street, with a light smattering of records, books, curios, the odd vintage clothes rail or piece of furniture, and food stalls. A Seafront Market, with book and craft stalls, runs at weekends from March

SHORTLIST

Best bookshops
- Book Nook (p158)
- City Books (p159)
- Kemptown Bookshop (p124)

Retro style
- Dig For Victory (p122)
- Jump The Gun (p84)
- Hope & Harlequin (p83)
- Get Cutie (p83)

Best for gifts
- Castor & Pollux (p98)
- Dowse (p159)
- Oh So Swedish (p124)
- Pussy (p84)

Statement accessories
- Irregular Choice (p83)
- Snoopers Attic at Snooper's Paradise (p85)

Best for kids
- Oddballs (p84)
- Poppets (p161)
- Rocket Science (p85)

Best for interiors
- Bert's Home Store (p69)
- Lollipop Shoppe (p70)
- Wood Store (p125)

Best intentions
- Fair (p70)
- Hisbe (p145)
- Infinity Foods (p83)
- It Is What It Is (p20)

Crafty things
- Mr Magpie (p84)
- Quilty Pleasures (p107)
- YAK (p85)

Best showroom cafés
- Compass Point Eatery (p114)
- Salvage Café (p157)
- Vine Street Vintage Brighton Market (p85)

DON'T MISS

to December (9am-dusk) on the Lower Esplanade by the West Pier. Down on London Road, the Open Market (see box p144) has been reborn as a covered space housing 45 permanent vendors – selling everything from fresh bread to beard oil, local wine to children's toys – and 12 arts and crafts studios. There are temporary stalls in the middle of the space and regular themed and seasonal fairs.

Record shopping

When in Brighton, go record shopping. The city's oldest independent record shop, Rounder Records, may have closed in 2012, brought down by downloads and the big online retailers. But that's all the more reason to support the traders that remain, and underpin the city's musical reputation. North Laine is your best starting point, with Wax Factor (24 Trafalgar Street, www.thewaxfactor.com), Rarekind (p84), Across The Tracks (110 Gloucester Road, www.acrossthe tracksrecords.com, 01273 677906), One Stop Records (p73) and Resident

(p84) all within minutes of each other. Further afield, check out Monkey Music Emporium (p145), near London Road, and Dance 2 (p70), on Western Road. At Record Album (p70), near the station, you can even get a copy of the folio to *Raiders of the Lost Ark* complete with rumbling boulder. The elderly owner, George Ginn, is a vinyl devotee. He will try to conceal his wince if you mention CDs.

Food & drink

One of Brighton's most famous shops is Infinity Foods (p83), often credited with starting the organic boom. It opened as a small shop in 1971, and today sells a vast array of wholefoods and organic produce from a large premises on the corner of North Road and Gardner Street. There's a bakery on site, but it faces increasingly stiff competition. When it comes to artisanal bread, Brighton is now spelt (little pun there) for choice, with four branches of Real Patisserie (p118), Sugardough (p157) in Hove, the bakery arm of no-waste restaurant Silo (p79), and a second

Record Album

Sage & Relish

DON'T MISS

branch of North Laine's Flour Pot Bakery (p77) just opened in Hanover (in a former brothel – that's Brighton for you).

The taste for alternative supermarkets started by Infinity has found its latest incarnation in Hisbe (p145; 'How it should be') on York Place. This 'ethical supermarket' was crowd-funded, and has eight basic principles: go local, choose seasonal, protect nature, support ethical, think welfare, save fish, end waste and avoid processed. Another local success story is Taj (p70), a large Middle Eastern and South Asian organic emporium on Western Road, where bhangra music and crates of vine tomatoes spill on to the pavement. On a smaller scale, Black Radish (p152) is a small new organic grocery store and café in Hove.

Specialist food and drink shops have proliferated, supported by the commitment of many cafés and restaurants to source local produce. Particular sources of civic pride include the Brighton Sausage Company (p80) and Boho Gelato (p93), whose ice-cream makers

recently invented a new flavour (banana custard with sweet cherry swirl) to raise money for a young people's reading project. There are several independent chocolatiers in the city, including the fantastical Choccywoccydoodah (p98) and the wonderfully old-fashioned Audrey's (p158), which recently introduced a line of chocolate buttons modelled on a box of buttons left to the owner by her own grandmother. Specialist international food shops include La Cave au Fromage (p159), E-Kagen Shop (p145), and Hove's new high-end Mediterranean deli, Sage & Relish (p161).

Brighton is also now home to the UK's first tea mixology company, Bluebird Tea (p80). Keep your seaside spirit up in winter with a cup of its candy floss tea.

There are few better ways to finish a day's shopping in Brighton than watching the sunset on the seafront. To do it in style, pick up a bottle from top local merchants Butler's Wines (p122), Quaff (p161) or Ten Green Bottles (p79), or from the new Bison Beer Crafthouse (p97), Brighton's first specialist beer shop.

Bleach

Nightlife

Pier, promenade, pavilion, pah! It's partying that brings so many to Brighton – a fine tradition upon which the town's very development rested, back in the days of the foxy Prince Regent (George IV).

Nightlife here comes in both alternative and mainstream versions, encompassing everything from vintage burlesque to arty happenings and the goings on at the Dungeon Bar (p71) – the UK's first fetish bar. There's also a vibrant comedy scene.

Live music

With Nick Cave, Norman Cook and international music festival the Great Escape (p37) calling the city home, Brighton hardly needs to prove its musical credentials. From grassroots to big names, this is a historic, vibrant and well-promoted scene. Promoters such as Melting Vinyl (www.meltingvinyl.co.uk) and Lout (www.loutpromotions.co.uk) are at the forefront in bringing cult, indie and just-about-on-the-radar bands to Brighton, as well as giving a break to home-grown talent.

But because this is a compact city, gig venues also live under permanent threat of the dreaded Noise Abatement Notice (RIP the semi-legendary Freebutt and Blind Tiger Club). The council is currently being petitioned to do more to protect long-established venues from complaints by new neighbours. Alternative music venues that do survive, such as the Prince Albert (p86), are duly treasured. Among more recent additions, Green Door Store (p86) is tucked under the railway arches and has the feel of a cellar speakeasy, while Sticky Mike's Frog Bar (p100) feels like the ultimate student common room. The Hope has just been reborn as Hope & Ruin (p63), with a downstairs restyle and unfussy but significant changes to the upstairs venue. All these venues are within a few minutes' walk from the station. So is Komedia (p86), a multi-arts venue with great live-music bookings.

Further afield, on Preston Circus, the new 150-capacity Bleach (p146) is keen to become a rite of passage for rising touring bands, while new pub the Joker (p138) has started programming in its upstairs venue, the Devil's Disco. In Hove, Grade II-listed the Old Market (p162) has a brilliant sound system.

Pubs with a long reputation for live music include the Greys (p115) in Hanover and the Brunswick (p162) in Hove, while the Verdict (p126) has recently brought a dedicated jazz programme to Kemp Town. On the seafront, listen out for bands playing at drinking dens Brighton Music Hall (p59), Fortune of War (p100) and new arrival the Tempest Inn (p97). The last has invited in Felix Buxton of Basement Jaxx to use its man-made cave system as a resonance chamber.

Bigger concerts are best enjoyed in the plush regency auditorium at the Brighton Dome (p86), where – it's obligatory to mention – Abba won the Eurovision Song Contest in 1974, or the smaller, neighbouring Corn Exchange (p86). Arena-sized pop acts play the Brighton Centre (p71). For gigs in more unusual spaces, check in with top local promoter Melting Vinyl, which has used local galleries, cinemas and churches.

Clubs

Does Brighton's clubbing scene belong to the ageing ravers, the EDM aficionados, the gay community, the students, or the visiting stags and hens? Or did resident superstar DJ Fatboy Slim blow such distinctions out

SHORTLIST

Alternative vibe
- Caroline of Brunswick (p136)
- Cowley Club (p146)
- Marlborough (p128)

For big names
- Brighton Centre (p71)
- Brighton Dome (p86)

Best gay venues
- Bedford Tavern (p58)
- Charles Street (p126)
- Legends (p117)

Best for jazz
- Komedia (p86)
- Old Market (p162)
- Verdict (p126)

Best sound
- Arch (p98)
- Brighton Dome (p86)
- Old Market (p162)

Best small venues
- Bleach (p146)
- Green Door Store (p86)
- Sticky Mike's Frog Bar (p100)

Best music pubs
- Brunswick (p162)
- Greys (p115)
- Prince Albert (p86)

Best for rising bands
- Concorde 2 (p126)
- Haunt (p100)
- Hope & Ruin (p63)
- Komedia (p86)

Cabaret & burlesque
- Brighton Ballroom (p125)
- Latest Music Bar (p126)
- Marlborough (p128)

Late licences
- Bulldog (p125)
- Coalition (p98)

Welcome to Thailand...
no passport required

Open 7 days a week 12 noon to 10.30pm
To book please call 01273 207444
5 & 20 Brighton Square, Brighton, Sussex, BN1 1HD
www.streetthai.co.uk

street
thai

สตรีทไทย

Special 2-course
menu £9.95

3-course menu
£11.95

(not available Saturday)

of the water when, in 2002, he played to 250,000 revellers (more than the city's population) on Brighton Beach?

Having given birth to Big Beat back in the early 1990s, for a while Brighton dance culture put its creative feet up and let the pissed-up hordes of West Street lead the way – usually to giant chain club Pryzm (formerly Oceana), or seafront 'VIP super club' Shooshh. But things are looking up, with two new seafront venues on some hallowed clubbing turf: Arch (p98), on the old site of Digital and the Zap, and Patterns (p126), formerly Audio. Expect big but credible names, and a more discerning crowd.

Of course, you don't have to go to a club to experience a great club night. Komedia is home to a raft of fun and credible regulars, including '60s femme pop and soul night Da Doo Ron Ron, and Spellbound ('the '80s club night for people who hate '80s nights). Green Door Store has nights dedicated to everything from '50s rock to sleazy Italian disco, and the Haunt (p100), Sticky Mike's Frog Bar and the Mesmerist (p100) are popular late-night venues too. The Cowley Club (p146) is renowned for its politically potent late nights. In 2014, Brighton even played host to its first breakfast rave, courtesy of pre-work party-starters Morning Gloryville.

LGBT nightlife

Brighton's famous LGBT scene is deep-rooted and dynamic. Kemp Town is Brighton's 'gay village', but there's no ghetto here. Rainbow politics, LGBT culture and the pink pound permeate most areas of city life. This is especially true of Brighton nightlife, which owes much of its spark and anything-goes character to the LGBT community.

Many clubs put on at least one gay night (look out for the flamboyant branding of prestigious party starters Wild Fruit), while at Revenge (p126), the biggest gay club on the south coast, you'll find as many straight as gay revellers dancing to cheese (or the latest *X-Factor* evictee). Kemp Town's Bulldog Bar (p125), on St James's Street, is popular for late-night drinking.

The Camelford Arms (p114) and Bedford Tavern (p58) offer a cosier scene. Keep your eye, too, on the Grosvenor (16 Western Street, 01273 770712), a small pub just off Western Road that recently changed hands. The plan is to put on cabaret, and develop a gay hub in Hove. Meanwhile, the Marlborough (p128) continues to grow in strength as a queer and leftfield artistic hub. This is where you'll find nights such as Steampunk Hidden Cabaret and Naked Boys Reading: a literary salon led by unclothed men.

Comedy & cabaret

Brighton is the comedy capital of the south-east, with its own annual comedy festival and comedy fringe. Komedia is the venue most closely associated with comedy, hosting four Krater Comedy Club shows a week and fostering future talent via Jill Edwards' standup comedy course (Jimmy Carr is a graduate). Komedia's production arm manages cult comic character Count Arthur Strong, now the subject of a TV sitcom. These days, cult comedians are more likely to be found at the Basement (p86), now being programmed by the Chortle Award-winning Otherplace Productions, and at the Caroline of Brunswick (p136). In addition, UK-wide promoter Laughing Horse Comedy runs a weekly Saturday night comedy club at the Quadrant (p66). Big-name touring comedians play the Theatre Royal (p88), Brighton Dome and Brighton Centre; the Brighton Ballroom (p125) is usually the first choice for dedicated cabaret and burlesque shows.

Fabrica p31

Arts & Leisure

When Costa-winning novelist Ali Smith guest directed the 2015 Brighton Festival, she talked about wanting to blur the boundaries between art forms. It's something the city, with its compact cultural scene, is particularly good at. Artists and performers in Brighton like to collaborate and experiment. The best venues have both core passions and open-minded programming policies. Audiences criss-cross between theatre and dance, visual art and live music. It's no surprise that Urban Playground, the first company in the world to fuse performance and parkour, was born on the terraces and balustrades of Brighton.

So the following subdivisions are a bit false. You'll sense this most strongly in May, during the Brighton Festival and Brighton Fringe. It's often hard to tell whether you're sitting on a bench or participating in an installation, chatting with an eccentric passer-by or engaging in an intimate piece of theatre, walking through a street or a stage set. Above all, when it comes to art and performance, Brighton rewards the explorer and the risk-taker.

Theatre & dance

Brighton's proximity to London means both a steady flow of touring productions, and a rich scene of resident artists who commute to the capital when needed, but love nothing better than performing on home turf. Interactive and digital theatre pioneers Blast Theory are based here, as are site-specific gurus Dreamthinkspeak, and groundbreaking Royal Court playwright Tim Crouch.

Theatre Royal Brighton

DON'T MISS

There are three new theatres, all founded by local artists: Emporium Brighton (p146), which has Alan Rickman as its patron; the Rialto (p71), home to local satirists the Treason Show; and Brighton Open Air Theatre (p108), an extraordinary legacy project. The Old Market (p162) arts venue was saved by local boys turned international sensations Stomp, and now has a dedicated and often daring theatre programme.

The Basement (p86) in North Laine is flushed with new blood following the arrival of Otherplace Productions, while programming at Brighton Dome's Studio Theatre (p86) is going from strength to strength. The Marlborough Pub & Theatre (p128) are now united and sparking creatively under one management.

At one time, the Theatre Royal Brighton (p88) received 'flying matinées' from London – West End shows that came down by train, casts, sets and all, and raced back to the capital for a show the same night. Now, this historic theatre

often serves as a launch pad for pre-West End shows. It is also a popular venue for touring dance companies, alongside Brighton Dome's Concert Hall and Corn Exchange (p86).

In September 2015, work will begin on the Dance Space (www. southeastdance.org.uk/dance-space), a new performance centre and choreographic hub for South East Dance. The Dance Space is at the centre of the Circus Street development (p110), and set to open in 2018.

But don't restrict yourself to permanent venues. Brighton Festival has a reputation for site-specific theatre staged everywhere from derelict shops to toilets, and Ragroof Players (www.ragroof players.co.uk) might hold their participatory vintage tea dances in a theatre, or in a seafront square. Meanwhile, one of Brighton's most innovative programmers, the Nightingale Theatre, built a set of old-fashioned bathing machines to host one-on-one performances, and has recently flown its nest above the Grand Central pub to become nomadic. Their slogan? 'Theatre can happen anywhere'.

Classical music & opera

Brighton Dome has the most substantial classical music and opera programme in the city, and its Concert Hall has a suitably impressive acoustic. It's also home to the respected Brighton Festival Chorus and Brighton Philharmonic Orchestra (www.brightonphil.org. uk), which puts on at least one performance a month. The London Philharmonic and Royal Philharmonic Orchestras are regular guests. Theatre Royal Brighton also hosts occasional opera, and serious fans can make the short train journey to Glyndebourne, near Lewes.

Every autumn, Brighton Early Music Festival explores early classical, folk, world and choral music, with a lively programme that throws up fascinating connections. The Tallis Scholars, Emma Kirkby and Red Priest have all performed here, and BBC Radio 3 broadcasts many of the concerts.

Visual art

Brighton attracts artists and arts students like moths to a flame, and its public galleries are vibey places with high footfalls and rapid turnovers of work. Phoenix Brighton (p128) is a huge building that hosts large-scale modern art exhibitions, provides studios for 100 artists, and holds events such as indoor market Art Junky. University of Brighton Art Gallery (p128), with its glass-frontage making exhibitions enjoyable from the street, is just down the road.

Fabrica (p31), based in a Regency church in the heart of the Lanes, commissions site-specific work in every media from light installations to grass lawns. The newer Gallery (p88) themes eye-catching exhibitions around environmental issues. Brighton Museum & Art Gallery (p73) hosts modern exhibitions, such as a retrospective of New York pop artist Jeff Koons, alongside its resident works.

Artists Open Houses (p35, p37) takes place twice a year and attracts a whopping 50,000 visitors. Started in 1982, it now sees 200 homes and studios thrown open to the public, who can snoop at random or follow 14 mapped trails.

Brighton is packed with commercial art galleries, which you'll find listed in this guide under Shopping. See Don't Miss Sights & Museums (pp8-15) for an overview of the city's public sculptures and street art.

Film

Brighton has a rich history of cinematography. William Friese-Greene, who had a studio in the city, was one of the pioneers of moving pictures. His friend Esmé Collings shot some of the earliest films here, with titles such as *Boys Scrambling for Pennies Under the West Pier* and *Ocean Waves in a Storm*, as well as what's thought to be the first erotic film, *A Victorian Lady in Her Boudoir*. The first film show here took place in 1896, and by 1900 Brighton had weekly shows of 'animated photography', many in St Ann's Well Gardens (p149).

At the height of the film industry's popularity, in 1940, there were 24 cinemas in the city. Now there are just four: Cineworld in the Marina, the Odeon on West Street, the Duke of York's Picturehouse (p146) and Dukes at Komedia (p88). These last two go a long way to making up for the loss of all the others. The Duke of York's, which celebrated its centenary in 2010, is one of the prides of Brighton, and its partnership with Komedia has created a brilliant little cinema in the North Laine.

For the last few years, a free beachfront cinema has screened films (such as *Jaws*) and big sporting events in June and July (www.brightonsbig screen.com). Brighton Open Air Theatre is also planning to host the odd screening from summer 2015.

Sport

Brighton is home to a picturesque racecourse (p110), the oldest cycle track in the country (in Preston Park, p135), a floodlit new skate park (the Level, p132), two watersports centres (at Hove Lagoon and Brighton Marina), and a cricket ground (p162), where you can watch matches from the comfort of a deckchair. You can play sandy beach volleyball at Yellowave (p128), join a bike ride at cycle café Velo (p143), hire a kayak (www.thebrightonwatersports.co.uk), hang out with longboarders at the Fortune of War (p100), or just play a tipsy game of crazy golf.

Best of all is watching local footie team Brighton & Hove Albion play at 'the best new sporting venue in the world': the Falmer Stadium (or, to give its official title, the American Express Community Stadium), a short train journey away near the University of Sussex. The Seagulls' home cost £100 million, opened in 2011, and scooped the international Stadium Business Award the following year.

So it seems churlish to mention Hove's King Alfred's Leisure Centre and those failed Frank Gehry redevelopment plans. The latest seafront leisure proposal, announced in March 2015 but yet to receive the go ahead, is for a £3-million heated saltwater pool inspired by Bondi beach. It's all water off a duck's back, though, to members of England's oldest swimming club, the Brighton Swimming Club, which has been hopping over the pebbles and plunging into the raw sea since 1863. Hundreds join them every year for the Christmas Day Swim.

The Brighton Marathon (p35) has been taking place every April since 2010, hot on the heels of the long-established Sussex Beacon Half Marathon (p35). It finishes on Madeira Drive, which also throbs with vintage engines during the famous Brighton Speed Trials (p33) and Mods & Rockers-themed Ace Café Reunion (p33).

There's no better encapsulation of Brighton's unique sporting spirit than Paddle Round The Pier (p38), a beach festival in which residents attempt to navigate round the West Pier on whatever outlandish object they can temporarily persuade to float.

Calendar

Colour Run p34

The following are the pick of the annual events that take place in Brighton and around. Further information and exact dates can be found nearer the time from the tourist information centres and at the websites listed. The major venues also have their own programmes that can be picked up across the city.

Autumn

Sept **Brighton Digital Festival**
Various venues
www.brightondigitalfestival.co.uk
A month of exhibitions, workshops and performances showcasing and forging connections within the city's strong digital culture.

Mid Sept **Ace Café Reunion**
Seafront
www.ace-cafe-london.com
Around 40,000 motorbikes descend on Brighton seafront in celebration of biking and the legendary Ace Café, a 1960s bikers' meeting place on London's North Circular Road.

Mid Sept **Japan Festival**
Various venues
www.brightonjapan.com
Japanese arts, food, film, theatre and performance – the largest event of its kind in the UK.

Mid Sept **Brighton & Hove Autumn Harvest Food & Drink Festival**
Various venues
www.brightonfoodfestival.co.uk
Seasonal festival of local producers, growers and retailers.

Late Sept **Brighton Art Fair**
Corn Exchange
www.brightonartfair.co.uk
Buy direct from the artists at the largest exhibition on the south coast, which brings together artists including painters, printmakers, photographers, sculptors and more.

Sept **Breakout Festival**
Brighton Racecourse
www.breakoutfestival.co.uk
First held in 2014, this outdoor rock and metal festival features over 30 bands across three stages.

Early-late Oct **Brighton Comedy Festival**
Brighton Dome & other venues
www.brightoncomedyfestival.com
Top comedians at venues across the city. Smaller and cult acts come courtesy of Brighton Comedy Fringe.

Mid Oct **Colour Run**
Madeira Drive
www.thecolorrun.co.uk
A 5k race in which thousands of participants are doused from head to toe in different colours at each kilometre.

Mid Oct-early Nov **Brighton Early Music Festival**
Various venues
www.bremf.org.uk
The UK's second-largest early music festival, with a lively and imaginative programme that crosses art forms. Many concerts are broadcast on BBC Radio 3.

Autumn (dates vary) **Colour Out of Space**
Various venues
www.colouroutofspace.org
Autumn festival of experimental music and film. Since 2006 it has played host to some of the most visionary musicians, sound artists and filmmakers of the last 40 years

Winter

Early Nov **London to Brighton Veteran Car Run**
www.lbvcr.com
This annual event commemorating the Emancipation Run of 14 November 1896 attracts hundreds of vehicles from the UK and abroad.

Mid-late Nov **MADE**
Corn Exchange
www.brightoncraftfair.co.uk
This friendly, accessible and high-quality design and craft fair attracts more than 100 creators.

Mid Nov-early Dec **CineCity Film Festival**
Various venues
www.cine-city.co.uk
Brighton's own film festival, featuring premières, previews, talks, workshops and film-themed art installations at locations across the city.

Nov-Dec weekends **Christmas Open Houses Festival**
www.aoh.org.uk
Explore more than 100 houses across the city, where you can see and buy the work of local artists, often over a mince pie and glass of mulled wine.

Burning the Clocks

Late Dec **Burning the Clocks – Winter Solstice Parade**
www.samesky.co.uk
Seafront
A stunning winter treat to mark the shortest day, as residents make and carry paper lanterns through the city, before burning them on the beach in conjunction with a fireworks display.

Late Jan **Brighton Tattoo Convention**
Hilton Brighton Metropole
www.brightontattoo.com
Artists who use the human body as their canvas.

Feb-Mar **Brighton Science Festival**
Various venues
www.brightonscience.com
A fun festival for kids, geeks and inquisitive adults, with workshops, demos and talks. Past events include dinosaur digs and build-your-own-games-console workshops.

Mid Feb **Brighton Half Marathon**
www.beaconhalf.org.uk
2015 marks the 25th anniversary of this annual charity seafront race.

Early-mid Mar **WhaleFest**
Brighton Centre and other locations
www.whale-fest.com
Celebration of wild whales and dolphins in aid of the World Cetacean Alliance, with celebrity speakers and life-size inflatable whales.

Early-mid Mar **Sussex Beer Festival**
Corn Exchange
www.sussexbeerfestival.co.uk
Great beers (and ciders), food, friendly staff and a fantastic atmosphere.

Mar **Sick! Festival**
Basement & other venues
www.sickfestival.com
Performances, films and talks exploring the physical, mental and social challenges of life and death.

Late Mar **VegFestUK**
Brighton Centre
www.brighton.vegfest.co.uk
Weekend event with vegan stalls, cookery demos, nutritional advice and, oddly, comedy and speed-dating.

Spring

Early Apr **Brighton & Hove Spring Harvest Food and Drink Festival**
Various venues
www.brightonfoodfestival.com.
Festival for local producers, growers and retailers, including the Big Sussex Market & Live Food Show, the Children's Food Festival and Brighton Fish Festival.

2nd week Apr **Brighton Marathon**
www.brightonmarathon.co.uk
The buzz around this 26-mile race gets bigger every year, with thousands lining the course from Preston Park through to Madeira Drive. The weekend also includes the Mini Mile Races, the BM10K and the Brighton Marathon exhibition.

Early May **Foodies Festival**
Hove Lawns
www.foodiesfestival.com
The largest celebration of food and drink in Britain, including a live-entertainment stage, cooking masterclasses and contributions from various local restaurants.

May **Brighton Festival**
Various venues
www.brightonfestival.org
An international programme of theatre, dance, music, books and debate, plus outdoor spectacles kick-started by the now famous Children's Parade. See box p39.

May **Brighton Fringe**
Various locations
www.brightonfestivalfringe.org.uk
The third-largest fringe festival in the world offers everything from theatre,

exhibitions and street performances to cabaret, comedy and club nights. See box p39.

See box p39.

Throughout May **HOUSE Festival**
Various locations
www.housefestival.org
A curated contemporary visual-arts festival featuring commissioned site-specific works by established artists.

Weekends in May **Artists Open Houses**
www.aoh.org.uk
Free visual arts event, in which many Brighton artists open their homes and studios, grouped around 14 trails. There's another Artists' Open Houses event in December.

Mid May **Great Escape**
Various venues
www.escapegreat.com
Music festival and industry showcase of rising bands (everyone from Adele to Brighton's own Royal Blood has played here) attended by thousands of international delegates alongside 13,000 regular music fans. See box p39.

Mid May **Heroes Run**
Brighton seafront
www.heroesrun.org.uk
Over 1,000 participants dress as super-heroes (or villains) and race for charity. There's also a Mini-Heroes 500m dash for children.

Mid-late May **Royal Escape Race**
Starts at Brighton Pier
www.royalescaperace.co.uk
Around 100 boats compete in this cross-Channel event commemorating the escape of Charles II to France from Cromwell and his forces.

Mid-late May **Elderflower Fields Festival**
Ashdown Forest
www.elderflowerfields.co.uk
A family-friendly music festival in the Sussex countryside.

Brighton Fringe p35

Summer

Early June Great Skinhead Reunion
Volks Bar
www.greatskinheadreunion.co.uk
The biggest gathering of skinheads in the UK, this weekend-long event is in its fifth year in 2015.

Early June Sussex Festival of Nature
Stanmer Park
www.brighton-hove.gov.uk
Formerly the Springwatch Festival, this free celebration of local wildlife includes stalls and activities such as sheep shearing.

Early-mid June World Naked Bike Ride
www.worldnakedbikeride.org/brighton
A seaside bike ride in the buff, usually leaving from the Level.

Mid June London to Brighton Bike Ride
www.bhf.org.uk/london-brighton
The annual 54-mile bike ride from the capital to the coast in aid of the British Heart Foundation. It's the UK's largest charity bike ride, with 27,000 riders taking part.

Mid June-July TAKEPART Festival
www.brighton-hove.gov.uk
The largest celebration of community sport and physical activity in the country, with two weeks' worth of displays and taster sessions.

Early July Paddle Round the Pier
www.paddleroundthepier.com
A free festival of beach culture, featuring urban and street sports, live music and family fun, and the central paddle-round-the-pier race.

Early July Kite Festival
Stanmer Park
www.brightonkiteflyers.co.uk
A family event that has been flying high for 35 years.

Mid July March of the Mermaids
Hove Lawns & seafront
www.facebook.com/mermaids.march
A fun dress-up event for all the family, with prizes for the best costumes and

Great Escape p37

The main event

Brighton gets festive in May.

Artists' Open Houses

Brighton & Hove doesn't do culture by the calendar – the arts here are lived and breathed year-round. But come May, you'll witness an explosion of events in and around the **Brighton Festival** (p35).

Founded in 1966, Brighton Festival is the biggest multi-artform festival in England, attracting more than 500,000 people to 200-plus events. These range from open-air Shakespeare to cutting-edge theatre, classical ballet to contemporary dance, vibey gigs to sophisticated author talks, and from big visual art installations to free family-friendly outdoor displays. Much of the work is commissioned, or here for its world or UK première.

In 2009, British Indian sculptor Anish Kapoor became the festival's first guest artistic director, a role that has helped reshape the festival afresh every May. The likes of Brian Eno, Vanessa Redgrave, Burmese democracy campaigner Aung San Suu Kyi, Children's Laureate Michael Rosen and novelist Ali Smith have all brought their own political and artistic passions to the role.

Brighton Festival is based at, but does not restrict itself to, the Brighton Dome complex. More broad-ranging, and more impish in spirit, is the **Brighton Fringe** (p35). This parallel festival originated in 1967 and now sprawls across the city (and beyond). Past venues for performances have included a *Spiegeltent*, a giant upside-down purple cow and a set of Victorian bathing machines. Unlike the Brighton Festival, Brighton Fringe is open to anyone who wants to put on a show, making the programme of around 4,000 performances more of a lucky dip. At weekends, the Fringe City showcase on New Road provides tasters of shows.

Other festivals have sprung up around the twin poles of the Brighton Festival and Brighton Fringe. **Artists' Open Houses** (p37) invites visitors into the homes of artists. And the **Great Escape** (p37) has also taken advantage of the spike in visitor numbers in May. It's billed as Britain's answer to SXSW and takes over most of the city's pubs and music venues for three days in the second week of May.

Loud and proud

Brighton Pride is now free only in spirit.

The city wears its LGBT heart on its sequined sleeve, so its hardly surprising that **Brighton Pride** (right) is a huge event, attracting around 50,000 revellers. Usually taking place on the first Saturday of August, and loosely themed around a different visual concept each year, the Pride parade sets off from Madeira Drive at 11am and is watched by thousands as it sashays through the city centre and along London Road to Preston Park.

The park itself undergoes a transformation, becoming a festival site with fairground rides, market stalls selling everything from pet accessories to sex toys, food vendors, bars and entertainment tents with DJs, cabaret and pop stars. Since 2011, the event has – controversially – charged entry.

As a result, many feel that the soul of Brighton Pride resides instead on St James's Street, where venues such as the Bulldog and Brighton Rocks have helped grow a grassroots street party. Cue even more controversy when, in 2014, prompted by a rise in numbers and police concerns, the decision was made to ticket the 'Pride Village Party' too. Entry is now only by wristband.

Clubs such as **Revenge** (p126), **Legends** (p117) and **Charles Street** (p126) keep the mood celebratory well into Sunday, with official and unofficial Pride parties. and after-parties.

crowns for Miss Brighton Mermaid and King Prawn.

Early Aug **August Festival**
Brighton Racecourse
www.brighton-racecourse.co.uk
Watch the races, sip champagne and admire all the hats on Ladies' Day.

Early-mid Aug **Brighton Pride**
www.brightonpride.org
The biggest Pride festival in the UK celebrates everything LGBT in a week of events and parties culminating in a spectacular parade through the city to Preston Park. See box left.

Mid Aug **Brunswick Festival**
Brunswick Square
www.brunswickplaceresidents.org.uk
An annual community festival in the Regency seafront square, featuring food and drink, street theatre and live music.

Mid Aug **Shakedown Festival**
Waterhall Brighton (2015)
www.shakedown.co.uk
The biggest electronic music festival on the south coast. Defected, Hospitality, Digital Soundboy and Supercharged are hosting stages in 2015.

Mid Aug-mid Sept **Big Screen on the Beach**
Beach by Madeira Drive
www.brightonsbigscreen.com
Free sport and blockbuster movies on the beach, with grandstand seating and a bar.

Late Aug **Brighton Mod Weekender**
www.newuntouchables.com
Mods and their Vespas descend on the seafront, with live music at the Volks.

Early Sept **Brighton Speed Trials**
Madeira Drive
www.brightonandhovemotorclub.co.uk
Britain's oldest motor-racing event, first staged in 1905.

Itineraries

Decadent Brighton

Ever since the profligate Prince of Wales swaggered down in 1783 with his entourage of gamblers, drunks and lovers, Brighton has had something of a 'nudge nudge, wink wink' reputation. Pocketed away from the rest of the country by the South Downs, it's perceived as a city with its own rules – or lack of them. People come here to break free, to party, and to rekindle that great British tradition of the dirty weekend. In return, Brighton behaves as if the sea, despite being too cold to dip your toe in for much of the year, somehow washes everything clean come 8am Monday morning. (Or make that 11am Tuesday if you're on North Laine time.)

This walk takes you from the Brighton that was the Prince's playground, via *Brighton Rock* and the battling mods and rockers, to its present-day status as a creative and alternative romping ground, with more restaurants per head here than anywhere else in the UK except London, and a watering hole for every day of the year. Depending on how much time you spend indulging in the latter, you can easily make a day of this tour.

The route begins at Britain's most extravagant and opulent regal residence: the **Brighton Royal Pavilion** (p73), aka the Prince Regent's party pad. On becoming Regent in 1811, Prince George had John Nash extend the building into a no-expense-spared fantasy, with twin exotic gateways, bulbous oriental-style domes, and joyous disregard for such things as thematic integrity or architectural codes. The chandelier in the banqueting room is worth the admission price alone – henceforth, no chandelier will truly impress you unless it's being borne in the claws of a huge fiery dragon.

Brighton Royal Pavilion

Choccywoccydoodah p46

In his later years, the Prince Regent liked to navigate the city unseen. An underground tunnel still runs from the Royal Pavilion to the current **Brighton Museum** (p73) and **Brighton Dome** (p86) complex in the pavilion gardens, originally his riding stables. Two other fabled passageways are more likely to be the products of the dirty local imagination: folklore has it that he had a subterranean route built to his lover Mrs Fitzherbert's house, and another to the Marlborough Hotel. Then a brothel, now a brilliant alternative pub and theatre, the **Marlborough** (p128) is located minutes from the Royal Pavilion, just off Old Steine – and a jewel in Brighton's assuredly skew-whiff tiara. Pop in for some of the city's most interesting nights (this was the birthplace of the vintage porn-based ArtWank). Urban legend has it that Virginia Woolf and Vita Sackville-West conducted their affair here. En route, look out for the statue of Queen Victoria overlooking the Pavilion in stern disapproval. Not

a big fan of Brighton, she stripped down the Pavilion and took the furnishings to London.

The landscaped gardens of the Royal Pavilion lead to pedestrianised New Road. The Prince celebrated his 33rd birthday here in 1795 with a vast firework display; in 1802, he bettered it with an exploding 'Mount Vesuvius'. Straight ahead is the **Theatre Royal Brighton** (p88). A backstage tour takes in the dressing room Marlene Dietrich once swept to calm her nerves, and the Single Gulp bar where actors could get some Dutch courage between scenes. Apparently, the barmaid liked to play the fruit machine during performances, and didn't always synchronise it too carefully with the audience applause.

It was the fashion for spas and sea bathing that led the Prince of Wales to Brighton, 'the Queen of the Watering Places'. The nobility had previously derided sea bathing, but changed their minds after the publication of snappily titled pamphlets such as the *Dissertation of the Use of Sea Water in the*

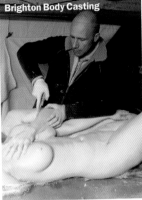

Brighton Body Casting

Diseases of the Glands (1750), by Lewes physician Dr Richard Russell. Wooden bathing machines were drawn into the sea by horses, and controlled by 'dippers' who touted for business along the 'season'. Some men chose to bathe nude, risking a fine if they were seen. (Today, a nudist beach exists further along Madeira Drive). The most famous dipper, favoured by the Prince himself, was Martha Gunn (1726-1815). Her stout portrait hangs in Brighton Museum.

Using the defence that sea bathing was an antidote for wanton living, London society decamped to Brighton for the 'season'. It was, of course, an excuse for wanton living: three months by the sea spent gambling, drinking, partying and parading. With the visitors came coffee houses, inns, lodging houses – and the first ever example of that peculiar Victorian engineering feat, the pleasure pier.

The first of three in Brighton, the Royal Suspension Chain Pier opened in 1823. By the time the trains arrived in 1841, it had become Brighton's most popular tourist destination. But it was brought down by a storm

in 1896, making way for the Palace Pier, now called **Brighton Pier** (p90), and reached from the Theatre Royal via North Street and the Old Steine. Opened in 1899, it featured freak shows, and haunted houses with mock executions. Today, its gaudy arcades still offer an archetypal seaside experience. To the west, you'll see the haunting remains of the **West Pier** (p58), burnt under suspicious circumstances in 2003, and its thrusting new companion, the **i360** (p55).

After exploring Brighton Pier, re-cross Grand Junction Road and turn left, before taking a right into East Street, West Street's slightly more mature sibling when it comes to late-night dancing, drinking and decadence. Newest on the scene is **Dirty Blonde** (p94), a speakeasy-themed cocktail bar where you can sip ten varieties of champagne from cut-crystal glasses – and buy a £300 vintage lighter or stuffed owl from the in-house pawn shop on your way out. Look out, too, for the **Bison Beer Crafthouse** (p97). The city's first dedicated craft beer store, it stocks 300 varieties – and funky cool bags handy for picnics on the beach.

If there's time, we recommend making use of the East Street taxi rank for a detour to Hove. Why? To get your bits artistically rendered in plaster, of course. Jamie McCartney of **Brighton Body Casting** (p162) is famous for creating *The Great Wall of Vagina*, cast from 400 different vulvas. But he's tackled most things fleshy, from pregnant bellies to the face of a Liechtenstein princess. You can get an arty cast done in as little as half an hour, he says – though obviously it rather depends on size. Best to book ahead, anyway.

Back on East Street, eagle-eyed *Quadrophenia* fans will recognise Pool Passage. This is the flint-walled alleyway where Jimmy and Steph managed a swift knee-trembler during the film's riot scenes. It's also a rare remaining glimpse of Brighton's old 'East End'. Incidentally, Brighton is also thought to be the birthplace of blue movies: *A Victorian Lady in Her Boudoir*, alternatively titled *Woman Undressing*, was made here by Esmé Collings in 1896, and deemed suitable only for 'gentlemen's smoking parties'. Nearby, at the **Old Police Cells Museum** (p90), beneath the Town Hall in Batholomew Square, between Prince Albert Street and East Street, you can still see graffiti left by the imprisoned mods and rockers who had fought in front of Palace Pier during the 'Battle of Brighton' in 1964.

Brighton's decline into a seedy seaside destination began much earlier than this. By the beginning of the 20th century, Brighton was tired. The *Daily Mail* called it an 'un-enterprising, unattractive and outdated holiday resort'. This was the Brighton Graham Greene portrayed in *Brighton Rock*, published in 1938 and first made into a movie in 1947. The film's opening salvo stated: 'Brighton today is a large, jolly, friendly seaside town in Sussex, exactly one hour's journey from London. But in the years

between the two wars, behind the Regency terraces and crowded beaches, there was another Brighton of dark alleyways and festering slums. From here, the poison of crime and violence and gang warfare began to spread, until the challenge was taken up by the police.' Brighton has changed so much, in fact, that the 2010 remake was actually filmed in Eastbourne.

Leaving the Old Police Cells Museum, walk along Prince Albert Street to the **Cricketers** (p94). This was Greene's favourite Brighton pub, and appeared directly in another of his works, *Travels With My Aunt*: 'I was surprised by the number of glasses my aunt could put down,' confesses the narrator, 'and feared a little for her blood pressure.' There's been a pub on the site since 1547, when the first landlord, Deryk Carver, was burnt as a martyr – the Bonfire Night celebrations in Lewes commemorate him and 15 others. It once housed Jack the Ripper suspect Robert Stephenson – and was certainly popular with prostitutes in the Victorian age, when there were more than 100 brothels in the city.

It was during the 1950s and '60s that Brighton shook off its exaggerated gangland reputation to became known as a cheap holiday destination. A key marketing feature of the time was the Promettes, smartly uniformed young women who appeared in newsreels across the world. One newspaper described them as 'walking information bureaux with sex appeal.' They were a great success.

For a more refreshing attitude to female sexuality, pop in to erotic boutique **She Said** (p98). Brighton's most celebrated sex shop now stands proud in a four-storey shop on Ship Street, at the far end of Prince Albert Street, offering Passion MOTs for individuals or couples, and 'Coffee, Cake and Kegel' workshops for women. She Said has done much to

She Said p45

literalise famous resident Julie Burchill's observation that 'Brighton looks like a town recovering from a multiple orgasm.' If you're feeling shy, use the excuse that you're 'here to see the art': it now hosts exhibitions.

From sex, obviously, to chocolate. Just round the corner in Meeting House Lane, **Choccywoccydoodah** (p98) has been baking fantasies for over 20 years, and now stars in its own reality TV show. If it had been around in the 1800s, the Prince Regent would doubtless have commissioned the Royal Pavilion to be made out of chocolate. The shop has recently introduced a Witches Kitchen, where you can learn to make your own chocolate skulls or dangly bits. 'Without Brighton,' founder Christine Taylor writes in her new recipe book, *Choccywoccydoodah: Chocolate, Cake and Curses*, 'Choccywoccydoodah would not exist. With our massive population of artists, gays, gangsters, good timers and chancers, Brighton is unshockable.'

Linger in the Lanes long enough for a cocktail. Still in Meeting House Lane, new addition **BYOC Brighton** (no.41, 020 3441 2424, www.byoc.co.uk/brighton) is a bar without a booze licence. You supply the alcohol, they supply the mixologist and a range of

homemade syrups. The candlelit drinking den is hidden, speakeasy-style, within the juice bar Juice People. Alternatively, slink down the yellow alleyway to **Twisted Lemon** (p97), with its 70-point cocktail menu, for a Dirty Sanchez.

In recent years, the city's reputation for decadence has been commodified for the stag and hen demographic, and naff burlesque shows and 'bespoke indulgence packages' abound. But Brighton's talent for coexistence extends to the past and present, the alternative and the mainstream. End your day in Regency Square, a beguilingly seedy seafront crescent opposite the West Pier and i360, and you can bed down where Bobby Gillespie partied at **Hotel Pelirocco** (p175), drink in the **Regency Tavern** (p66), an 18th-century inn with a disco ball in the loo, dine on a 'dirty fish burger' at hip new restaurant the **Set** (p67), and have a swing (in one or two senses of the word) at fetish bar, **Dungeon** (p71).

We turn again to *Brighton Rock* for the final word:
Rose: People change.
Ida: I've never changed. It's like those sticks of rock. Bite one all the way down, you'll still read Brighton. That's human nature.

Paddling pool at Kings Road Playground

A Family Day Out

An aquarium with sharks, a pier with seven thrill rides, a toy railway that isn't a toy and a huge palace built by a spoilt young man named George, just because he felt like it. There's so much in Brighton to capture young imaginations, your challenge is likely to be fitting it all in. This itinerary can be split over two days or crammed into one, depending on ages and attention spans. But you'll want to leave space for a few random surprises: whether that's a skateboarding dog, the bird-whistle man in the tweed cap impersonating blue tits, or the starlings performing synchronised acrobatics over the skeleton of the West Pier.

In decent weather, there's no better starting place than the seafront. **Brighton Pier** (p90) opens at 10am in summer months. Alternatively, **Kings Road Playground** near the West Pier (p58) is open all hours, and overlooked by the new **Bucket & Spade Café** (p59), serving breakfast from 9am. This stretch of beach is also home to the **i360** (p55) and the New Cultural Quarter in the renovated West Pier Arches. The little low-ceilinged shops here sell everything from children's clothing to paper-cut artworks.

Things get gaudier back towards Brighton Pier, where you'll find the merry-go-rounds and giant trampolines in summer and several permanent sculptures. The pier itself exerts a magnetic pull on both kids and their pocket money. Decide who's buying the candy floss with a family play-off on the Dolphin Derby. The **Mechanical Memories Museum** (p90), nearby, has a working selection of vintage arcade machines.

Brighton Beach is many things, but sandy isn't one of them. This can be a sticking point if all one of your party wants to do is to build a sandcastle. At

Mechanical Memories Museum p47

Jubilee Square

Yellowave (p128), the little ones can play in a large sandpit equipped with buckets and spades, while the big ones have a game of beach volleyball. Between March and September, you can reach Yellowave via the **Volks Electric Railway** (p112), which trundles east from near the **Sealife Centre** (p112) to Brighton Marina. Along the way, tell them about maverick Victorian inventor Magnus Volks' other creation, the Daddy Long Legs. This train on stilts travelled through the water via tracks on the seabed. They can hunt for the remaining sleepers at low tide on the beach nearest Rottingdean.

Yellowave is next to an adventure golf course and **Peter Pan's Playground**, an enclosed and well-equipped play park with great views of the sea and Madeira Arches. In the post-war years, a straw-boatered and bow-tied gent known as Uncle Jack ran a children's talent contest here every summer. Carol White (later of *Cathy Come Home* fame) was one of the young star turns to be rewarded with a lollipop.

Get the Volks back in to town for lunch. **Bill's** (p74) on North Road is the safe option. For something new, try **Curry Leaf Café** (p94) in the Lanes. Its kids' menu includes softly spiced chicken makhani, and a scoop of beetroot and cardamom or cinnamon and carrot ice-cream. Parents can enjoy spicier Indian street food and the craft beer.

From Bill's, stroll via **Jubilee Square**, now programmed as an outdoor space by innovative arts venue the **Basement** (p86). Look out for pop-up performances and installations. On rainy days, the **Jubilee Library** (Jubilee Street, 01273 290800) is a godsend, with its lively children's area decorated with the ceramic 'Wall of a Thousand Stories'. There's a graphic novel selection for older kids, spacious baby-changing facilities and great coffee.

Cross Church Street for New Road and the entrance to **Pavilion Gardens**, where you can point out the statue of famous local music hall comedian Max Miller (and embarrass them with one of his 'cheeky chappy' routines). Tell them there's a chippy across town that displays a selection of his flamboyant suits (it's Bardsley's). The red ropes inside the Royal Pavilion itself can be frustrating for eager explorers. But there's plenty to enjoy on the outside. This is a popular busking spot, and toddlers love running round the Gardens, with their low fences and leafy hiding places. And the palace itself is a fantastical creation that looks as if it was made from giant iced gem biscuits. Beat that, Disney. **Brighton Museum** (p73) shares the gardens, and is free. Popular exhibits for younger visitors include the Punch & Judy booth, table football and, of course, the Prince Regent's enormous breeches. Listen out for Brumel, the giant fibreglass museum cat, who sits audibly snoozing in the entrance.

Loop back to Church Street, and in to the heart of North Laine. Children love the street art in this area, where brightly coloured murals and curious characters surprise you from almost every turn. On café-lined Gardner Street, you'll find a run of toy and baby shops, sweet shop **Cybercandy** (no.15; www.cybercandy.co.uk) and **Komedia** (p86), which programmes regular children's theatre and films. It's recently sprouted a huge pair of can-can legs. On cobbled Kensington Gardens, you'll find skateboard, scooter and juggling emporium **Oddballs** (p84); **Snooper's Paradise** (p85), a huge fleamarket with a high turnover of vintage toys; and **Get Cutie** (p83), where you can pick up a mini Dr Seuss dress or space rocket shirt. Follow the flow of shoppers on to Sydney Street, home to **Dave's Comics** (p83). Turn right down Trafalgar Street to reach crafty toy shop **Rocket Science** (p85).

The new **Open Market** (p145) is a few minutes' walk along London Road, and houses permanent cafés and creative shops as well as pop-up fairs and food stalls. There are often free children's workshops and demos here, and a choice between artisanal ice-cream or a gloriously un-reconstructed 99. Pick up Greek or Goan, falafel wraps or Real Patisserie pastries as you cross the Open Market on your way to the **Level** (p132) for a picnic tea in the park. **Bardsley's** (p135), with the Max Miller memorabilia, is just around the corner if only fish and chips will do.

Summer afternoons at the newly renovated Level are a more recent Brighton pleasure. The landscaped park – with its skate park, pétanque area and run-through water fountains, plus a playpark with seagull ride-ons and a shark in the sandpit – is a good place to retreat to when the seafront gets rowdy.

As the evening draws in, check out the programme at **Emporium Theatre** (p146), housed in an old church back on London Road. The shabby-chic café-bar is large, atmospheric and welcoming, with cosily furnished nooks, picturebooks and hot chocolates. Recent family-friendly shows have included a new musical adaptation of *The Jungle Book*. Alternatively, catch a bus or taxi up to Seven Dials, where popular family pub-restaurants include the **Dyke** (p105) and **Good Companions** (p106). Have a quick sniff round the eccentric and evocatively musty **Booth Museum** (p102), with its beady-eyed taxidermy, Sussex dinosaur bones and 'merman', before crossing the road to **Dyke Road Park**.

With its safe children's play area and elevated views of the sea, this has always been a popular spot to catch the last of the day's rays. Now you can enjoy sundown looking over the sea from the lawned terraces at the **Brighton Open Air Theatre** (p108), where shows run from May to September up to five nights a week.

ITINERARIES

London to Brighton Bike Ride

Biking Brighton

Bikes and Brighton aren't exactly new lovers: this, after all, is a city of students, families, Green voters, and MAMILs (middle-aged men in lycra). It's always been a popular spot for cycling races and meets, too. The London to Brighton Bike Ride, which celebrated its 40th anniversary in 2015, brings 28,000 cyclists from the capital to the coast every June. Most summers you can watch the World Naked Bike Ride wending its way from the Level to the naturist beach, a wonderfully carefree if occasionally wince-inducing sight.

But there's never been a better time to explore the city on two wheels. Brighton Station now has a £1.5-million Cycle Hub, incorporating smartcard-secure storage for 500 bikes, a spinning gym, a café and a workshop offering everything from a quick tune-up to a full rebuild. The city's first bike café, **Velo** (p143), has

established itself as a community hub at the centre of renovated park the Level, welcoming an influx of riders from London. The city even has a nationally acclaimed bike train, which runs stewarded rides to the retro boomings of the ghetto blaster wedged in the leader's bicycle basket. The Greens, meanwhile, have steadily been improving road safety, with a 20mph city-centre speed limit and new cycle lanes all over the city.

Sure, Brighton is also known for its big fat hills. But head for the seafront and you can revel in nine miles of glorious flatness in the form of the National Cycle Network Route 2 (NCN2). This stretches right across Brighton & Hove, from Rottingdean to Shoreham Harbour, taking in the piers, cafés and crowds of Brighton beach, as well as a dramatic stretch of coastline usually hidden from tourists.

If you're arriving by train, and bringing your own wheels, check

Arriving by train

buy, or accessorise, you'll find the first of many independent bike shops a few paces down Trafalgar Street: **Velo Vitality** (p85). A little further down Trafalgar Street you'll pass **Magazine Brighton** (p84), a new shop dedicated to independent magazines – pop in for the latest copy of beautiful British cycling mag *Rouleur*.

Whatever you're riding, launching down Trafalgar Street is an excellent way to test your brakes. This is Brighton's steepest cycle lane – too steep for horses, in fact, which is why a special route had to be built in the mid 1800s for horse-drawn cabs to access the station. (The cobbled road still exists, but is closed off and locked behind doors opposite the Prince Albert pub.)

Emerging from Trafalgar Street opposite St Peter's Church, pick up the cycle lane that runs parallel to the church and left towards the Level (keeping an eye out for the owner of nearby independent shop **Baker Street Bikes**, p144, who rides a green 'tall bike'). At the Level, you can pull in to Velo Café for an all-round pitstop. On Saturday mornings, up to 90 cyclists of all abilities gather here for ride-outs, though on weekdays you're more likely to be sharing the scene with kids on stabilisers.

Many cycle north from here along Lewes Road to Stanmer Park (a popular destination for mountain bikers), or to nearby **Preston Park** (p135), with its historic outdoor velodrome. Constructed in 1877, it's thought to be the UK's oldest cycle track, and in its 1950s heyday attracted crowds of 5,000 to watch top cyclists such as Olympic medalist Reg Harris. Rising star Felix English used to train here, and there's currently a local campaign to save racing at the track.

Instead, cross the Level and turn down Grand Parade towards the sea. This area, known as Valley Gardens,

your bike in to the new Cycle Hub while you breakfast at station refreshment rooms the **Cyclist** (p61). No dry sandwiches and dreary coffee here: from 9am you can fuel up for your ride on smoked cod with poached eggs, rice salad and curry dressing – or just grab a sausage bap and a Small Batch coffee and be on your way.

If you're looking to hire, there are three main bike rentals in the city, including **Brighton Sports Company** (p61) next to Brighton Pier, and **Cyclelife Electric** (p186) at the Marina. Opened in late 2014, the latter is the only specialist ebike shop in Brighton, and a sound bet if you want to extend your comfort zone or level up your ability when cycling as a group. Closest to the station is **Brighton Cycle Hire** (p186), specialising in Dutch Amsterdammers. Turn left out of the concourse down Trafalgar Street and you'll find them under the station arches, alongside the Green Door Store music venue, Café Moksha and a vintage market. If you're looking to

ITINERARIES

is next in line for rejuvenation: an approved scheme will include improved cycle lanes and bike parking. Pick up the cycle path bang opposite Brighton Pier, turning left along Madeira Drive towards the bobbing masts of the Marina. On your left stretch the historic Madeira Arches, ornamental cast-iron arches supporting zig-zagging promenade terraces on which 50,000 people gathered during the 2014 Tour of Britain. You'll pass the Madeira Café (famous meeting point for bikers of the motorised variety) and the birthplace of big beat, Concorde 2, and can cycle in leisurely parallel with the **Volks Railway** (p112). Its cute ticket kiosk now neighbours the miniature **Brighton Sports Café**, a kiosk where cyclists can order a coffee or ice-cream without disembarking. There's a handy pump outside too.

Pedal on to the **Marina** (p163), passing Britain's first nudist beach – opened in 1980 and protecting its modesty with big banks of pebbles. For most daytrippers, the Marina, with its chain restaurants, cinema and bowling alley, is the end of the line. In fact, it's a portal to one of the area's most unexpected and inspiring attractions: the **Undercliff Walk** (p165). Reopened in 2013 and popular with cyclists, this seafront path runs along a seawall built between 1930 and 1935 to hold back the erosion of the chalk cliffs. It winds right out to Saltdean, famous for its art deco lido (p167), which is now being reopened. But closer by is a gap in the cliffs just big enough to accommodate **Rottingdean**, a charming village known for its 18th-century smugglers, and once home to Rudyard Kipling.

On sunny days, the bright white of the cliffs is intense. In colder weather, with the sea roaring and crashing unpredictably beneath you, it's like walking a battlement. At low tide,

clamber on rockpools, and try to spot the remaining tracks of the old Volk's Electric Sea Railway (or Daddy Long Legs), protruding like fossils from a fantastical past age. At high tide, you can play a game of daredevil with the waves as they throw themselves up at the wall, sometimes splashing right over the pathway. Just a curve or two of cliff-face behind you, Brighton city centre suddenly feels centuries away.

If you smell bacon, you're nearing **Ovingdean Beach Café**, a kiosk with chairs nestled between cliff and beach. You can order a bacon butty or slice of home-made cake here, joining the odd assortment of dog-walkers, families and thinkers who come to sit companionably and stare at the sea. Or you can push on to the Rottingdean Gap, for lunch at the **Plough Inn** (Vicarage Lane, 01273 390635) next to the village pond and Kipling's old house.

Turning towards the city again, you can make a day of it by following the other arm of the NCN2 out to **Shoreham-by-Sea** (p165), with its atmospheric estuary and arty houseboats. Or pedal just as far as **Hove** (pp148-161), relaxing your pace as the promenade widens for the pastel beach huts and expansive seafront lawns, and stopping before you reach the more industrial contours of Portslade, with its working port. Hove Lagoon, home to Norman Cook's Big Beach Café, is a handy boundary marker. Turn inland here and you can have dinner at the **Urchin** (p159), Hove's new shellfish and craft beer pub, whose boats fish the same waters your senses have been communing with all day.

A quick word on staying over: Brighton's boutique townhouse accommodation isn't always so handy for bikes, but the new **YHA Brighton** (p178), in the fancy former Royal York Hotel, has bike storage – and even the odd double with a roll-top bath, perfect for a post-ride soak.

Brighton by Area

West Pier

City Centre

It may seem strange, but Brighton's city centre is often unappreciated. The sea exerts a magnetic pull on day-trippers, who stream from the station straight down Queens Road and West Street to the beach, and there's a tendency to view everything else within a ten-minute walk of the Clock Tower, at the junction of West Street, North Street and Western Road, as merely a commercial zone.

Certainly, this area is dominated by the crowded shopping areas of **Western Road** and **Churchill Square** (a three-storey mall with more than 80 chain stores including a big new Topshop), and the clubbing destination of West Street. The latter is a vortex of hen and stag parties where the scent of Lynx Pulse seems to steam up from the pavements. But turn an unassuming corner or climb a steep residential hill and Brighton's city centre reveals

plenty of character. Step left or right off Western Road and you'll find yourself in a different world, with many of the city's best pubs, small independent theatres and restaurants. There's the odd architectural surprise, too: look out for the cartoonishly Gothic Wykeham Terrace (a refuge for fallen women in the 1830s). Just across the street, at the foot of Dyke Road, is the **Rialto Theatre**, which opened in 2014 in another Grade II-listed Gothic building.

The section between Western Road and the sea is also home to most types of cuisine, from fish restaurants overlooking the West Pier to atmospherically windswept cafés and the takeaway joints of Preston Street. In this area you'll find the original **Gingerman**, modest birthplace of the nationally acclaimed Gingerman Restaurants group, and nook-and-cranny filled

Brighton Bandstand

Clock Tower

19th-century pub the **Lion & Lobster**. It became Brighton's most expensive pub in 2014 when it was bought by a London company for £4.5 million.

After a period in the doldrums, **Western Road** itself is picking up steam. Local vegetarian success stories **Foodilic** and **Iydea** have opened second eateries here, **Small Batch Coffee** has arrived on the border with Hove, and a desultory old lighting shop is now home to large independent ice-cream emporium **Jo Jo's Gelato**. **Queens Road**, too, has found new purpose, now spoiling you for choice with small stylish coffee shops.

But the big city centre news is down at the seafront, where the **i360** is the focus of a £5 million regeneration project that also encompasses the **West Pier Arches**, a section of the Victorian Kings Road Arches that had fallen into disuse. At the time of writing, work had begun on the 530-foot-tall observation tower, set to open in summer 2016. In summer 2014, ten new shops, including **Artist Anon** and the **Lollipop Shoppe**, opened in 26 beautifully renovated, cream-panelled arches. But until the tower is completed, it is still the skeletal remains of the **West Pier** that draw the eye.

This is also the location of the restored **Brighton Bandstand**, where you'll often spot couples taking their wedding vows (it's an approved venue for ceremonies). The Bandstand Café beneath may not have the greatest reputation for service, but its terrace is a good place to enjoy the concerts and bands with a beer or wine.

For the purposes of this guide, we are defining the city centre as the area bounded by Western Street, Norfolk Square and Norfolk Road to the West; West Street to the East; and roads leading north from Western Road. You'll also spot a cluster of steep, mostly residential roads to the west of the station, home to several little-known pubs handy for a pre-train pint.

West Street features an eight-screen Odeon and superclub Pryzm.

City Centre

© Copyright Time Out Group 2015
Contains OS data © Crown
copyright & database right 2015

0   200 m
0   200 yds

NEW ENGLAND QUARTER & PRESTON pp 129-147

SEVEN DIALS, MONTPELIER & CLIFTON HILL pp 101-108

HOVE pp 148-162

Brighton Station

TERMINUS ROAD

Brighton Toy & Model Museum

Royal Alexandra Hosp.

St Ann's Well Gardens

SEVEN DIALS

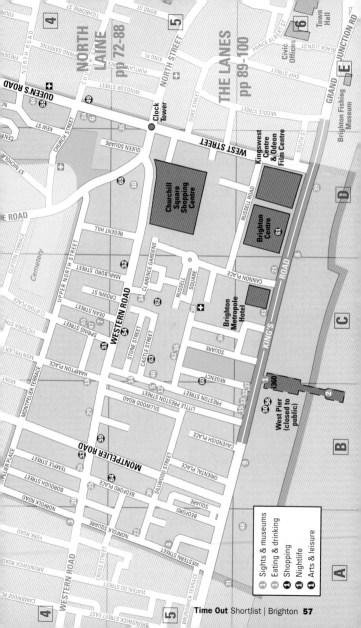

FOUR

TICHBORNE ST

BOND ST

NORTH ROAD

4

5

6

Town Hall

PRINCE ALBERT ST

NORTH LAINE pp 72-88

THE LANES pp 89-100

CHURCH STREET

FREDERICK GARDENS

FREDERICK PLACE

NORTH ROAD

QUEEN'S ROAD

KING PL

WINDSOR STREET

PORTLAND ST

NORTH STREET

Civic Offices

BLACK LION ST

SHIP STREET

MIDDLE STREET

DUKE STREET

LION ST

49

KEW ST

9

28

Clock Tower

QUEEN SQUARE

QUEEN SQUARE

WEST STREET

Kingswest Centre & Odeon Film Centre

GRAND JUNCTION RD

E

CENT

ST NICHOLAS

CHURCH STREET

35

65

10

Churchill Square Shopping Centre

RUSSELL ROAD

SOUTH ST

Brighton Fishing Museum

ROAD

REGENT HILL

39

D

CLIFTON TERRACE

Cemetery

UPPER NORTH STREET

MARLBORO STREET

CLARENCE GARDENS

62

Brighton Centre 61

CLIFTON PLACE

VICTORIA STREET

CROWN ST

DEAN STREET

34

RUSSELL SQUARE

29

CANNON PLACE

21

KING'S

8

C

MONTPELIER TERRACE

MONT

HAMPTON PLACE

SPRING STREET

WESTERN ROAD

STONE STREET

CASTLE STREET

42 16

38

Brighton Metropole Hotel

SQUARE

41

15 51

64

40 12 13

REGENCY

36

ROAD

Regency

LITTLE PRESTON STREET

PRESTON STREET

45 33 32 37

1

West Pier (closed to public)

i360

50 56

2

B

MONTPELIER ROAD

SILLWOOD ROAD

CAVENDISH PLACE

9

MONTPELIER PLACE

63

TEMPLE STREET

BOROUGH STREET

BEDFORD STREET

SILLWOOD STREET

ORIENTAL PLACE

53

26

52

30

20

NORFOLK ROAD

BEDFORD PLACE

BEDFORD SQUARE

3

YORK ROAD

NORFOLK STREET

WESTERN STREET

CROSS STREET

48

A

WESTERN ROAD

BRUNSWICK STREET EAST

WATERLOO STREET

CAMBRIDGE ROAD

BRUNSWICK TERRACE

51

4

5

Legend box:

1. Sights & museums
2. Eating & drinking
3. Shopping
4. Nightlife
5. Arts & leisure

Time Out Shortlist | Brighton **57**

We don't list them in this guide, but if you want them, you can't miss them.

Buses

Venues in this chapter are easily reached on foot from Brighton station. Bus 77 is the only bus that runs along the seafront; it operates at weekends and bank holidays throughout the year, and daily from April to September. Seafront destinations can also be reached by Western Road buses with a short walk. See p184 for a list of Western Road and Brighton station buses.

Sights & museums

i360

NEW *Kings Road (www.brighton i360.co.uk).* **Map** p57 C6 ❶
See box p60.

West Pier

Kings Road, BN1 2FL (www.westpier. co.uk). **Map** p57 B6 ❷
For many, the ruins of the old West Pier are the ultimate Brighton image – made still more iconic by the starlings that swoop around it at dusk. Which explains why the i360 (see box p60) at the pier's head is proving so controversial. The West Pier was built in 1866. It included a pavilion and a large glass-panelled concert hall, and by World War I had become one of the country's leading pleasure piers. But changing holiday habits caused it to fall into neglect after World War II, and it closed in 1975. In the 1980s, it was sold for £100 to the newly formed West Pier Trust, which pleaded for funding to repair it – right up until the storm of 2002 and fire of 2003 that left it in a state of permanent, progressive, and highly poetic ruin. Despite the arrival of the i360, the Trust remains (hopelessly?) attached to the idea of a new West Pier.

Eating & drinking

Roasting sensation **Small Batch Coffee** (see box p155) has a branch at 111 Western Road (01273 731077, www.smallbatchcoffee.co.uk), while the Western Road outpost of **Foodilic** (p96) is at no. 163 (01273 760190, www.foodilicbrighton.co.uk).

Bankers

116A Western Road, BN1 2AB (01273 328267, www.bankers-restaurant.co.uk). **Open** 11.30am-10pm daily (9pm Sun in winter). **££**. **Fish & chips**. **Map** p57 A4 ❸
A standard order averages around a tenner at this large, old-fashioned chippy, but then it does have a chandelier. Takeaways (many destined to be eaten on the beach) queue to the right, while eat-in diners sit at wooden tables; a bar sells bottled beers, liqueurs and Irish coffees. Saturday evenings sees pensioners in tweed suits linger over jelly puddings.

Bedford Tavern

30 Western Street, BN1 2PG (01273 739495). **Open** noon-midnight Mon-Thur, Sun; noon-1am Fri, Sat. **Pub**. **Map** p57 A5 ❹
There are few things more joyful than Sunday piano bingo at this 200-year-old pub. It has been restored to glory as a mainly gay and lesbian but super-straight-friendly local. Think country pub – with occasional drag acts. It has kept many of its original features, including exposed beams, a fireplace and – if the ghost stories are to be believed – even some of yesteryear's clientele. Luckily, they don't seem to mind landlord Adam Brooks encouraging singalongs from *The Jungle Book*.

Binari

31 Preston Steet, BN1 2HP (01273 567004, www.binarikorean.com). **Open** 11.30am-3.30pm, 5.30-10.30pm Mon-Thur; 11.30am-10.30pm Fri-Sun. **££**. **Korean**. **Map** p57 B5 ❺

An authentic Korean restaurant where dishes such as *jjigae* (a spicy tofu stew, here served with brown rice) and *bibimbap* (mixed rice with vegetables and various seasoned meats) arrive in stone bowls, and home-made ice-cream comes in flavours such as plum or ginseng. There are six set menus, each a mini-education in the cuisine.

Blue Man

8 Queens Road, BN1 3WA (01273 726003, www.bluemanbrighton.com). **Open** 10am-11pm Mon-Wed, Sun; 10am-midnight Thur; 10am-2am Fri, Sat. **££. Café-bar/North African**. **Map** p57 E4 ⑥
The Blue Man was one of Brighton's best-kept secrets in its former premises on Edward Street and then Little East Street. Now, the North African restaurant has arrived on the main drag of Queens Road, with an inviting upstairs café-bar and a beautifully lit basement venue. Dishes such as Algerian spicy lamb sausages are all served with dips, bread and fragrant mixed salads. The basement is a Brighton Fringe venue and hosts intimate live music, comedy and spoken word.

Brighton Beer Dispensary

NEW *38 Dean Street, BN1 3EG (01273 710624, www.brightonbier.com).* **Open** noon-11pm Mon-Thur, Sun; noon-midnight Fri, Sat. **Pub**. **Map** p57 C4 ⑦
Kemp Town brewery Brighton Bier Company have gone into partnership with London's Late Knights to open their first pub – so you'll find two beers from each on the pumps at any one time, with choices changing twice a day at busiest times. Other ales are 'gravity dispensed' straight from casks to the left of the bar, giving proceedings an earthy feel. It's a lovely little local, filled with light from the greenhouse-style back room.

Brighton Music Hall

NEW *126-137 Kings Road Arches, BN1 2FN (01273 747287, www.brighton musichall.co.uk).* **Open** *Winter*

10am-5pm daily. *Summer* 9am-midnight daily. Closing times can vary; sometimes 2am. **££. Bar**. **Map** p57 D6 ⑧
The largest heated beach terrace in Brighton is the main draw at this seafront music bar, which spans eight of the Kings Road Arches and sucks up passing traffic in the summer months like plankton by a whale – just as Gemini did on the same site until 2011. Run by the people behind OhSo Social, with a restaurant and cocktail bar upstairs, it has continued with its precessor's live music tradition. Bands play on the outside terrace from April to September when the sun shines.

Bucket & Spade Café

NEW *26-28 Kings Road Arches, BN1 2LN (01273 220222, www.bucketandspade cafe.co.uk).* **Open** 9am-5pm daily. Later summer hours. **£. Café**. **Map** p57 B6 ⑨
A popular spot for breakfast, this cosy café with cute arched windows is also a favourite with families using the seafront playground. In summer 2014, new owners freshened things up and doubled the amount of seating inside and out. They serve burgers, salads, sandwiches, milkshakes and several kids' options.

Café Arcadia

15B Imperial Arcade, BN1 3EA (01273 326600, http://cafearcadia.com). **Open** 8.30am-6pm Mon-Sat; 9am-6pm Sun. Closed some Suns. **£. No credit cards.** **Café**. **Map** p57 D5 ⑩
This independent tearoom has its entrance in the Imperial Arcade and a large window on to Dyke Road. Baked potatoes, prawn salads, macaroni cheese and teacakes are served beneath photos of the Brighton of yesteryear by waitresses you nostalgically imagine spending their earnings on the pier.

Café Coho

83A Queens Road, BN1 3XE (01273 719126, www.cafecoho.co.uk). **Open** 7am-6.30pm Mon-Fri; 9am-6pm Sat, Sun. **£. Café**. **Map** p56 E3 ⑪

Towering over the past

Brighton's dramatic new seafront attraction.

A futuristic 530-foot-high observation tower located on the seafront, at the head of the derelict West Pier, is Brighton's latest dramatic attraction.

In 1866, Brighton's West Pier (p58) opened to the public with the futuristic-sounding invitation to 'walk on water'. In summer 2016, the **i360** (p58) will launch with an invitation to 'walk on air' in what, for lack of a precedent, is being called a 'vertical cable car'.

Taller than the London Eye (and from the same architects, Marks Barfield), the i360 is a vertical viewing platform affording visitors 360-degree views from 450 feet above sea level. They will reach these dizzying heights not in an elevator but in a ring-shaped pod that will travel up and down a slender stem, carrying up to 200 passengers at a time. In early projections it looks rather like a steel tornado.

Even as work began on the tower in July 2014, locals remained divided as to whether the i360 would be an eyesore or icon. The Brighton Wheel (p111), installed along Madeira Drive in 2011, has already changed the seafront view to the east. This build is all the more controversial for taking place on the site of the skeletal but still beloved West Pier. It involves restoring and reinstating the pier's old Victorian tollbooths, while part of its cast-iron supporting structure will be used in the new visitor centre. The West Pier's 'sea island', though, will be left well alone.

The i360 is expected to attract at least 70,000 visitors per year, and generate 440 new full-time jobs. And it has already been the catalyst for the restoration of the West Pier Arches, now filled with a variety of independent outlets and craft studios that together make up a whole new cultural quarter.

One thing's for sure: when the 17 steel cans for the tower arrive across the North Sea from Holland in summer 2015, delivered direct on to the beach by barge, the whole city will be watching.

Coho's other premises on Ship Street in the Lanes feel more characterful and buzzy, but this café is extremely handy for the station and offers the same beautifully treacly house espresso and pancake-tower breakfasts. The narrow space has been made stylish with a now very familiar formula: blackboards, dangling lighting and exposed brick.

Casalingo

29 Preston Street, BN1 2HP (01273 328775, www.casalingorestaurant.com). **Open** 5-11pm daily. **££**. **Italian**. Map p57 B5 ⑫

Visitors seeking authentic Italian food are lucky if they stumble on Casalingo. It's always had a casual air (including a wall of approving customer graffiti), but this cosy restaurant takes its cooking seriously. The menu is divided into familiar pasta and risotto, meat and fish options; chef's specials have included spaghetti with clams, garlic and chilli.

Caxton Arms

36 North Gardens, BN1 3LB (01273 380232, www.caxton-arms.com). **Open** 4-11pm Mon; 4pm-midnight Tue-Thur; noon-1am Fri, Sat; noon-10pm Sun. **Pub**. Map p56 E3 ⑬

Concealed down a street of pretty white Regency cottages, this pub is named after William Caxton, who introduced the printing press to England. The left-hand bar is furnished with old books and a fireplace; the right-hand bar, with its white tables and snug, has great Thai food. There are also cocktails, a heated garden and a pool table in the cellar.

Chequers

45 Preston Street, BN1 2HP (01273 220855, www.chequersbrighton.co.uk). **Open** 11am-midnight Mon-Thur; 11am-2am Fri, Sat; noon-midnight Sun. **Pub**. Map p57 C5 ⑭

The log fire and lovely bar staff have, since a refurbishment and change of management in 2013, made this little pub an excellent refuge from the busy shops on Western Road. In February 2015, it changed hands again. Hopefully the new owners will keep the DJ and open mic nights – and the takeaway beach basket service for picnicking on the beach.

China Garden

88-91 Preston Street, BN1 2HG (01273 325124/325065, www.chinagarden. name). **Open** noon-11.30pm daily. **££**. **Chinese**. Map p57 B6 ⑮

A 150-seat Chinese restaurant just off the seafront, with a harsh black frontage giving way to a warm, carpeted space framed by sofas and with a tinkling piano. Try squid cakes and turnip paste from the imaginative dim sum menu between noon and 4pm, and East Sussex-sourced Ying Yang dover sole for dinner.

Cocktail Shack

34 Regency Square, BN1 2FJ (01273 321196, www.cocktailshackbrighton. co.uk). **Open** 5-11pm Mon-Thur, Sun; 5pm-midnight Fri, Sat. **Bar**. Map p57 C5 ⑯

This isn't the sort of cocktail bar where people wear heels – some even take their shoes off, the better to enjoy the living-room ambience. Following a 2015 refurb, the Artist Residence hotel's in-house drinking den is now homelier than ever, with cushions, lamps, a rug and incense burning. A new drinks menu includes bar manager Dean's signature, the Hoptical Illusion (hops, green tea, grapefruit and gin). The Shack is now dehydrating its own ingredients and making its own purées, with bar snacks such as Kentucky fried rabbit and scallops sliders provided by the hotel's new restaurant, the Set (p66).

Cyclist

NEW *Brighton Train Station, Queens Road, BN1 3XP (01273 724879, www.thecyclistbrighton.co.uk).* **Open** 9am-10.30pm Mon-Fri; 9am-10pm Sat, Sun. **££**. **Café/bar/modern British**. Map p56 E2 ⑰

BRIGHTON BY AREA

Inspired by old-fashioned train station refreshment rooms, this spacious new station restaurant and bar takes its design cues from its location. It has a suitcase-lined bar, vintage waiting-room sofas, and lighting sourced from an old train station in Europe. The broad daytime menu is supplemented by a fancier dinner menu: herb-crusted chicken and wild mushroom risotto, or pork loin with bubble and squeak.

Estia

3 Hampton Place, BN1 3DA (01273 777399, www.estiabrighton.com). **Open** 6pm-late Mon-Sat. **££**. **Greek**. **Map** p57 C4 ⑱

This family-run Greek-Cypriot restaurant is a popular place for parties, with fairy lights behind its white cottage windows and a range of traditional Greek dishes such as souvlaki, plus the likes of sirloin steak in Metaxa brandy.

Evening Star

55-56 Surrey Street, BN1 3PB (01273 328931, www.eveningstar brighton.co.uk). **Open** noon-11pm Mon-Thur, Sun; noon-midnight Fri; 11.30am-midnight Sat. **Pub**. **Map** p56 E3 ⑲

A rustic haven for real-ale types, this pub was the birthplace of the fabulous Dark Star brewery, which vacated its basement to expand in 2001. Several Dark Star creations are always on offer, alongside guest pumps and a host of unpronounceable Flemish bottles. Seasonal ales include the Winter Meltdown, brewed with chocolate in a cask conditioned with ginger.

La Florentina

50 Norfolk Square, BN1 2PA (01273 774049). **Open** noon-3pm, 6-10pm Tue-Sun. **££**. **Italian**. **Map** p57 B4 ⑳

Holding out barnacle-like against the fast-food places and estate agents along this stretch of Western Road, this tiny Portuguese-run Italian restaurant is a 1970s timewarp: chicken kiev and melon balls, white textured walls that look as if someone hoed up a wedding cake, and coffee and a mint to finish. Trendy, thankfully, it ain't.

GB1 at the Grand

97-99 Kings Road, BN1 2FW (01273 224300, www.grandbrighton.co.uk). **Open** 12.30-4pm, 5-10pm Mon-Sat; 1-4pm, 5-10pm Sun. **£££**. **Seafood**. **Map** p57 C6 ㉑

The daddy (or, rather, rich maiden aunt) of the seafront hotels updated its restaurant in 2013. GB1's *raison d'être* is seafood, and its centrepiece is a circular bar where 20 diners can sip champagne and slurp oysters while watching the chefs up close. The crisp white linen, marble pillars and brushed steel bar all say 'luxury', but chef Andrew White thinks enjoying the local catch shouldn't be an exclusive experience. Alongside the £150 beluga caviar and the lobster platter is a £40 midweek menu for two.

Gingerman

21A Norfolk Square, BN1 2PD (01273 326688, www.gingermanrestaurants. com). **Open** 12.30-2pm, 7-10pm Tue-Sun. **£££**. **Modern British**. **Map** p57 A5 ㉒

The original Gingerman (the family also owns three local gastropubs) is squeezed into a townhouse down from Norfolk Square and specialises in hearty modern British dishes. Indulgent dinner options might pork belly with crumble, black pudding, pressed potato and burnt quince, followed by rhubarb soufflé, ice-cream and custard. Set lunches are good value. The decor got an update in early 2015, with exposed brick, copper-top tables and more spacious seating.

Grocer & Grain

1 Surrey Street, BN1 3PA (01273 823455). **Open** 7am-7.30pm Mon-Fri; 8am-7.30pm Sat; Sun 9am-7pm. **£**. **Deli**. **Map** p56 E3 ㉓

Local fruit and veg is piled artfully in crates outside, and when it's not fresh enough to sell they turn it into delicious cakes or frittatas – in fact, Jamie Oliver turned to this deli for a programme about food upcycling. Grains and oils line the shelves, spices and nuts are stacked in small reusable tubs, and there's organic shandy in the chiller cabinet. It's a good place to grab a fresh baguette and a slice of chocolate orange vegan cake on your way from the station to the beach, or there's some crate seating under an awning on the pavement.

Hope & Ruin

NEW *11-12 Queens Road, BN1 3WA (01273 235793).* **Open** noon-midnight Mon-Wed, Sun; noon-2am Thur-Sat. **Bar**. **Map** p57 E4 ㉔

Formerly the Hope, this bar and venue just down from the station earned its place in music fans hearts for the quality and intimacy of the gigs (Bonnie Prince Billy, The Strokes and Adele have all passed through) rather than the stylishness of the experience. And quite right, too. But in its new guise as the Hope & Ruin, it's doing both. Upstairs, the stage is bigger and higher, you no longer have to traverse the entire audience to reach the bar, and the capacity has gone up to 150. Happily, the disco ball remains. Downstairs, they've turned a bath into a sofa, propped a table on a washing machine, and converted half a caravan into a kitchen serving poutine and hotdogs. Will bands want to play anywhere else?

Iydea

105 Western Road, BN1 2AA (01273 965904). **Open** 9.30am-10pm Mon-Sat; 9.30am-5.30pm Sun. **£**. **Vegetarian**. **Map** p57 B4 ㉕

Regular winners of vegetarian food awards, this reasonably priced and speedy canteen-style café has hit on a winning concept. Once you've picked your main course (enchilada, say, or a crisp mushroom and broccoli filo pie), your plate is stacked with seasonal salads and vegetables and drizzled with your choice of 11 toppings. This is

the sibling of the original North Laine café, serving double the diners over two spacious floors, and it gets to stay up late – well, past 5.30pm anyway.

Jo Jo's Gelato

NEW *123-124 Western Road, BN1 2LB (01273 771532, www.jojosgelato.co.uk).* **Open** 7am-11pm daily. **£**. **Ice-cream**. **Map** p57 B4 ㉖

Artisan ices and organic gelatos are all very well. But sometimes you just want your ice-cream to be fun. This early-opening and late-closing ice-cream parlour has the biggest and most colourful selection in town, including blue bubble gum, Ferrero Rocher and fig and ricotta. There's even a Red Bull sorbet (for parents hosting the popular children's parties?). There are sundaes in garish glasses, and the hot waffles are popular in winter. Spread over three floors with banquettes as bright as some of the scoops, this is the new venture from the people behind popular local grocers' Taj (p70).

Julien Plumart

48 Queens Road, BN1 3XB. (01273 777412, www.julienplumart.com). **Open** 7am-6pm Mon-Fri; 8am-7pm Sat, Sun (takeaway only for first half hour). **££**. **Pâtisserie**. **Map** p56 E3 ㉗

Raymond Blanc-trained chef Julien Plumart uses French Grand Cru chocolate and sprinklings of gold dust to produce stunning little mousse cakes, eclairs and *galettes des rois*. His signature, the *macaron*, can also be purchased in colourful gift boxes. The place also serves an excellent French onion soup – but the savoury menu is hardly the point.

Kindlewood Pizza

NEW *Brighton Station forecourt, Queens Road, BN1 3XP (no phone).* **Open** varies. **£**. **Pizza**. **Map** p56 E3 ㉘

This mobile pizzeria, in a vintage 1969 Citroën H van, serves ten-inch pizzas from its Bushman wood-fired oven, with a 90-second service promise. Varieties range from a classic margarita to the Kindlewood Blue (mozzarella, smoked pancetta, brighton blue cheese and rosemary), and there's a choice of bases too. Most people take their pizza away but you can pull up a stool and eating from the serving shelf.

Koba

135 Western Road, BN1 2LA (01273 720059, www.kobauk.com). **Open** 8am-7pm Mon-Wed; 8.30am-late Thur-Sat. **££**. **Café/cocktail bar**. Map p56 B4 ②

This independent cocktail joint has expanded into a four-tiered café-bar in exposed brick, steel and wood. There are six seating areas, from the communal picnic tables out front to the private upstairs rooms. By day, it's a popular place for shoppers to relax with a coffee and panini. By night, the long, well-priced cocktail menu rules, featuring both classics and innovations.

Lion & Lobster

24 Sillwood Street, BN1 2PS (01273 327299, www.thelionandlobster.co.uk). **Open** 11am-1am Mon-Thur; 11am-2am Fri, Sat; noon-midnight Sun. **££**. **Pub/British**. Map p57 B5 ③

One of the most popular pubs in Brighton, and not just because of the frisky cross-species signage. Downstairs it's all local drinkers, model ships and dark corners. The first floor is a Regency-style restaurant, divided into four rooms. Climb up more warren-like stairs and you'll find the fantastic two-tier roof terrace, with tastefully concealed televisions and a wood-burning stove. There's food from noon daily, with a late-night menu from 10pm, and live jazz every Sunday evening. In 2014 the pub was bought by London's City Pub Company for a whopping £4.5 million – but it's promising no change.

Meeting Place Café

Promenade, Kings Road, opposite Western Street, BN3 2WN (01273 206417, www.themeetingplacecafe.co.uk). **Open** 7am-sunset daily. No credit cards under £5. **£**. **Café**. Map p57 A5 ③

Ice-cream, toasties, baked potatoes, fish and chips, coffees and eccles cakes – to be enjoyed the windswept way. This seafront café, run by the same family since 1977, sits bang on the seafront between Brighton and Hove, just opposite the peace statue, and affords one of the best views in the city. Think twice about meeting here if you've just had your hair done.

Melrose

132 Kings Road, BN1 2HH (01273 326520, www.melroserestaurant.co.uk). **Open** 11.30am-10.30pm daily. **££**. **Seafood**. Map p57 B6 ③

Although not as prestigious as the Regency Restaurant (p66), probably because of the 1970s-style decor, this seafood restaurant is just as good as its neighbour and picks up much of its overspill. A more narrowly drawn menu makes it the more popular choice for many fish connoisseurs.

New Club

133-134 Kings Road, BN1 2HH (01273 730320, www.thenewclub brighton.com). **Open** 9.30am-10pm Tue-Sun. **££**. **Diner**. Map p57 B6 ③

One of the city's favourite spots for its first meal of the day, thanks in no small part to its 'breakfast burger', replete with fried egg and 'hangover cure dressing'. Also on the menu at this New York-style diner is a series of 'hard brunch beverages' including a Chorizo Bloody Mary and something called a Corpse Reviver that involves an absinthe rinse. The lofty interior, with retro diner chairs and a photo backdrop of NY apartments, is more laid-back homage than cheap imitation.

Pull & Pump

1-2 Clarence Gardens, BN1 2EG (01273 328263). **Open** noon-midnight Mon-Thur, Sun; noon-1am Fri, Sun. **Pub**. Map p57 C5 ③

clockwise from top left: Cyclist p61; Queensbury Arms p66; Talk of Tea p67; Lion & Lobster

Tucked just off Western Road along from Brighton Little Theatre, this candlelit pub is not as old-fashioned as it first appears. It has a surprisingly huge stock of tequila: 64 different types, from blue agave to whatever it is they serve with the spicy tomato chaser. Pop-up kitchen Brighton Burger often does its gourmet burger thing here too.

Quadrant

12-13 Queens Road, BN1 3FA (01273 733238). **Open** 11am-midnight Mon-Thur; 11am-2am Fri, Sat; 11am-midnight Sun. **Pub**. Map p57 E5 ㉟
This grade-II listed pub opposite the Clock Tower, dating back to 1864, is a dark and masculine affair popular with real-ale drinkers as well as shoppers breaking for a quick refresher. The low-ceilinged upstairs lounge hosts gigs, open-mic nights and the Laughing Horse comedy club every Saturday.

Queensbury Arms

Queensbury Mews, BN1 2FE (01273 328159). **Open** noon-11pm Mon-Thur, Sun; noon-midnight Fri, Sat. **Pub**. Map p57 C5 ㊱
The smallest pub in Brighton (it just has room for a plaque) is a cosy, gay-friendly retreat for theatrical types round the back of the Hilton. The bar is lined with signed black-and-white photos, and legend has it that Sir Laurence Olivier once drank half a bottle of champagne here in disguise.

Regency Restaurant

131 Kings Road, BN1 2HH (01273 325014, www.theregencyrestaurant. co.uk). **Open** 8am-11pm daily. **££**. **Seafood**. Map p57 B6 ㊲
The red-and-cream-fronted Regency has become synonymous with the 'Brighton experience', and is still the standard recommendation for seafood. It has expanded to meet demand (with a menu that includes pasta, roasts and veggie options), meaning its corner of Regency Square is always heaving. The menu changes according to the catch,

and fish is served in good-sized portions with chips, new potatoes or salad.

Regency Tavern

32-34 Russell Square, BN1 2EF (01273 325652). **Open** noon-11pm Mon-Thur; 11am-midnight Fri, Sat; noon-11pm Sun. **££. Pub/pub food**. Map p57 C5 ㊳
Where else could you find six real ales on tap and a disco ball in the urinal? Tucked in the twitten between two squares, this Shepherd Neame pub is a pocket of seaside baroque, with striped silk wallpaper, gilt mirrors and gold cherubs. The not-for-profit Cherub's Kitchen serves daily, with a very popular Sunday lunch, and there's classical and cabaret-style music from the piano.

Riddle & Finns

139 Kings Road Arches, BN1 1FN (01273 821218, www.riddleandfinns. co.uk). **Open** noon-late Mon-Sat. **£££**. **Seafood**. Map p57 D6 ㊴
The table at the little arched first-floor window is one of the most romantic spots in town. Riddle & Finns is a classy seafood restaurant in the sea-front arches; its terrace is a great place to enjoy the music from neighbouring Brighton Music Hall (p59). Unlike the original Riddle & Finns in the Lanes – a champagne and oyster bar where diners sit on stools and communal tables – this is a more traditional restaurant: you can book, for one thing, and there are individual tables. Local fishermen of yore look down from black and white photos as you pick through crab or lobster platters or linger over a pan-fried fillet of local bream with sultana couscous.

Royal Sovereign

66 Preston Street, BN1 2HE (01273 323289, www.royalsovereign.pub). **Open** noon-midnight Mon-Thur; noon-1am Fri-Sun. **Pub**. Map p57 C5 ㊵
It can get very busy in this townhouse pub – especially for Sunday roast. But if you time it just right, the roaring fires, red velvet window banquettes, candles and chandeliers still make

it a great place to escape the shops or the rain. There's a good range of craft beers, bottled and on draft, at the friendly island bar.

Salt Room

NEW *106 Kings Road, BN1 2FU. (01273 929488, www.saltroom-restaurant. co.uk).* **Open** noon-10.30pm daily. **£££. Seafood.** Map p57 C6 ⓷

The Hilton Metropole's had a £3.75 million refurb, and with it comes this new seafood restaurant from the people behind the acclaimed Coal Shed (p94). Like its sister restaurant, the Salt Room's sustainable, seasonal menu features the freshest catch, from spiced monkfish with pickled cauliflower, yoghurt and ginger to a fruits of the sea sharing board, or a whole fish grilled over charcoal (charcoal also having been a key word, one suspects, on the designer's mood board). The place has swanky floor-to-ceiling windows and a shaded and heated terrace (open March to October).

The Set Restaurant

NEW *33 Regency Square, BN1 2GG (01273 324302, http://artistresidence brighton.co.uk).* **Open** 12.30-3pm, 6-9.30pm Tue-Thur; 12.30-3pm, 6-10pm Fri, Sat. **££. Modern British.** Map p57 C5 ⓸

A fresh concept (three set menus, running side by side and evolving every week) and two kick-ass cooks: Dan Kenny, formerly head chef at the Gingerman (p62), and Simone Bonner, formerly at the helm at the Ginger Pig (p156). In the basement of the Artist Residence hotel (and with plenty of modern art on display), this new restaurant features an open kitchen, industrial touches of concrete and corrugated iron, and tables made from bits of the old West Pier. Dinner might include octopus with bacon and seaweed broth and black onions; lunch could be soy-glazed trout with grapefruit marmalade and tempura chillies. The Set's open kitchen also services

the hotel's new café, the Set of Scales, so pop next door if you're after a casual fish slider and beer.

Sunoso

NEW *55 Queens Road, BN1 3XD (01273 739776, www.sunoso.co.uk).* **Open** 11am-9pm Mon-Sat. **Pan-Asian.** Map p56 E3 ⓸

High-speed, healthy Asian food-to-go has arrived on Queens Road. Grab a cup of glass noodles in chicken broth, a 'fish lover' sushi tray with beautiful salmon, prawn and tuna bundles, or a box of donburi rice with tofu and mushroom curry – all devised in consultation with a local nutritional therapist. Most people buy takeaway, but there are a few seats along the wall.

Sussex Yeoman

7 Guildford Road, BN1 3LU (01273 327985). **Open** noon-11pm Mon-Sat; noon-9pm Sun. **Pub.** Map p56 E3 ⓸

Poll the city on its favourite Sunday roast, and the Sussex Yeoman often comes out top. A small corner pub in one of the steep residential roads to the right as you exit the station, it specialises in traditional pub grub served to high standards, in decent-sized portions. The tasteful touches of pink and green don't seem to have put off the liquid-only locals.

Talk of Tea

26 Spring Street, BN1 3EF (01273 748444, www.talkoftea.co.uk). **Open** 10am-6pm Mon-Sat; noon-5pm Sun. *Games night* 7-10pm Thur. **Tea shop.** Map p57 C4 ⓸

Fancy a tea break? This east European-inspired tea house hidden in a residential street may have space for only 24 inside, but it serves over 60 different brews, including rum- and vanilla-flavoured black tea and a white-tipped tea from the foothills of Mount Kilimanjaro. You can also order afternoon tea at any time of the day. Thursday is games night, with backgammon, carrom, chess and cards from 7pm to 10pm.

top: Bert's Homestore;
bottom left: Fair p70;
bottom right: Eden p70

Sustainable Fashion

MAN

PERFUME £35
REFILL £23

£15

£15

www.thefairshop.co.uk

Taylor St

28 Queens Road, BN1 3XA (01273 735466, www.taylor-st.com). **Open** 7.30am-5.30pm Mon-Fri; 8.30am-6pm Sat; 10am-5pm Sun. **£**. **Café**. **Map** p57 E4 46

Taylor St distinguishes itself on the increasingly caffeine-rich Queens Road. Its rather gloomy L-shaped interior is lifted by bright red chairs and friendly service. The excellent breakfasts and brunches also make it a good spot to end an all-nighter before the morning train. Taylor St is a small chain and this is the only branch outside London. It sometimes stays open late on Thursdays.

Tookta's Café

30 Spring Street, BN1 3EF (01273 748071). **Open** 6-10pm Tue-Sat. **£**. No credit cards. **Thai**. **Map** p57 C4 47

The Thai menu at the Office pub in North Laine is always picking up praise, but many aren't aware that the food there is cooked by Tookta – the convivial owner of this cosy purple restaurant-café just off Western Road. There are no surprises on the menu: stir-fries, curries and noodle soups, and crispy starters served with sweet chilli sauce. But the flavours are far from standard. The tofu in particular is unusually tasty, and service always comes with added zing.

World Famous Pump Room

121-122 Kings Road Arches, BN1 2LN (no phone). **Open** May-Sept 9am-9pm daily. Oct-Apr 10am-5pm daily. **£**. **Café**. **Map** p57 A6 48

This seafront pit stop is, as you can see from its name, adept at blowing its own trumpet. But it's hard to argue with the 22 flavours of farm-made ice-cream (from amaretto to ginger and honey), coffee courtesy of Redroaster Coffee House (p118) and location just opposite the volleyball court. It's a traditional place to break a long seafront walk – and is even open on Christmas Day and New Year's Day.

Shopping

Ackerman

124 Queens Road, BN1 3WB. (01273 739942, www.ackermanmusic.co.uk). **Open** 10am-6pm Mon-Sat; 11am-5pm Sun. **Map** p57 E4 49

Ackerman stocks the largest orchestral instrument and sheet music collection in Sussex. These expanded premises now house a big digital piano range (replete with a slightly eerie cardboard cut-out of Jools Holland).

Artist Anon

NEW *50-51 West Pier Arches, BN1 2LN. (01273 739964, www.artistanon.com).* **Open** Summer 10.30am-5.30pm daily. Winter 10.30am-5.30pm Mon, Tue, Thur-Sun. **Map** p57 B6 50

One of ten retail units housed in the newly refurbished West Pier Arches, this is home to local urban designer Artist Anon, who takes his name from his old 1980s graffiti crew. He specialises in paper-cut artworks and hand-printed T-shirts, and on quiet days you can watch him work. Locally resonant designs include a Brighton beach hut.

Bert's Homestore

155-156 Western Road, BN1 2DA (01273 774212, www.bertshomestore. co.uk). **Open** 9am-6pm Mon-Sat; 11am-5pm Sun. **Map** p57 C4 51

This homegrown homewares store is packed with everything one could need to kit out a home in a vaguely retro-kitsch fashion, from cake-stands to cute lunchboxes, bright pink cocktail glasses to shabby-chic breadbins, plus more standard kitchen and bathroom stuff. There are now two further stores, one in North Laine and another in Hove.

C&H Fabrics

179 Western Road, BN1 2BA (01273 321959, www.candh.co.uk). **Open** 9am-5.30pm Mon, Wed-Sat; 9.30am-5.30pm Tue. **Map** p57 C5 52

An old-fashioned department store with three floors' worth of craft materials, homewares, upholstery, handbags, fancy-dress outfits, gifts, children's toys and boardgames, and wedding hats. There's also an in-store café that wouldn't look out of place in a Victoria Wood sketch.

Dance 2
129 Western Road, BN1 2AD (01273 220023, www.dance2.co.uk). **Open** 10am-6pm Mon-Sat. **Map** p57 B4 ⑤
A specialist vinyl store and leading audio equipment supplier, where DJs can pick up the latest bass releases and have a protracted conversation about slip mats with the expert staff. Dance 2 can supply everything you need to start a party, from smoke machines to lighting rigs.

Eden
NEW *69 Western Road, BN1 2HA (01273 722030, www.edenperfumes. co.uk).* **Open** 10am-6pm Mon-Sat; 11am-6pm Sun. **Map** p57 C5 ⑤
This clean white space with optic bottles lining the walls looks like the future of perfume. The staff will help you design your own scent, using natural ingredients, ranging from jasmine and passionfruit to saffron and sandalwood. Or tell them you like Gucci and they'll work on a match. Perfumes are organic, vegan, and use only real flowers, and the refill option is eco-friendly too.

Fair
21 Queens Road, BN1 3XA (01273 723215, thefairshop.co.uk). **Open** 10am-6pm Mon-Sat. **Map** p57 E4 ⑤
The emphasis is on women's fashion – funky banana-fibre frocks, chunky jewellery made from recycled magazines, and some very chic work dresses and jackets – at this fair-trade boutique for shoppers who care both about design and provenance. It also stocks Little Green Radicals childrenswear and toys.

Lollipop Shoppe
NEW *54-55 West Pier Arches, BN1 2LN (01273 945300, www.thelollipop shoppe.co.uk).* **Open** 10am-5.30pm Mon-Sat; 11am-5pm Sun. **Map** p57 B6 ⑤
Lollipop is all about beautiful, innovative design – whether for mugs, tote bags and cushions, or a three-grand-and-upwards Swedish modernist armchair. This is a homecoming for the store, which began in Brighton, moved to London's Spitalfields, and was lured back by the newly refurbished West Pier Arches.

Record Album
8 Terminus Road, BN1 3PD (01273 323853, www.therecordalbum.com). **Open** 11am-4.30pm Mon-Sat. No credit cards. **Map** p56 E3 ⑤
This tiny corner store behind the train station has been selling original film soundtracks and other records since 1948, and should be on the radar of every vinyl geek in the country. Octogenarian owner George Ginn is a true gent. The window display always seems to change according to which films are on TV that week.

Taboo
2 Surrey Street, BN1 3PA (01273 263565, www.tabooshop.com). **Open** 9am-8pm Mon-Sat; 11am-6pm Sun. **Map** p56 E3 ⑤
There's something old-fashioned about Brighton's most famous sex shop, with its small misted-out window. But that doesn't preclude a pleasant welcome, whether you're after DVDs, the latest adult toys, sexy lingerie or perhaps just a 'spank me' ruler.

Taj the Grocer
95 Western Road, BN1 2LB (01273 735728). **Open** 8am-9pm daily. **Map** p57 B4 ⑤
Seasonal vegetables spill out on to the pavement, unusual cereals, pulses and puddings line the shelves, and bhangra music is the soundtrack at Brighton's Middle Eastern and South

Asian organic grocery emporium. Taj also has a deli counter serving home-cooked Lebanese dishes and curries to take away.

Nightlife

See also p58 **Blue Man** for live music, spoken word and DJs; p59 **Brighton Music Hall** for bands on the terrace in summer, and p64 **Quadrant** for gigs, open-mic nights and comedy.

Dungeon Bar

🆕 *12A Regency Square, BN1 2FG (01273 747685, www.dungeonbar brighton.co.uk). Open Summer* 6pm-2am Mon-Sat. *Winter* 6pm-2am Fri, Sat. **Map** p57 C5 ⑥⓪
Brand spanking new, Brighton's only fetish club occupies an intimate basement. Unusually, it's fine to wonder in off the street, and the merely curious can mingle with the hardcore. Equipment includes a coffin and a medieval-style hanging cage alongside an old-school desk and cane. At the helm is Kitten Skye, sex blogger and hostess of Brighton Killing Kittens sex parties – the local wing of the infamous orgy planners.

Arts & leisure

Brighton Centre

Kings Road, BN1 2GR (01273 290131, www.brightoncentre.co.uk). **Map** p57 D6 ⑥①
The Brighton Centre has a standing capacity of more than 5,000 – enough to draw big mainstream touring acts, as well as large-scale events and exhibitions. Following a £1 million facelift in 2012, the concrete exterior looks slightly less like it's been cast from a multi-storey car park, but the look and vibe is still 'big corporate conference centre'.

Brighton Little Theatre

9 Clarence Gardens, BN1 2EG (01273 777748, www.brightonlittletheatre.com). **Map** p57 C5 ⑥②

Lively amateur theatre company the BLT is now in its seventies, and continues to programme everything from Shakespeare to Sondheim, Noel Coward to *The Jungle Book*, at its premises in a former church just off Western Road.

Castle Street Snooker & Leisure Club

22-23 Castle Street, BN1 2HD (382246, www.castlesnookerclub.com). Open 10am-11pm daily. **Map** p57 C5 ⑥③
The 13 full-size snooker tables are brushed after every session and ironed after every six hours of play. If this information excites you, so will the prices – starting at a fiver for an hour. New managers have installed pool tables, fruit machines, a kids' club, an extended bar and a pie-based menu. It's a members' bar, but joining is simple, and only costs £10 a year.

New Venture Theatre

Bedford Place, BN1 2PT (box office 808353, 746118, www.newventure. org.uk). **Map** p57 B5 ⑥④
This attractive community theatre has been putting on amateur productions of popular works since 1956, and now hosts more experimental productions in the smaller downstairs studio. The large Theatre Upstairs reopened as a flexible, modern space in 2013 after a fundraising campaign. Quality varies, but you can have fun listening in on the luvvies in the bohemian saloon bar, which sometimes hosts cabaret performances.

Rialto Theatre

🆕 *11 Dyke Road, BN1 3FE (725230, www.rialtotheatre.co.uk).* **Map** p57 D5 ⑥⑤
This Grade II-listed building has been many things – including a school for the poor, and most recently the New Hero nightclub. It now provides a home for itinerant local satire legends the Treason Show (and a new role as artistic director for their mastermind, Mark Brailsford). The theatre also hosts new plays, musicals and comedy. Downstairs, Bacall's Bar hosts cabaret turns.

Kensington Gardens

North Laine

It's easy to confuse North Laine with the Lanes. But there is a world of difference between the upmarket area of the Lanes (pp89-100) and North Laine, the heart of alternative Brighton, which can be reached by turning immediately right out of the station, then doubling back down steep Tralalgar Street as it goes down under the station forecourt. In this rainbow maze of partially pedestrianised streets you can stock up on Native American spirit flutes, Ninja rope grapples and nu-rave babygros, drink guarana smoothies and eat blissfully happy chickens. The North Laine may not have the exclusive on independent galleries and record shops, salvage yards and vintage stores, but where else would a café (**Inside Out** in Gloucester Road) equip its toilet with a one-way mirror (so loo users can see what's going on outside but people can't see in)?

In the early 19th century, the North Laine was a sprawl of slums and slaughterhouses. Now, it's rarely mentioned without the prefix 'trendy' or 'boho', and at weekends the narrow streets fill with vintage rails and alfresco diners.

Heading down Trafalgar Street past the **Prince Albert** music pub and **Brighton Toy Museum** (nos.52-55, 01273 749404, www.brightontoy museum.co.uk), home to 10,000 toys and models, all – frustratingly for many visiting children – behind glass, most visitors turn left on to Sydney Street, then Kensington Gardens, Gardner Street, Bond Street, and thus to North Street. This route takes in **Komedia**, **Snooper's Paradise**, and two shops long used as bywords for the area's kookiness: the **Brighton Bead Shop** (21 Sydney Street, www.beadsunlimited.co.uk) and **Vegetarian Shoes** (12 Gardner Street, www.vegetarian-shoes.co.uk).

But it's worth exploring the area more fully. This was how Douglas McMaster stumbled upon the perfect site for the UK's first no-waste restaurant. **Silo** is on Upper Gardner Street, which is a great spot for antique-hunting and hosts **Brighton Street Market** every Saturday.

Remember, too, that some of Brighton's best shops are inside others. **Cloth of Habit** (90 Trafalgar Street, 01273 609006, www.clothofhabit.co.uk) sells second-hand designer menswear within DVD shop Timeslip. **One Stop Records** (30 Sydney Street, 01273 123456) is accessed via vintage clothing store Wolf & Gypsy. **Punker Bunker** (34 Sydney Street, 01273 608382) is a tiny punk shop in the basement of Immediate Clothing. And you'll only find cocktail bar **Valentino's** and Japanese restaurant **E-Kagen** if you know where to look.

These streets lead to the sudden Regency splendour of the **Royal Pavilion**, and the neighbouring **Brighton Museum** and **Brighton Dome** arts complex, home of the Brighton Festival (p35). This is the area officially dubbed the city's cultural quarter (though one of Brighton's most exciting live-arts venues, the **Basement**, is back along Kensington Street). The looping **Pavilion Gardens**, home to an outdoor café that was saved from demolition in 2014 following a public backlash, offers a rest-point for shoppers emerging between North Laine and the Lanes. The now pedestrianised New Road (home to the historic **Theatre Royal**) and Jubilee Square (housing the Jubilee Library) are also popular spots to pause and people-watch, and often host pop-up markets and performances.

Buses

All the venues in this chapter are easily reached on foot from Brighton station. No buses run in North Laine.

For a list of North Street and Brighton station buses, see p184.

Sights & museums

Brighton Museum & Art Gallery

Royal Pavilion, 4-5 Pavilion Buildings, BN1 1EE (0300 029 0900, www. brightonmuseums.org.uk). **Open** 10am-5pm Tue-Sun. **Admission** free. **Map** p75 C4 ❶

Located in Pavilion Gardens, this idiosyncratic museum has a grand central gallery (overlooked by the café balcony) filled with 20th-century home design, including a lip-shaped Salvador Dali sofa. A Grayson Perry vase heralds a gallery of 'popular pottery' collected by founder Henry Willet. Upstairs, the history of fashion is traced from George IV's enormous breeches to Fatboy Slim's Hawaiian shirt, and a rather eerie performance gallery includes Vietnamese water puppets and opera masks. Pop a coin in Brummel, the giant snoring cat, on your way out (though sadly he hasn't said thank you for years).

Brighton Royal Pavilion

4-5 Pavilion Buildings, BN1 1EE (0300 029 0900, www.royalpavilion.org.uk). **Open** *Apr-Sept* 9.30am-5.45pm daily. *Oct-Mar* 10am-5.15pm daily. **Admission** £11; £6 reductions. **Map** p75 C4 ❷

King George IV's pleasure palace is a sort of pocket Taj Mahal built for orgies rather than love, and the wonderfully preposterous glacé cherry on Brighton's architectural cake. John 'Marble Arch' Nash designed it between 1815 and 1822 with a free mix of Indian, Chinese and Gothic notes, expressly in pursuit of ornate excess. Inside, the domed Music Room is lit by nine lotus-shaped chandeliers and decorated with dragons, and the Great Kitchen (a favourite with kids thanks to the fake food) pillared with palm trees. The garden hosts a pop-up ice rink and restaurant-bar every winter (www.royalpavilionicerink.co.uk).

See also p86 **Prince Albert**. Restaurants and cafés listed elsewhere with branches in North Laine include **Iydea** (p63; 17 Kensington Gardens, 01273 667992); **Moksha** (p140; Trafalgar Arches); **Small Batch** (see box p155; 17 Jubilee Street, 01273 697597), and **Real Patisserie** (p118; 43 Trafalgar Street, 01273 570719).

Basketmakers Arms

12 Gloucester Road, BN1 4AD (01273 689006, www.thebasketmakersarms. co.uk). **Open** 11am-11pm Mon-Thur; 11am-midnight Fri, Sat; noon-11pm Sun. **Pub. Map** p75 C2 ❸

This neighbourhood pub has eight real-ale hand-pulls, a low-ceilinged sense of history, and a corner for drinkers to spill out on in summer. The tobacco tins lining the walls aren't just vintage gimmicks: open one and you'll find messages and poems left by drinkers of yesteryear; you are welcome to post one of your own.

Bill's

The Depot, 100 North Road (01273 692894, www.bills-website.co.uk). **Open** 8am-11pm Mon-Sat; 9am-10.30pm Sun. **££. Global. Map** p75 C3 ❹

A popular spot for brunch, Bill's originated in a Lewes greengrocer's (p166) and has its Brighton base in a former bus depot. It has survived a corporate buy-up and UK roll-out with some soul, and at weekends there are still enthusiastic queues for fancy fish-finger sandwiches with a glass of Hedgerow Fizz.

Bond St Coffee

NEW *15 Bond Street, BN1 1RD (no phone, www.bondstcoffee.co.uk).* **Open** 8am-6pm Mon-Sat; 10am-5pm Sun. **Café. Map** p75 B4 ❺

The choice of some of the most discerning buyers in Brighton, including Silo (p79) and Semolina (p143), the family-run Horsham Coffee Roaster now has its own stylishly stripped-back coffeehouse. In the cup: single-origin coffees from across Africa and South America.

Burger Brothers

97 North Road, BN1 1YE (01273 706980). **Open** noon-11pm Tue-Sun. **£. Burgers. Map** p75 C3 ❻

The most tweeted burger in Brighton. One 'brother' takes your order, the other pounds the meat and cooks it from scratch. Within five minutes, and starting from a fiver, you'll have a burger so brilliant they don't even bother doing chips. Juicy is a key word, so make use of the window seats.

Chilli Pickle

17 Jubilee Street, BN1 1GE (01273 900383, www.thechillipickle.com). **Open** noon-3pm, 6-10.30pm Mon, Wed-Sat; noon-3pm, 5-10pm Sun. **££. Indian. Map** p75 B3 ❼

The founder of this restaurant trained at Brighton's City College before learning to differentiate his *kolumbu* from his *kachooris* in the kitchens of Dubai. So there's a lot of love for Chilli Pickle (and its life-size painted cow), though mains such as tandoori pheasant breast with orange and chestnut pilau, clove-smoked malai sauce, saffron riatta and ginger chutney don't come curryhouse-cheap. For lunch, try a Railway Tray – available to take away in typically beautiful packaging.

Chocaffinitea

NEW *103 Gloucester Road, BN1 4AP (01273 690515, www.chocaffinitea. co.uk).* **Open** 10am-6pm Mon, Wed-Sat; 11am-6pm Sun. **£. Café. Map** p75 B2 ❽

This new café aims to unmask the raw flavours and nutritional benefits of single-origin and ethically sourced coffee, tea and chocolate.

Coffee @ 33

33 Trafalgar Street, BN1 4ED (01273 462460). **Open** 11am-5.30pm Mon-Fri; 11am-5pm Sat. **Café. Map** p75 B1 ❾

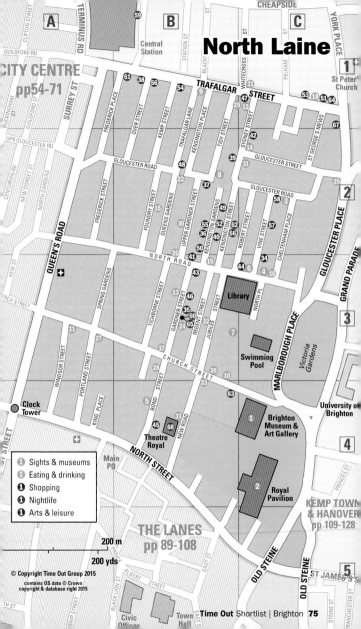

North Laine

CHEAPSIDE

A TERMINUS RD **B** **C** YORK PLACE

59

Central Station

CITY CENTRE
pp54-71

St Peter Church

1

GUILDFORD RD
CLIFTON ST
SURREY ST

61 38 56 54 9 TRAFALGAR STREET 21 53 18 51 64

BUCKINGHAM ST
GUILDFORD RD
UPR GLOUCESTER RD

FREDERICK PLACE
OVER STREET
KEMP STREET
TRAFALGAR LANE
KENSINGTON PLACE
TIDY STREET
WHITECROSS ST
SYDNEY STREET
PELHAM
ST PETER CHURCH

29 47 17 42 14

ST GEORGES MEWS
67

CENTURION RD
NEW DORSET ST
NORTH GARDENS

GLOUCESTER ROAD 48 8 39 31 GLOUCESTER STREET

22 37 GLOUCESTER ROAD 58 3

2

QUEEN'S ROAD

FREDERICK STREET
FOUNDRY STREET
QUEENS GARDENS
UPPER GARDNER STREET

15 49 55 62 57
36 40 66
50 19 44 6 34 16
41
43

KENSINGTON GARDENS
KENSINGTON STREET
ROBERT STREET
VINE STREET
CHELTENHAM PLACE

NORTH ROAD 20

GLOUCESTER PLACE
GRAND PARADE

KEW ST
SPRING GARDENS

13 46
35 60
24 65

TICHBORNE STREET
GARDNER STREET
REGENT STREET
JUBILEE STREET

Library

NORTH PL

3

CHURCH STREET

11 27 17 28 26 10
23
63

WINDSOR STREET
PORTLAND STREET
KING PLACE
BOND STREET
NEW ROAD

7

Swimming Pool

MARLBOROUGH PLACE

Victoria Gardens

University of Brighton

Clock Tower

45 68 33
Theatre Royal

1 **Brighton Museum & Art Gallery**

4

Main PO NORTH STREET

2 **Royal Pavilion**

KEMP TOWN & HANOVER
pp 109-128

1 Sights & museums
1 Eating & drinking
1 Shopping
1 Nightlife
1 Arts & leisure

THE LANES
pp 89-108

OLD STEINE
ST JAMES'S

5

200 m
200 yds

© Copyright Time Out Group 2015

contains OS data © Crown
copyright & database right 2015

ALBERT STREET

Civic Offices

Town Hall

Time Out Shortlist | Brighton **75**

top: Burger Brothers p74;
bottom: Flour Pot Bakery

This minimalist café with a sack-cushioned window seat was one of the first in Brighton to 'do coffee properly', and is friendlier than it looks. You'll find a smattering of snacks on the counter.

Côte

115-116 Church Street, BN1 1UD (01273 687541, www.cote-restaurants. co.uk). **Open** 8am-11pm Mon-Fri; 9am-11pm Sat; 9am-10.30pm Sun. **££. French. Map** p75 B3 ⑩

Brighton took it surprisingly lightly when this big French chain moved into the site of the Old Music Library opposite Brighton Dome – perhaps because it serves dependable classics in a sparkly bistro setting at fair prices. The thickly curtained entrance lends a sense of drama to arrivals.

Earth & Stars

26 Windsor Street, BN1 1RJ (01273 722879). **Open** noon-midnight Mon-Thur, Sun; noon-1am Fri, Sat. **Pub. Map** p75 A3 ⑪

Brighton's first organic pub is a rustic hideaway powered by a solar panel. Meat eaters are well catered for alongside vegans and gluten-avoiders. Central but chilled, it's a popular meeting point for clubs.

E-Kagen

22-23 Sydney Street BN1 4EN (01273 687068, http://ekagen.mitsu-hide.com). **Open** 11.30am-6pm Tue, Wed; 11.30am-3.30pm, 6.30-10pm Thur, Fri; 11.30am-4pm, 6.30-10pm Sat; noon-6pm Sun. **£. Japanese. Map** p75 C1 ⑫

A modest cantina with wallet-friendly but fresh sushi (and a mean crispy chicken *katsu*). A welcome contrast to the glossiness of most sushi joints.

FilFil

21 Gardner Street, BN1 1UP (01273 696289, www.fil-fil.co.uk). **Open** 10am-7pm Mon-Fri, Sun; 10am-8pm Sat. **£. Middle-Eastern. Map** p75 B3 ⑬

Authentic falafel, and it's the best in town. Grab a simple wrap, eat in with a Lebanese flat bread, or grab a table on the street, order a beer, and share a mezze plate laden with houmous, baba ghanoush, vine leaves, *labneh* and olives. It sometimes closes early in winter.

Flour Pot Bakery

NEW *40 Sydney Street, BN1 4EP (01273 621942, www.flour-pot.co.uk).* **Open** 8am-7pm Mon-Sat; 9am-5pm Sun. **£. Bakery/café. Map** p75 C2 ⑭

A bakery with a promo video of a tattooed young man tossing flour. Who knew bread could be so hip? In the shop window, sourdough loaves are displayed like sculptures. Behind stretches the Nordic-style café, with plain wood benches on which to enjoy a fennel and pork sausage roll or slice of pistachio-studded polenta cake. Flour Pot started out as suppliers to Small Batch (see box p155), and looks likely to enjoy a similar trajectory of success. In early 2015, they opened a second bakery on Elm Grove.

Foundry

13-14 Foundry Street, BN1 4AT (01273 697014). **Open** noon-11.30pm Mon-Thur; noon-12.30am Fri, Sat; noon-midnight Sun. **Pub. Map** p75 B2 ⑮

Hidden down a residential street off North Road, this tiny pub (more than 20 people and it's a squash) is often forgotten. Which makes it a great place to hole up in winter, when a real fire crackles beside the deep red sofas. There's just room for the Sunday roasts.

Fountainhead

101-102 North Road, BN1 1YE (01273 628091, www.drinkinbrighton.co.uk/ fountain-head). **Open** noon-9pm Mon-Thur; noon-8pm Fri-Sun. **Pub. Map** p75 C3 ⑯

A friendly, medium-sized pub just where you need it for a North Laine lunchbreak, with light-funnelling window seats, open fires, big wooden tables and highchairs. Plus a big gold Buddha head. The food is tasty if slightly pricey.

BRIGHTON BY AREA

Gelato Guso

2 Gardner Street, BN1 1UP (01273 673402, www.gelatogusto.com). **Open** 11.30am-6pm Mon-Fri; 11am-6pm Sat, Sun. **£. Ice-cream. Map** p75 B3 ⑰

A stylish Italian gelateria that makes its own gelato and *sorbetto* daily in the upstairs kitchen. Flavours include dark Ecuadorian chocolate and mojito. In summer, you'll see its slim waffle cones being licked all over North Laine.

Great Eastern

103 Trafalgar Street, BN1 4ER (01273 685681). **Open** noon-midnight Mon-Thur, Sun; noon-1am Fri, Sat. **Pub. Map** p75 C1 ⑱

Tourists slope straight past this shabby-looking boozer near the bottom of Trafalgar Street. But inside it's a cosy, candlelit scene with scuffed wooden tables and big bookshelves; it's a haven for whisky and bourbon drinkers.

Grow 40

NEW *40 Kensington Gardens, BN1 4AL (01273 622519, www.grow40.com).* **Open** 8.30am-11pm Tue-Sat; 8.30am-6pm Mon, Sun. **££. French. Map** p75 B3 ⑲

We've smelt plenty of herb wafting around Kensington Gardens before – but it's not usually rosemary. At this new French restaurant on a busy corner, there's an emphasis on local sourcing, and herbs and leaves come from the roof-top garden. There are omelettes, open sandwiches and croque monsieur for lunch, and local cheese and charcuterie boards. The sommelier runs a monthly wine club in a 'wine snug' upstairs.

Heart & Hand

75 North Road, BN1 1YD (01273 683320). **Open** noon-11pm Mon-Thur, Sun; noon-midnight Fri, Sat. **Pub. Map** p75 B3 ⑳

Sealed behind a green-tiled façade and stained-glass windows, with posters for gigs long past and a battered old jukebox playing Rolling Stones vinyl, this pub is in its own little world. It occupies a particular soft spot with mods and rockers.

H.en

NEW *87-88 Trafalgar Street, BN1 4ER. (01273 671004, www.henrestaurant. com).* **Open** 10am-11pm daily. **££. Chicken. Map** p75 C1 ㉑

Brighton's first ethical chicken restaurant. The birds all come from Brookland Farm in Surrey, which describes its rearing methods as 'a step back in time but a leap forward in quality'. Eat them grilled or fried, with sweet potato chips, corn on the cob, sauerkraut, onion rings or salad.

La Choza

36 Gloucester Road, BN1 4AQ (01273 945926, www.lachoza.co.uk). **Open** 11.30am-4pm Mon; 11.30am-10pm Tue-Sun. **£. Mexican. Map** p75 B2 ㉒

Mexican street food that's as lively on your tastebuds as the pink paint and floral skull motifs are on your eyes. La Choza keeps this corner buzzing with friends and families cramming down burritos in slightly chaotic fashion. It's fun, filling and great value. Naturally, there's tequila. It now runs the kitchen at the Hare & Hounds (p137) too.

Mash Tun

1 Church Street, BN1 1UE (01273 684951, www.drinkinbrighton.co.uk/ mash-tun, www.burgerkult.co.uk). **Open** noon-2am Mon-Thur, Sun; noon-3am Fri, Sat. **Pub/burgers. Map** p75 B4 ㉓

All paths seem to lead to this turquoise boozer with the pedestrianised New Road as its unofficial beer garden. The crowd blends with that of popular neighbouring pub Fitzherbert's, and there's no spot more animated on a Saturday night. The Mash Tun is even better since the arrival of Burger Kult. Ask for a Chuck Satan: the Remix.

Namul

49 Gardner Street, BN1 1UN (01273 973878). **Open** 11.30am-9pm Mon-Fri; 11am-9pm Sat; noon-7pm Sun. **£. Korean. Map** p75 B3 ㉔

Korean bibimbap prepared to order in a café with one indoor table and more outside. Choose from tofu, mushroom, beef, calamari, sashimi, eel or tuna, add a homemade sauce, then stir with your choice of rice.

North Laine Pub & Brewery

27 Gloucester Place, BN1 4AA (01273 683666). **Open** noon-12.30pm Mon-Wed; noon-2.30am Thur, Fri; 11am-2.30am Sat; 11am-11.30pm Sun. **Pub.** **Map** p75 C2 ㉕

More on the scale of a beer hall, and furnished with long benches and barrels, this pub and microbrewery is in a former nightclub – and still turns up the volume with DJs and live bands at weekends. The steel barrels behind the bar have produced 12 cask beers to date. Laine's Best is a nutty traditional bitter.

Pompoko

110 Church Street, BN1 1UD (07796 001927, www.pompoko.co.uk). **Open** 11.30am-11pm daily. **£.** No credit cards. **Japanese.** Map p75 B3 ㉖

A cheap BYOB Japanese restaurant opposite the Corn Exchange – a perfect location for a pre-show meal or post-pub hangover-buster. The menu includes noodles, curries, teriyaki dishes, salads and highly moreish starters, all under a fiver.

Pop Pie

25 Church Street, BN1 1RB (01273 206294, www.pop-pie.co.uk). **Open** 8am-6pm Mon-Fri; 9am-6pm Sat; 10am-6pm Sun. **£. Greek.** Map p75 A3 ㉗

This Greek-run pie and pastries shop reckons it's a UK first. Try the sesame dough sticks with potato and olives, or a filo and feta *tyropita*. There's even a pastry-based cheeseburger.

Riki Tik

18a Bond Street, BN1 1RD (01273 683844). **Open** noon-2am Mon-Wed, Sun; noon-3am Thur-Sat. **Bar.** Map p75 B3 ㉘

Previously a place to top up your boozy late-night buzz to a background of loud beats, Riki Tik has changed management and is now a Jamaican music bar with tropical-island murals and rasta-hatted stools. It still hits its stride as a venue well after 10pm, though. A sister seafront rum bar opened in 2014 (p100).

Rock*Ola

29 Tidy Street, BN1 4EL (01273 673744, www.rockolacoffeebar.com). **Open** 10.30am-4.30pm Mon-Fri; 9.30am-4.30pm Sat. **£. Diner.** Map p75 B1 ㉙

The free-play jukebox stacked with rockabilly classics and breakfast plates stacked with buttermilk pancakes make this American diner-style café the perfect place for a cheery wake-up call. Even better, it's owned by – and has hidden access to – Wax Factor records next door. On Fridays staff sometimes run a Rock*Ola Burger Bar from 6pm to 9pm.

Silo

NEW *39 Upper Gardner Street, BN1 4AN (01273 674259, www.silobrighton.com).* **Open** 9am-5pm Mon-Wed; 9am-8.30pm Thur-Sat; 11am-5pm Sun. **££. Modern British/bakery.** Map p75 B2 ㉚

See box p81.

Solera

42 Sydney Street, BN1 4EP (01273 673966, www.solera-brighton.co.uk). **Open** noon-10pm Mon-Thur, Sun; noon-11pm Fri, Sat. **££. Spanish.** Map p75 C2 ㉛

A cosy tapas place with wooden stools and steamy windows, where friends chat expansively and dates spark to the sizzle of chorizo and the slosh of rioja. The food's nothing special, but the atmosphere is. There's a sister restaurant, Bodega D Tapas, on Church Street.

Ten Green Bottles

9 Jubilee Street, BN1 1GE (01273 567176, www.tengreenbottles.com). **Open** 11am-10pm Mon, Tue; 11am-11pm

Wed-Sat; noon-9pm Sun. **Wine bar**. **Map** p75 B3 ㉜

A classy but unpretentious drink-in wine shop specialising in European wines from small producers, including a fair splosh of English offerings. There are nibbles and larger plates to match your chosen vintage, and a range of seating to suit your occasion.

Valentino's

Above El Mexicano, 7 New Road (01273 727898, www.elmexicano. co.uk/valentino). **Open** 5pm-late Mon-Sat; 6-11pm Sun. **Cocktail bar**. **Map** p75 B3 ㉝

Visible from the street only as an iron balcony neighbouring the Theatre Royal, this cocktail bar almost justifies a 'best-kept secret' tag. The loungey interior is rather dated and staff enthusiasm variable, but it's impossible not to enjoy knocking back daiquiris overlooking the trees of Pavilion Gardens.

Shopping

Bert's Homestore (p69) has a branch at 10 Kensington Gardens (01273 675 536).

Beyond Retro

42 Vine Street, BN1 4AG (01273 671937, www.beyondretro.com). **Open** 10am-6pm Mon-Wed, Fri, Sat; 10am-7pm Thur; 11am-6pm Sun. **Map** p75 C3 ㉞

The biggest and best-organised, if not the best-value, vintage shop in Brighton. The local branch of the international chain fills a former bus depot, with everything from fur coats to cropped silk shirts carefully batched by style and colour.

Bluebird Tea

NEW *41 Gardner Street, BN1 1UN (01273 681792, www.bluebirdteaco. com)*. **Open** 10.30am-6pm Mon-Fri; 10am-6.30pm Sat, Sun. **Map** p75 B3 ㉟

The UK's first tea mixology company now has its own shop, selling over 50

of its own blends. There are teas to perk you up or help you sleep, boost your metabolism or make you feel Christmassy, covering every flavour and leaf base from rhubarb and custard rooibos to green gingersnap. All are blended on site, beautifully packaged and sold by weight.

Boy Parker

6 Kensington Gardens, BN1 4AL (01273 687768, www.boyparker.com). **Open** 10.30am-5.30pm Mon-Wed; 10.30am-6pm Thur, Fri; 10am-6pm Sat; 11am-5pm Sun. **Map** p75 B2 ㊱

For many Brighton males, clothes shopping consists simply of popping into this independent T-shirt store and seeing which witty new design catches their eye. A cult books range (including a beautifully minimalist *The Great Gatsby*) has recently reinvigorated the stock. Nearby Tee Pony (92 Gloucester Road) has some lovely designs too.

Brighton Sausage Company

28A Gloucester Road, BN1 4AQ (01273 676677, www.brightonsausageco.com). **Open** 11am-7pm Mon-Fri; 10am-7pm Sat; 11am-5pm Sun. **Map** p75 B2 ㊲

There are pork, beef, lamb, game and continental sausages here in endless varieties, such as piri-piri boerewors or pork, pear and stilton, plus wheat- and gluten-free options. There's also a deli counter packed with cheeses, cured meats, pickles and olives, and sausage rolls for a quick snack. An ideal place to stock up for a beach barbecue.

Café Del Golfo

NEW *45 Trafalgar Street, BN2 6LH (07988 775366, www.cafedelgolfo. com)*. **Open** 7.30am-4pm Mon-Sat. **Map** p75 B4 ㊳

The smallest coffee house in Brighton, with standing room for one customer and barista. Squeeze in to buy Italian extra-virgin olive oil and Brazilian coffee (roasted in Naples).

Waste not, want not

Silo shows the way – by not throwing away.

A jam jar containing roughly five millilitres of waste will be guest of honour at **Silo**'s first birthday celebrations in October 2015. That's the sum total said to have been produced by the North Laine's most revolutionary new presence: a restaurant that refuses to throw anything in the bin except the rules.

Your average eaterie, shockingly, chucks away half of what it buys in. As the UK's only zero-waste restaurant, Silo mills its own flour, churns its own butter, and has fermented its own cider from 2.6 tonnes of pears intercepted on their way from Sainsbury's to landfill. Dishes arrive on plates made from recycled plastic bags, and the toilets flush with water from the coffee machine. A gleaming composter sits in pride of place, converting 60 kilogrammes of food scraps in 24 hours.

But young founder and head chef Douglas McMaster isn't here to preach. 'I want to lead by example and create a pre-industrial food system people can taste and smell and see and hear,' he says. 'You can hear the flour milling, see the animals coming in on the farmer's shoulder. I'm not trying to be some cool dude pulling gimmicks out of my sleeves. This is just common sense.'

Originally from Sheffield, McMaster learnt his trade at the likes of London's St John and Copenhagen's Noma, before road-testing the no-waste concept in Melbourne. Dishes such as jerusalem artichoke with goat's cheese sauce and fermented red cabbage, or poached chicken with warm violet potato salad tossed in homemade apple jam and mustard, show considerable skill. But he thinks elitism and perfectionism have traumatised the food industry. 'With a lot of chefs, you get all this glitter on a plate,' he says. 'For me, it's about spending time on the foundational elements of food.' There are only ever five seasonal items on Silo's menu, including whatever swam into the fisherman's net that day.

The dream is to set up several specialist Silo satellites: a 'bean-to-bar' chocolate café would use Venezuelan cacao imported by zero-carbon ship. But McMaster wants to take things slowly: he enjoys having the time to pop out from the pass and introduce diners to the house-made 48-hour sourdough.

A restaurant where you can taste the seasons and reconnect with real food production, Silo isn't about virtuous show. Eating here is romantic and a bit of a revelation.

top: Irregular Choice;
bottom: Jump the Gun p84

Dave's Comics

5 Sydney Street, BN1 4EN (01273 691012, www.davescomics.co.uk). **Open** 10am-6pm Mon, Tue, Thur, Fri; 11am-7pm Wed; 9.30am-6pm Sat; 11am-5pm Sun. **Map** p75 B2 ❸❾

In situ long before the rise of graphic novels to common consciousness and literary acclaim, Dave's Comics is a two-floor treasure trove of cult and children's classics, and Marvel, DC and manga titles. *Tintin* and Maurice Sendak's *Wild Things* brighten the entrance, and the geeks come out in force for New Comic Day on Wednesdays. Two doors down is Dave's Books, specialising in back issues and collectibles.

Get Cutie

33 Kensington Gardens, BN1 4AL (01273 688575, www.getcutie.co.uk). **Open** 10.30am-5.30pm Mon-Fri; 10am-6pm Sat; 11am-5pm Sun. **Map** p75 B2 ❹❶

Skulls and red roses, gun- and guitar-toting cowgirls, and Frida Kahlo complete with moustache: the retro-inspired dress cuts are flattering, but it's the bold illustrated fabrics that make this independent boutique a firm Brighton favourite. Men, how about a naval-tastic shirt in 'All at Sea'?

Guitar, Amp & Keyboard Centre

76-81 North Road, BN1 1YD (01273 665142, www.guitarampkeyboard.com). **Open** 9.30am-5.30pm Mon-Sat; 11am-4pm Sun. **Map** p75 B3 ❹❶

Behind its grungy yellow front the GAK is a veritable superstore of guitars, basses, amps, recording equipment, songbooks and stompboxes, and has probably done more for Brighton's live music scene than any other institution. There is also a drum shop at no.66.

Hope & Harlequin

32 Sydney Street, BN1 4EP (01273 675222, www.hopeandharlequin.com). **Open** 10.30am-6pm Mon, Wed-Sat; 11am-5pm Sun; by appointment Tue. **Map** p75 C2 ❹❷

This high-end vintage boutique has taken second-hand to a glamorous new level. Cashmere jumpers, swing coats and ball gowns are picked for its 'collection' each season, and it offers in-house tailoring as well as bespoke re-creations of originals. The latter service is especially popular with brides-to-be. Wolf & Gypsy, next door, offers a similarly chic edit of 1960s and '70s items.

Infinity Foods

25 North Road, BN1 1YA (01273 603563, www.infinityfoodsretail.co.uk). **Open** 9.30am-6pm Mon-Sat; 11am-5pm Sun. **Map** p75 B3 ❹❸

Workers co-operative Infinity Foods was championing the delights of organic vegetarian and vegan eating long before anyone else in town. This large shop sells wholefoods, confectionery, fruit and vegetables, baby and body-care products, and bread from an on-site bakery. Infinity also has a health-food café at 50 Gardner Street.

Ink-d

96 North Road, BN1 1YE (01273 645299, www.ink-d.co.uk). **Open** 10am-6pm Mon-Sat; noon-4pm Sun. **Map** p75 C3 ❹❹

The antithesis of sterile, whitewashed contemporary art spaces, this commercial gallery opposite Brighton Dome looks more like a tattoo parlour. Inside, you'll find several floors' worth of paintings, prints, sculptures and installations, ranging from the enjoyably obscure to big-name exhibitions from the likes of Peter Blake and Radiohead lino-cutter Stanley Donwood.

Irregular Choice

38 Bond Street, BN1 1RD (01273 777120, www.irregularchoice.com). **Open** 10am-6pm Mon-Sat; 11am-5pm Sun. **Map** p75 B4 ❹❺

You can now buy Irregular Choice footwear at outlets from Covent Garden to Hong Kong, but this is its creator's hometown store. You'll find loud-patterned shoes decorated with bunches of grapes and peacock wings, or with garden gnomes for heels. Designs are getting kitschier by the minute.

Jump the Gun

36 Gardner Street, BN1 1UN (01273 626333, www.jumpthegun.co.uk). **Open** 10am-6pm Mon-Sat; noon-5pm Sun. **Map** p75 B3 ④⑥

There's often a vintage moped parked outside this gentlemen's boutique specialising in mod tailoring. If you can't afford a new suit, sharpen up with a trilby, target cufflinks, button badge or branded comb. Their plain shirts, which span the rainbow, will make a dapper man of any office drone.

Magazine Brighton

NEW *22 Trafalgar Street, BN1 4EQ (01273 687968, www.magazine brighton.com).* **Open** 11am-5pm Tue-Fri; 10am-6pm Sat; noon-4pm Sun. **Map** p75 C1 ④⑦

A minimalist shop dedicated to independent magazines, from the slow journalism of *Delayed Gratification* and leftfield football writing of *88* to design journal *Uppercase* and Parisian children's fashion bible *Milk*. There's even the first issue of *Paracetamol*, a feminist magazine by a local 14-year-old. The owner is a life-long fan of the medium, which he reckons is enjoying a resurgence on a par with vinyl. If he's right, this brilliant store with over 200 titles will be a key player.

Mr Magpie

94A Gloucester Road, BN1 4AP (01273 958603, www.mr-magpie.com). **Open** 10am-5pm Mon-Sat; 11am-4pm Sun. **Map** p75 B2 ④⑧

This little shop could probably only subsist in a city filled with both vintage-lovers and graphic designers. It specialises in old-fashioned printing equipment, from hand-carved Victorian letterpress blocks to 1970s Mecanorma transfer sheets. Mr Magpie sometimes closes on Sundays for workshops.

Oddballs

24 Kensington Gardens, BN1 4AL (01273 696068, www.skateboardsin brighton.co.uk). **Open** 10am-6pm Mon-Sat; 11am-5.30pm Sun. **Map** p75 B2 ④⑨

Oddballs has been keeping the city supplied with skateboards (and scooters, and rollerblades, and unicycles) for over 20 years. Regulars here include kids, crusties and even commuters. It also sells juggling balls and diabolos for those all-night circus skills sessions on the beach (it happens).

Pussy

3A Kensington Gardens, BN1 4AL (01273 604861, www.pussyhome boutique.co.uk). **Open** 10am-6pm Mon-Sat; 11am-4pm Sun. **Map** p75 B2 ⑤⓪

No, not a sex shop. A North Laine fixture since 1997, Pussy is a homewares boutique into which both men and women will happily enter, with plenty to entertain children too. The stock is carefully edited with style and genuine wit. Among the Tove Jansson books and Moomin crockery, you'll find bunny-baby lamps, prints by local artist Stereotypist and 'UNT' mugs with a cunningly placed handle.

Rarekind

104 Trafalgar Street, BN1 4ER (01273 818170, www.rarekind records.co.uk). **Open** 11am-6pm Mon-Sat. **Map** p75 C1 ⑤①

As charted in the documentary *South Coast*, there's a surprising hip hop scene in the UK's nethermost seaside towns. Key to Brighton's is this shop allied to the Rarekind graffiti crew, specialising in funk, soul and hip hop vinyl. Local contemporary house label Well Rounded opened a store on the first floor in 2013. On the second, you'll find the self-explanatory RK Bass.

Resident

28 Kensington Gardens, BN1 4AL (01273 606312, www.resident-music. com). **Open** 9am-6.30pm Mon-Sat; 10am-6pm Sun. **Map** p75 B2 ⑤②

Since the demise of Rounder, Resident has become the place to go for new music and gig tickets. A modest independent record store run by serious music-lovers, it's more about quality and well-arranged staff recommendations than exhaustive stock. The cut-price 'Every Home Should Have One' rack is addictive, and there are some great names squashing in for in-store gigs. In 2014 it won *Music Week*'s Independent Retailer of the Year award.

Rocket Science

100 Trafalgar Court, BN1 4ER (01273 757718). **Open** 10am-5pm Tue-Sat; noon-3pm Sun. **Map** p75 C1 (53)

A narrow little children's shop packed with the choicest wooden and scientific toys, Djeco craft kits, picture books, colouring sets and magazines. Lovely cards and wrapping paper too.

Sirene

37 Trafalgar Street, BN1 4ED (01273 818061, www.sirene-boutique.com). **Open** 10am-6pm Mon-Sat; noon-5pm Sun. **Map** p75 B1 (54)

The owner of this women's clothing boutique near the station regularly ransacks Paris so you don't have to. Best-selling brands include French labels Des Petites Hautes and Bensimom, Essential from Antwerp and new Danish collection Stella Nova – all relatively affordable and tricky to come by in the UK. Sirene has an eye, and a feel, for smart, stylish and soft designs that make you feel special for years.

Snooper's Paradise

7-8 Kensington Gardens, BN1 4AL (01273 602558, www.snoopersattic.co.uk). **Open** 10am-6pm Mon-Sat; 11am-4pm Sun. **Map** p75 B2 (55)

The pricing makes it a regular target of local comedians' jokes. But you can spend pleasurable hours exploring the rails of fur coats, shelves full of retro homewares, and rooms dedicated to individual furniture and craft concessions. Climb the twisting stairs near the shop front for Snooper's Attic, a vintage boutique sensuously draped with lace underwear, 1920s fascinators and bird-skull jewellery. Local girl Bat For Lashes probably bought most of her stagewear here.

Velo Vitality

44 Trafalgar Street, BN1 4ED (01273 699184, www.velovitality.co.uk). **Open** *Summer* 10am-6pm Mon-Sat. *Winter* 10am-6pm Tue-Sat. **Map** p75 B1 (56)

This cycling shop is filled with handsomely painted bicycles on whose handlebars you can imagine carrying your lover round Europe (with a bottle of red in the rattan basket). 'We like to think of our bikes as sidekicks to their owners,' say the helpful husband-and-wife owners. Decide your two-wheel personality from an international range including Reid, Bobbin, Tokyo, Pelago, Foffa, Brooklyn and Pure City cycles.

Vine Street Vintage Brighton Market

NEW *Unit 3, 13-16 Vine Street, BN1 4AG (07724 866301).* **Open** 7.30am-6pm Mon-Fri; 9am-6pm Sat; 10am-5pm Sun. **Map** p75 C2 (57)

A vintage market specialising in lighting and furniture with a French or industrial edge, from bomb-proof floor-lamps to tastefully distressed farmhouse tables. You can also sit down to coffee and cake or a bowl of seasonal soup. Housed beneath Vine Street Studios (p180) and just along from Beyond Retro, it's helping turn Vine Street into a little retro hub.

YAK

NEW *16 Gloucester Road, BN1 4AD (01273 679726, www.yarnandknitting.com).* **Open** 10am-6pm Tue-Sat; 11am-4pm Sun. **Map** p75 C2 (58)

Opened in early 2015 as 'a space for knitters', this big, warm hug of a shop stocks yarns in every hue and blend, some locally dyed, and hosts knitting and crochet workshops. You'll also find jewellery made from knitting needles courtesy

BRIGHTON BY AREA

of Yellow Bear Wares. The owner blogs about new patterns, and hosts a drop-in Knit Knight every Thursday. Craft fans should also check out Brighton Sewing Centre (68 North Road, 01273 621653, www.brightonsewingcentre.co.uk).

Nightlife

Green Door Store

Trafalgar Arches, BN1 4FQ (07944 693214, www.thegreendoorstore.co.uk). **Open** varies. **Map** p75 B1 **59**

Tucked under the railway arches and with the feel of a cellar speakeasy, this is one of the live music scene's greenest shoots. It hosts, among other things, the best small noisy bands, and discerning music-lovers' club nights dedicated to jazz, African music and successful Brighton soul and funk label Tru Thoughts. The free entry after 11pm makes it popular too.

Komedia

44-47 Gardner Street, BN1 1UN (01273 647101, www.komedia.co.uk). **Open** varies. **Map** p75 B3 **60**

Part of Brighton's entertainment history, Komedia began life as a theatre and cabaret bar in 1994, promoting the young and still-edgy Graham Norton, Al Murray and Sacha Baron Cohen. It has been in these premises – where it now extends warren-like behind a welcoming café-bar and box-office frontage – for over 15 years. The intimate Studio Bar has its entrance on neighbouring Regent Street, and it now also houses a cinema (Dukes at Komedia, p88). The theatre side of things has fallen away rather, though this is still one of the few places booking regular children's shows. Krater Comedy is now the signature night, but can feel factory-like with four shows a weekend. Instead, Komedia is a great place to catch music: there's a solid deck of club nights, a new monthly residency from ILuvLive (the London night that helped launch Jessie J and Emeli Sande), and a regular supply of touring bands.

Prince Albert

48 Trafalgar Street, BN1 4ED (01273 730499). **Open** noon-midnight Mon-Thur, Sun; noon-12.30 Fri, Sat. *Gigs* vary. **Map** p75 B1 **61**

One of Brighton's longest-surviving alternative venues, graffitied with portraits of music legends and Banksy's famous kissing policemen. Neneh Cherry recently played two very sweaty nights in the tiny upstairs venue: smaller bands play here as a rite of passage, and big acts by choice. Downstairs, the fireplace, knick-knacks, small wooden tables and series of homely backrooms make it a popular meeting place, with the noise from the regular DJ nights thumping down the staircase. See the venue's Facebook page for details of upcoming acts.

Arts & leisure

See also left **Komedia**.

Basement

24 Kensington Street, BN1 4AJ (01273 699733, www.thebasement.uk.com). **Map** p75 B2 **62**

Housed in an exposed-brick basement, Brighton's best alternative performance venue is underground in every sense. Cult comedians such as Daniel Kitson and Kim Noble, famous performance artists and international theatre collectives have all tested boundaries and blown minds here. The original team now focuses on the provocative Sick! festival so, in January 2015, Otherplace Productions took over the night-to-night programming. Formerly of the Chortle-award-winning Upstairs At Three And Ten venue, and responsible for pop-up Brighton Fringe theatre the Warren, Otherplace doesn't just have its finger on the creative pulse – it's the pacemaker. Cheap bar and tickets, too.

Brighton Dome

Church Street, BN1 1EE (01273 709709, www.brightondome.org). **Map** p75 B4 **63**

top: Dukes at Komedia;
bottom: ONCA Gallery

This multi-arts complex runs the Brighton Festival (p35) and consists of three year-round venues: the Concert Hall and Corn Exchange (both on Church Street) and Studio Theatre (round the corner on New Road). Funding has been secured to reconnect these buildings, which are all part of the royal estate. The main building on Church Street also houses the big, bright and contemporary Foyer Bar and flexible Founders Room (where you'll often find free exhibitions). It also links through to Brighton Museum. The Concert Hall started life as the Prince Regent's flamboyant stables, and gained a flowering art deco ceiling in the 1930s, making it a striking venue for big classical and pop concerts, dance and circus. The neighbouring Corn Exchange, with an arched ceiling, hosts mid-scale performance. Round the corner on New Road, where you'll also find the box office, the Studio Theatre is the most intimate venue, hosting alternative theatre, talks and the odd band.

Chutima

106 Trafalgar Street, BN1 4ER (01273 682129, www.chutimatherapy.co.uk). **Open** 10am-9pm Mon-Sat; 10am-5pm Sun. **Map** p75 C1 ①

If you're after an authentic Thai massage, and aren't a stickler for fancy waiting rooms, this exclusively Thai-run parlour squeezed into a narrow townhouse at the foot of Trafalgar Street is excellent.

Dukes at Komedia

44–47 Gardner Street, BN1 1UN (0871 9025728, www.picturehouses.com). **Open** from 10am daily. Closing times vary. **Map** p75 B3 ⑥

The addition of a pair of can-can legs to the exterior of Komedia in 2012 could mean only one thing: a partnership with the Duke of York's Picturehouse (see box p147), now resident in the venue's upper storeys. There are two screens with comfy seats and sofas, served by a café-bar that majors in Brighton Sausage Company hotdogs.

Lighthouse

28 Kensington Street, BN1 4AJ (01273 647197). **Open** varies. **Map** p75 B2 ⑦

Brighton's digital culture agency is the place to catch cutting-edge digital art and moving image – such as the recent Joseph Popper commission that reimagines the IRA bombing of Brighton's Grand Hotel as if viewed from a drone, or a talk by Brighton's own eerie electronicist Gazelle Twin.

ONCA Gallery

14 Saint George's Place, Brighton BN1 4GB (01273 958291, www.onca.org.uk). **Open** noon-7pm Wed-Fri, 11am-6pm Sat, Sun. **Map** p75 C1 ⑧

Sticking its neck out creatively, politically and geographically (it's on the outer edge of North Laine, near Old Steine), this lovely, imaginative gallery opened in 2012 with the aim of marrying art and conservation. It's been hung with jellyfish sculpted from plastic bottles, filled with snow made by hole-punching old Christmas paper, and disguised as a supermarket stocked with litter collected from the beach. The events programme is creating a real community hub too. When Ali Smith guest directed the 2015 Brighton Festival, she hung out here chatting every weekend.

Theatre Royal Brighton

35 Bond Street, BN1 1SD (0844 871 7627, www.ambassadortickets.com). **Map** p75 C4 ⑨

This doyen of faded Regency glamour once played host to the likes of Marlene Dietrich and Laurence Olivier. (The latter would down whiskeys between scenes at the 'gulp bar', which you can see for yourself on a guided backstage tour.) Ambassadors, the current owner, has kept it plugged with uninspiring touring shows. However, it does now have an in-house production company, Theatre Royal Brighton Productions, which is feeding shows (such as a recent English Touring Theatre co-production of Tom Stoppard's *Arcadia*) to the West End.

The Lanes

Their pedestrianised prettiness belies the analogy, but the Lanes are kind of like the bowels of Brighton. Sometimes called the South Lanes, this warren of twisting alleyways can be accessed by a narrow opening next to Ape records on the arterial North Street. It tumbles together some of the city's best restaurants, from vegetarian fixtures **Food for Friends** and **Terre à Terre** to buzzing new South Indian street-food joint **Curry Leaf Café,** and hot booking **64 Degrees**.

The twinkly jewellers and smart commercial art galleries here are much of a muchness, and so compact they're best recommended en masse. Also noteworthy, but not unmissable, are several celebrity ventures. Seafood brasserie **Fishy Fishy** (36 East Street, 01273 723750, www.fishyfishy.co.uk), owned by TV presenter Dermot O'Leary, and **VBites** (14 East Street, 01273 747371, www.vbites.com), the centrepiece café

of Heather Mills' vegan empire, are tucked among the high-end clothing and beauty chains on East Street. The area is also home to a branch of **Jamie's Italian** (11 Black Lion Street, 01273 915480, www.jamie oliver.com) and Liam Gallagher's clothing store **Pretty Green** (15 Dukes Lane, 01273 22 7117, www.prettygreen.com).

The Lanes date back to the 16th century, having grown out of pathways between allotments and gardens. Many of the buildings you see today came later, but the **Cricketers** pub is original. Look out too for the Grade II-listed Hippodrome on Middle Street, a Victorian circus-theatre that once played host to the Beatles. It recently escaped a bid to turn it into a cinema and restaurant complex, and could still be restored to its former glory.

For the purposes of this guide, we've also included the length of seafront between Brighton Pier and West Street (where there's a handy if unsanitary subway). The stretch of the Kings Road Arches here houses the Fishing Quarter, a cluster of studio-galleries, and a set of nightclubs including promising new addition the **Arch**. When it comes to clubbing, the windswept seafront queues are an initiation ceremony in themselves. Happily, you can now retreat from the storm (meteorological or musical) at the **Tempest Inn**, a pub with its own cave system.

Old-school seafront diversions include the **Mechanical Memories Museum**; 'clairvoyant to the stars' Eva Petulengro, who has a booth in the arches; and posing for a photo pretending to take a bite out of the bronze seafront sculpture on the groyne next to Brighton Pier. The official name of Hamish Black's artwork is *Afloat*, but Brightonians call it the Doughnut (and, occasionally, the Bum Hole).

Buses

Venues in this chapter are easily reached on foot from Brighton station. Most Lanes venues are also served by buses running along North Street – the main thoroughfare through the town centre – which we're including in this section. Seafront destinations are served by bus 77, which operates at weekends and bank holidays throughout the year, and daily from April to September. For a list of North Street and Brighton station buses, see p184.

Sights & museums

Brighton Fishing Museum

201 Kings Road Arches, BN1 1NB (01273 723064, www.brightonfishing museum.org.uk). **Open** 10am-6pm daily. **Admission** free. **Map** p91 B3 ❶
The hub of Brighton's Fishing Quarter, this quaint museum traces the town's maritime history, with a traditional Sussex fishing boat as its centre-piece. A more recent Seaside Gallery records the contributions of Brighton Swimming Club, the West Pier and Punch & Judy shows to beach life.

Brighton Pier

Grand Junction (01273 609361, www. brightonpier.co.uk). **Open** *Winter* 11am-5pm daily. *Summer* 10am-10pm daily. May vary with weather . **Map** p91 D3 ❷
There's something about the smell of frying doughnuts licked by sea spray that says 'Great British seaside' like nothing else. Pass through gaudy games arcades and round flashing fairground rides, trying not to be snagged by the karaoke at Horatio's Bar. The Super Booster rollercoaster goes from 0 to 60 in less than three seconds. For gentler thrills, we recommend the Dolphin Derby. Gentler still, the free deckchairs.

Mechanical Memories Museum

250 Kings Road Arches, BN1 1NB (01273 608620, www.mechanical memoriesmuseum.co.uk). **Open** noon-6pm Sat, Sun & school hols. **Admission** free. **Map** p91 C3 ❸
A vintage penny arcade paying homage to automated entertainments circa 1900-1960. Buy old-fashioned pennies (you get ten goes for £1.50) to play on fortune-tellers, horse-racing games and one-armed bandits. The museum closes in bad weather.

Old Police Cells Museum

Town Hall, Bartholomew Square, BN1 1JA (01273 291052, www.oldpolice cellsmuseum.org.uk). **Open** (pre-booked tours only) *Apr-Oct* 10.30am Tue-Sat. *Nov-Mar* 10.30am 1st & 3rd Sat of the mth. **Admission** free. **Map** p91 C2 ❹
Located in the basement of the town hall, these old police cells were in use between 1830 and 1967, and still have graffiti left by the battling mods and rockers of 1964. The small museum charts the city's criminal history, including the murder

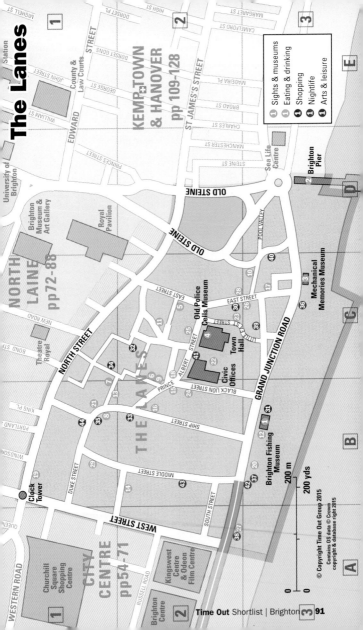

The Lanes

Michael St · Station

KEMPTOWN & HANOVER pp 109-128

Key
- ① Sights & museums
- ① Eating & drinking
- ① Shopping
- ① Nightlife
- ① Arts & leisure

University of Brighton

Brighton Museum & Art Gallery

Royal Pavilion

NORTH LAINE pp 72-88

Theatre Royal

NORTH STREET

THE LANES

Old Police Cells Museum

Town Hall

Civic Offices

GRAND JUNCTION ROAD

Mechanical Memories Museum

Brighton Pier

Sea Life Centre

OLD STEINE

Clock Tower

WEST STREET

CITY CENTRE pp 54-71

Churchill Square Shopping Centre

Kingswest Centre & Odeon Film Centre

Brighton Centre

Brighton Fishing Museum

200 m
200 yds

© Copyright Time Out Group 2015
Contains OS data © Crown copyright & database right 2015

top: Brighton Fishing Museum p90; bottom: Old Police Cells Museum p90

of the chief constable in 1844, and the Grand Hotel bombing of 1984.

Eating & drinking

Restaurants and cafés reviewed elsewhere with branches in the Lanes include **Café Coho** (p59) at 53 Ship Street (01273 747777); the **Giggling Squid** (p154; 11 Market Street, 01273 737373); **Julien Plumart Boutique & Salon de Thé** (p63; 27-29 Duke Street, 01273 208997) and **Riddle & Finns** (p66; 12B Meeting House Lane, 01273 323008).

42 Juice
19 Market Street, BN1 1HH (01273 710165, www.42juice.com). **Open** 8.30am-6pm Mon-Fri; 9am-6pm Sat; 11am-5pm Sun. **£**. **Juice bar**. Map p91 C2 ❺
A café serving raw, organic, cold-pressed juices as well as smoothies, wheatgrass shots and nut mylks. With names such as I Am Healing Green, I Am Buzzing and I Am Hungover, the extensive menu is easy to navigate.

64 Degrees
53 Meeting House Lane, BN1 1HB. (01273 770115, www.64degrees.co.uk). **Open** noon-3pm, 6-11pm. **££**. **Modern European**. Map p91 C2 ❻
A small restaurant with a big reputation. There are no waiting staff to mediate between the sweaty chefs and buzzy diners, and no rules to structure your order. Treat it like fine-dining tapas and choose small £6 plates from a changing menu: the likes of whelk, daikon and tabasco, maybe; followed by knodel, cabbage and smoked butter; and finishing with wings, kimchi and barkham blue cheese.

Angel Food Bakery
20 Meeting House Lane, BN1 1HB (01273 208404, www.angelfoodbakery. co.uk). **Open** 10am-6pm Mon-Sat; 11am-5pm Sun. **£**. **Bakery/café**. Map p91 B1 ❼
Choose from 13 types of freshly baked cupcake, including banoffee, cherry bakewell and honeycomb-dotted and coffee-crusted devil's food. At the new Angel Food Kitchen studio, round the corner in Brighton Square, you can take a baking class. Gluten-free cupcakes are also available.

Blackbird
30 Ship Street, BN1 1AD (01273 249454, www.blackbirdtearooms.com). **Open** 8.30am-6pm daily. **££**. **Tearoom**. Map p91 B1 ❽
This classy traditional English tearoom opened in 2012. But with its mahogany shelves lined with vintage china and tea tins, and its white-lace tablecloths, you could be forgiven for thinking it has been serving scones since before the war. A buttered teacake wouldn't have cost £3.10 back then, mind.

Bohemia
54-55 Meeting House Lane, BN1 1HB (01273 777770, www.bohemiabrighton. co.uk). **Open** 9am-1am Mon-Thur, Sun; 9am-3.30am Fri, Sat. **££**. **Café/bar**. Map p91 B2 ❾
This multifaceted three-floor hangout isn't a bad place to end up if you can't get in at 64 Degrees next door. Fish and chips come in edible newspaper and cocktails are made with dry ice and air pumps. There's a turfed and topiaried roof garden and live jazz every Thursday.

Boho Gelato
6 Pool Valley, BN1 1NJ (01273 727205, www.bohogelato.co.uk). **Open** 11am-6pm daily. **£**. **Ice-cream**. Map p91 C3 ❿
Apricot frangipane sorbet, Thai green tea and cinnamon chocolate pretzel are among the latest flavours of Italian-style ice-cream handmade here daily. One of Brighton's best (and smallest) ice-cream parlours.

Brighton Burger
11A Market Street, BN1 1HH (01273 205979). **Open** *Summer* noon-6pm Wed-Sat; noon-4pm Sun. *Winter* noon-4.30pm Wed-Sat; noon-4pm Sun. **£**. No credit cards. **Burgers**. Map p91 C2 ⓫

This small stand with seating under the awning is brilliant value and far from bog-standard: the Memphis Hot, inspired by the owner's Stateside travels, includes satay spread and a tiger bun.

Brighton Smokehouse

197 Kings Road, BN1 1NB (www. brightonfishingmuseum.org.uk). **Open** daily; times vary with weather. **£.** No credit cards. **Seafood. Map** p91 B3 ⑫
Retired fisherman Jack Mills and his wife Linda have been cooking local catch in a self-built smokehouse on the beach for over a decade. This hasn't escaped the notice of Nigel Slater, the Radio 4 Food and Farming Awards (who named it 'best takeaway' in 2011), or the tourists queuing along the boardwalk for hot mackerel sandwiches.

Casa Don Carlos

5 Union Street, BN1 1HA (01273 327177). **Open** 6-10pm Mon-Fri; noon-10pm Sat, Sun. **££. Spanish. Map** p91 B1 ⑬
This isn't one of those tapas joints where you'll pay a fiver for a titchy plate with three *boquerones*. The portions of *patatas bravas* and chorizo sizzling in brandy are as generous as the welcome. Quality can dip at peak times, though.

Coal Shed

8 Boyce's Street, BN1 1AN (01273 322998, www.coalshed-restaurant.co.uk). **Open** noon-4pm, 6-10pm Mon-Thur, Sun; noon-4pm, 6-10.30pm Fri, Sat. **£££. Steak & seafood. Map** p91 B2 ⑭
The 35-day, dry-aged Scottish beef is centre stage at this steak and seafood restaurant. The dark, simple interior is handsome and stylish, and you determine the cut and weight of the meat. New sister restaurant the Salt Room (p67) emphasises fish.

Cricketers

15 Black Lion Street, BN1 1ND (01273 329472, www.goldenliongroup.co.uk). **Open** 11am-midnight Mon-Thur; 11am-2am Fri, Sat; 11am-11pm Sun. **Pub. Map** p91 B2 ⑮

Graham Greene's favourite pub has renamed its upstairs bar the Greene Room in honour of the author of *Brighton Rock* (and framed some of his letters to the landlord on its walls). It feels suitably historic, with red banquettes, pots hanging from beams, and a cobbled courtyard where bands sometimes play.

Curry Leaf Café

NEW *60 Ship Street, BN1 1AE (01273 207070, www.curryleafcafe.com).* **Open** noon-3pm, 5.30-9.30pm Mon-Thur; noon-3pm, 6-10.30pm Fri, Sat; noon-3.30pm, 5.30-9.30pm Sun. **South Indian. ££. Map** p91 B2 ⑯
This brilliant café specialises in South Indian street food and craft beer, and has a greenhouse-style ceiling and plants to bring the outside in. It's particularly popular for Sunday brunch, thanks to the 'full Indian' fry-up of spiced omelette, dosai, thali, lentil doughnuts and slow-cooked biriyani. There's a children's menu too.

Dirty Blonde

NEW *75-79 East Street, BN1 1NF (01273 727494, www.dirtyblonde brighton.com).* **Open** 5pm-midnight Mon-Wed; noon-1am Thur; noon-3am Fri, Sat; noon-11pm Sun. **££. Bar/ American. Map** p91 C3 ⑰
From the street, Dirty Blonde looks like a high-end junk emporium. In fact, this is a carefully styled front for a bar and restaurant that takes its inspiration from the speakeasy. There's plush seating and booths, and the highest odds in the city of encountering a footballer. The name comes from a New York cocktail, and the food (grills, burgers, Maryland crab cakes) is also American.

Food for Friends

17-18 Prince Albert Street, BN1 1HF (01273 202310, www.foodforfriends.com). **Open** noon-10pm Mon-Thur, Sun; noon-10.30pm Fri, Sat. **£££. Vegetarian. Map** p91 C2 ⑱
The city's first vegetarian restaurant has been serving globally influenced

top: 64 Degrees p93;
bottom: Bohemia p93

dishes such as open saffron ravioli, or colcannon potato cake with carrot and star anise purée, since 1981. Don't let familiarity breed contempt. The dishes are, without exception, delicious, as are the organic wines.

Foodilic

60 North Street, BN1 1RH (01273 774138, www.foodilic.com). **Open** 8am-9.30pm Mon-Sat; 8am-6pm Sun. **£**. **Mediterranean/Middle Eastern**. Map p91 B1 ⑲

A healthy all-you-can-eat buffet for £6.95: help yourself to fresh, simple and imaginative salads (mange tout with walnuts and orange zest, or blueberry and red chard with rocket and mint), piled high in artfully stacked bowls. The vegetarian menu is so good, you may forget there are meat options too. A second branch has opened on Western Road (no.163), with counter service instead.

Lucky Beach

183 Kings Road Arches, BN1 1NB (01273 728280, www.luckybeach.co.uk). **Open** 9am-4.30pm Mon-Fri; 8.45am-5.30pm Sat, Sun. **£**. **Burgers**. Map p91 B3 ⑳

Crowded benches outside a beachfront establishment aren't always a guarantee of good grub. But this burger bar is a cut of organic, locally reared beef above. The Sussex Longhorn burger includes fig jam, toasted hazelnuts, smoked streaky bacon, cheddar and rocket. There's also a breakfast menu until noon for early walkers and strung-out clubbers, and a great drinks menu.

Marwood Café

52 Ship Street, BN1 1AF (01273 382063, www.themarwood.com). **Open** 9am-8pm Mon-Sat; 10am-8pm Sun. **£**. **Café**. Map p91 B1 ㉑

Where did Brighton residents go to loll on mismatched furniture, huddle over novels, make one coffee last the course of an existential debate or just enjoy

a lovely brownie before Marwoods came along? People started staying so long it introduced a kitchen, serving the Dr Seuss-inspired Green Eggs & Ham (scrambled with pesto) and a hash dish called Ken Dodds Dads Dogs Dinner. The owners have now opened Presuming Ed on London Road (p141).

Moshimo

Opticon, Bartholomew Square, BN1 1JS (01273 719195, www.moshimo.co.uk). **Open** noon-11pm daily. **££**. **Japanese**. Map p91 C2 ㉒

The originators of conveyer belt sushi in the UK, this brilliant Japanese restaurant is spearheading the Fishlove campaign for sustainable fishing. But what you'll notice first is the building: a modernist cube designed to float like a lantern in Bartholomew Square and slide open in summer.

Northern Lights

6 Little East Street, BN1 1HT (01273 747096, www.northernlightsbrighton.co.uk). **Open** 5pm-midnight Mon-Thur; 3pm-2am Fri; noon-2am Sat; 3pm-midnight Sun. **Bar/Scandinavian**. Map p91 C2 ㉓

A Scandinavian bar in a former fisherman's cottage, twinkling with fairy lights and glowing with bottles of flavoured vodka. You can accompany these with sharing platters of pickled herring, house-cured gravadlax and sautéed reindeer.

Pho

12 Black Lion Street, BN1 1ND (01273 202403, www.phocafe.co.uk). **Open** noon-10pm Mon-Thur, Sun; noon-10.30pm Fri, Sat. **£**. **Vietnamese**. Map p91 B2 ㉔

The Brighton branch of the small, Vietnamese street-food chain is one of the best places in the city for a cheap, healthy meal. There's a great range of seating in the large, low-lit urban-style interior. Order a steaming bowl of pho, a zingy rice noodle soup to which you add your own handfuls of fresh herbs.

Plateau

1 Bartholomews, BN1 1HG (www. plateaubrighton.co.uk, 01273 733085). **Open** noon-4pm, 6-10pm Mon, Wed-Sun; noon-4pm, 6-10.30pm Thur-Sat. **£££**. **French**. Map p91 C2 ㉕

This French restaurant specialises in sharing plates, based on the safe assumption that you'll want to pool your excitement over a wooden board loaded with slow-roasted pork belly, spiced quail, venison empanada and merguez sausage. There are similar offers for fish-lovers and veggies. The chic and moody styling, seriously good cocktails, wines (many or them organic and biodynamic) and monthly turntable playlist complete a pretty perfect – if pricey – picture.

Scoop & Crumb

5-6 East Street, BN1 1HP (01273 202563, www.scoopandcrumb.com). **Open** 10am-6pm Mon-Fri, Sun; 10am-7pm Sat. **£**. **Ice-cream**. Map p91 C3 ㉖

A two-minute stroll from Brighton beach, this faintly retro two-storey ice-cream parlour has 20 flavours including rhubarb crumble and custard and Super Cool Coconut Chocolate Crunch. There are also sorbets, sundaes and waffles, and sauces and toppings from hard-setting Belgian chocolate to chewy worms. If you can't chose, try a five-scoop cone for £6.50.

Tempest Inn

NEW *161 Kings Road Arches, BN1 1NB (01273 770505).* **Open** 11am-1pm Mon-Thur, Sun; 11am-3am Fri-Sat. **Pub**. Map p91 A2 ㉗

This brand new seafront pub has a genuine USP: it's in a warren of lantern-lit caves. Some are available for private booking, and there are supper clubs on the cards to supplement beer from the local Laine Brewery, bread from Brighton baker Flourpot and locally caught fish. There's also an upstairs Ariel Bar with sea views, and an all-weather seafront patio. Be sure to wreck your ship here.

Terre à Terre

71 East Street, BN1 1HQ (01273 729051, www.terreaterre.co.uk). **Open** noon-10.30pm Mon-Fri; noon-11pm Sat; noon-10pm Sun. **£££**. **Vegetarian**. Map p91 C2 ㉘

Vegetarianism as indulgence rather than abstinence is Terre à Terre's mantra – and lifelong veggies visiting this laid-back restaurant for the first time have been known to groan with pleasure. Each item on the menu is a compilation of unusual ingredients, and gluten-free and vegan options are plentiful. To experience the full range of invention, we recommend the £23 tapas plate.

Twisted Lemon

NEW *41 Middle Street, BN1 1AL (01273 945800).* **Open** noon-midnight Mon-Sat; noon-11pm Sun. **Cocktail bar**. Map p91 B1 ㉙

Squeezed down a bright-yellow alleyway, this no-frills cocktail bar is so homely you might be reminded of distant nights with your friends' parents' drinks cabinet. That's no comment on the quality, however. Summer evening? Try a frozen vanilla margarita. Feeling under the weather? How about a Modern Sacrifice with pressed apple, ginger syrup, fresh lemon and Abuelo rum? At current count, there are 73 cocktails on the menu. No, we're not seeing double.

Shopping

Bison Beer Crafthouse

NEW *7 East Street, BN1 1HP (www. bisonbeercrafthouse.co.uk).* **Open** 10am-7pm Mon-Sat; 11am-5pm Sun. Map p91 C2 ㉚

Brighton now has its first specialist beer shop, selling over 300 varieties from across the globe. There are iPads so you can find something suitable to match your evening meal. They're also the first in the city to sell growlers: a US invention that uses a counter-pressure filling system to keep three-and-a-half pints of the good stuff fresh for weeks.

Castor & Pollux

164-166 Kings Road Arches, BN1 1NB.
(01273 773776, www.castorandpollux.
co.uk). **Open** 10am-5pm daily. **Map**
p91 B3 **31**

The best, biggest and most actually-
open of the numerous seafront galleries, packed with cool design books and
magazines, jewellery, prints, homewares and giftcards, including Modern
Toss, Tatty Devine, Charley Harper
and Rob Ryan, and plenty more you'll
be glad to discover.

Choccywoccydoodah

3 Meeting House Lane, BN1 1HB (01273
329462, www.choccywoccydoodah.com).
Open 10am-6pm Mon-Sat; 11am-5pm
Sun. **Map** p91 C2 **32**

The towering, flower-crusted cakes in
the window of Choccywoccydoodah
look as if they've sprouted organ-
ically from the surface of another
planet. Relocated from Duke Street,
this famous Brighton chocolatiers has
a café and new workshop space (the
Witches Kitchen) upstairs. No icing or
marzipan trickery here – the fantastical decorations are all crafted entirely
from chocolate.

Jeremy Hoye

22A Ship Street, BN1 1AD (01273
776097, www.jeremy-hoye.com). **Open**
10am-5.30pm Mon-Sat, occasional Sun.
Map p91 B2 **33**

You can buy a silver deckchair and
Royal Pavilion charms (if you've got
£50 to spare) at Brighton's best-known
jeweller. His contemporary collection
(and store) has attracted attention the
world over, and he's big with celebrities.

Pecksniff's

45-46 Meeting House Lane, BN1 1HB
(01273 723292, www.pecksniffs.com).
Open 10am-5pm Mon-Sat; 10.30am-4pm
Sun. **Map** p91 C1 **34**

Always crammed before Christmas
and Mother's Day, this independent
local perfumery has been blending
fragrances and pamper products for

over 30 years. For £295 they'll design
a scent just for you.

She Said

32 Ship Street, BN1 1AD. (01273
777811, www.shesaidboutique.com).
Open 10am-6pm Mon-Sat; 11am-5pm
Mon, Sun. **Map** p91 B1 **35**

Sex shops may be common in Brighton,
but She Said is on another level: an erotic
boutique selling everything from heart-
shaped red crystal nipple tassles to
ornamental-looking glass flower dildos,
and covering all bases from corsetry to
couples' toys, bridalwear to bondage.

Nightlife

Arch

NEW *187-193 Kings Road Arches, BN1*
1NB (01273 208133, www.thearch.club).
Open 11pm-6am Fri, Sat; 11am-5am Tue.
Map p91 C3 **36**

This club has been the Zap (legendary), Digital (brilliant) and most
recently Coliseum (meh). So there
are big hopes for latest incarnation
the Arch, which hopes to 'bring the
dance music vibe back to Brighton
seafront'. The new owners' first act
was to revamp the bespoke 12KW
Funktion-one Dance Stack soundsys-
tem. The Arch opened in March 2015
with German techno duo Pan-Pot and
Tinie Tempah, and regular nights will
include commercial mashup Party
& Bullshit on Fridays, and the long
running See You Next Tuesday.
Opening days are likely to extend.

Coalition

171-181 Kings Road Arches, BN1 1NB
(01273 722385, www.coalitionbrighton.
com). **Open** noon-5am Mon-Fri; noon-
7am Sat; noon-4pm Sun. **Map** p91 B3 **37**

The best of the city's larger clubs,
Coalition yawns under those brick
arches and lolls out on to the beach
for daytime drinking. Pete Tong-sized
DJs, big touring indie bands, and tech-
house every Saturday from 3am courtesy of 'Brighton's after-party', Blow.

Fabrica p100

Fortune of War

156-157 Kings Road Arches, BN1 1NB (01273 205065). **Open** 11am-midnight Mon-Thur, Sun; 11am-2am Fri; 11am-3am Sat. **Map** p91 A2 **38**

The ship-shaped Fortune of War is the ancient mariner of Brighton pubs. Around since 1882, it has porthole windows, creaking timbers and, we wouldn't be surprised, the odd barnacle in its toilets – though it has undergone a recent paint job. One of the management team co-owns local funk and soul label Tru Thoughts, so expect quality live sounds and DJs.

Funfair Club

12-15 Kings Road, BN1 1NE (01273 757447, www.funfairclub.com). **Open** 10pm-4am Thur-Sat. **Map** p91 C3 **39**

This small, circus-themed club is run by the people behind London's brilliant Bathhouse clubs, and has a Punch & Judy DJ booth. So we're sticking with it despite chequered form. Just be aware: attractions such as the adult ball-pit and bed of nails are often booked out, and there's a one-in-one-out policy at its busiest.

Haunt

10 Pool Valley, BN1 1NJ (01273 736618, www.thehauntbrighton.co.uk). **Open** varies. **Map** p91 C3 **40**

A dark, dank club where the bar takes a diagonal bite out of the atmosphere. Nevertheless, the Haunt (and especially its balcony, which practically overhangs the stage) is one of the best places to catch hotly tipped acts. George the Poet, Biopolar Sunshine and Perfume Genius have all played here. The sound's ace, and its big on alternative '80s and '90s club nights.

Mesmerist

1-3 Prince Albert Street, BN1 1HE (01273 328542, www.drinkinbrighton.co.uk/mesmerist). **Open** noon-1am Mon-Thur, Sun; noon-2am Fri, Sat. **Map** p91 C2 **41**

If this venue were a person, it'd have a moustache and a porkpie hat, take classes in lindy hopping and taxidermy, and spend weekends DJing at a circus. It's trying very hard to be different. But there's plenty of straightforward fun to be had at Saturday's Juke Joint Jamboree, plus theatrical surprises at midnight. Food is served noon-9pm daily.

Riki Tik Beach Bar

NEW *169-170 Kings Road, BN1 1NB (01273 725541, www.drinkinbrighton.co.uk/RikiTikBeachBar).* **Open** noon-2am Thur; noon-3am Fri, Sat; noon-midnight Sun. **Map** p91 B3 **42**

Brighton beach now has its own rum shack, and never you mind the weather. Eighty different rums, Caribbean food, guest DJs and even a wee record shop courtesy of Bond Street's shotknocking Jamaican joint Riki Tik.

Sticky Mike's Frog Bar

9-12 Middle Street, BN1 1AL (01273 749465, www.drinkinbrighton.co.uk/stickymikesfrogbar). **Open** 6pm-2.30am Mon-Thur; 6pm-3.30am Fri-Sat; 6pm-midnight Sun. **Map** p91 B2 **43**

Upstairs: Pizzaface pizzas (p157), Slush Puppy cocktails, colourful murals by local illustrators, screenings, spoken word, and DJs playing just about everything. Downstairs: a small live-music venue hosting some of the best alternative bands and club nights. Look out for the little arched glass doorway.

Arts & leisure

Fabrica

40 Duke Street, BN1 1AG (01273 778646, www.fabrica.org.uk). **Open** noon-5pm Wed-Sun during exhibitions. **Map** p91 B1 **44**

This contemporary art gallery and arts centre in a Regency church has been sewn with grass, strung with shirts and hosted a kaleidoscopic light installation by Brian Eno. It commissions site-specific work and thinks up interesting ways to explore exhibitions further – talks, workshops, even the odd dance. There are some late openings until 7pm.

St Nicholas

Seven Dials, Montpelier & Clifton Hill

The painter John Constable may have written off the hilly land stretching inland from Western Road as 'hideous masses of unfledged earth', but visitors have always welcomed the opportunity to stand back from the city centre and breathe.

The **Clifton & Montpelier** conservation area developed in the mid 19th century, with impressive stucco-clad terraces and villas, enticing residential squares and crescents, and architectural curios at every turn. It even has its own summer arts festival (www.cmpca online.org.uk), based around two historic churches: **St Nicholas** on Dyke Road, the oldest building in Brighton, and **St Michael's & All Angels** on Victoria Road, famed for its stained glass by William Morris. The fancy **Clifton Terrace** also offers one of the most striking views of the sea – framed by high rises Chartwell Court and Sussex Heights.

Upper North Street and its westerly extension, Montpelier Place, continue to attract idiosyncratic shops and cafés. In this area, you'll find great independent cafés **Mr Wolfe** and the **Nowhere Man**, the only non-London premises of the **Craft Beer Company**, and bespoke tote-makers **Brand New Bags**. Neighbouring Victoria Street is now home to **Four Candles**, a furniture and fashion workshop co-owned, in keeping with Brighton's propensity for weird celebrity associations, by the daughter of Ronnie Corbett.

To the north, **Seven Dials** (a quaint name for what is essentially a big roundabout) is a compact alternative shopping spot dotted with restaurants, gift shops, delis and, increasingly, gastropubs. In 2013, improvements were made to the pedestrian functioning of the roundabout, so that it's no longer a feat of courage, cunning and arcane local knowledge to cross. In the well-to-do residential north-east area of Seven Dials known as Port Hall, Upper Hamilton Road is now home to an award-winning café, gastropub and several interesting shops.

You'll get another surprising glimpse of sea from the maze-like hedged rose gardens and playing field up at **Dyke Road Park**. Following a long campaign, its disused bowling green is now the site of Brighton's first dedicated open-air theatre, **BOAT**, which will seat 425 people in a grass amphitheatre.

For this chapter, we have taken Upper North Street, Montpelier Terrace and Montpelier Place, and the opening stretch of Old Shoreham Road, extending north along Dyke Road to include Dyke Road Park, as our southern and northern boundaries. Go further west than York Road/York Avenue and you're technically in Hove. The eastern boundary zig-zags down Howard Place above the station, the long, commuter-populated Buckingham Road, and the section of Dyke Road that's home to St Nicholas Church.

Sights & museums

Booth Museum of Natural History

194 Dyke Road, BN1 5AA (03000 290900, www.brighton-hove-rpml.org. uk). Bus 14, 27. **Open** 10am-5pm Mon-Wed, Fri, Sat; 2-5pm Sun. **Admission** free. **Map** p103 A1 ❶

A wonderfully old-school, 'dead things in glass cases'-style museum built to house the collection of Victorian ornithologist (and gun enthusiast) Edward Booth. Behind the old red doors, you'll find over half a million insects, animal skeletons, and stuffed birds posed – rather ghoulishly to modern eyes – in re-creations of their natural habitats.

Its most popular exhibits include the 'Merman' (a Victorian fake cobbled together from a fish and a monkey) and the 140-million-year-old bones of a Sussex dinosaur. The floor-to-ceiling displays are perfect for small children – look out for the new tortoises beneath your feet.

St Nicholas Church & Rest Garden

41 Dyke Road, BN1 3LJ (www. stnicholasbrighton.org.uk). Bus 14, 18, 27, 37, 47. **Open** 9.30am-2.30pm Mon, Tue; 9.30am-1.30pm, 2-4pm Wed. **Admission** free. **Map** p103 C5 ❷

Perched on a hill overlooking the city centre is Brighton's 'ancient mother church', dedicated to the patron saint of sailors and fishermen. There has been a church on this site since the times of the Domesday Book, and even in its current incarnation it is the oldest building in Brighton, with a Norman font of Caen stone carved around 1170. Just across the road, through iron gates that shut at dusk, St Nicholas Rest Garden is an extension of the cemetery (including 14 Victorian vaults) and a beautiful, secluded spot to take a break on your way down to Western Road or up to Seven Dials.

Eating & drinking

There is a branch of **Small Batch Coffee** (see box p155) at 108A Dyke Road (01273 711912, www.small batchcoffee.co.uk).

Almond Tree Café

109C Dyke Road, BN1 3JE (01273 729505). Bus 22, 56. **Open** 8am-5pm Mon-Sat; 10am-4pm Sun. **£**. **Vegan café**. **Map** p103 B3 ❸

Seven Dials has taken this vegan café and the friendly young Italian couple who run it to its heart. Their vegan alternatives to cooked breakfasts and Sunday roasts are especially popular, and they also make (and sell) their own jams and chocolate-hazelnut spread.

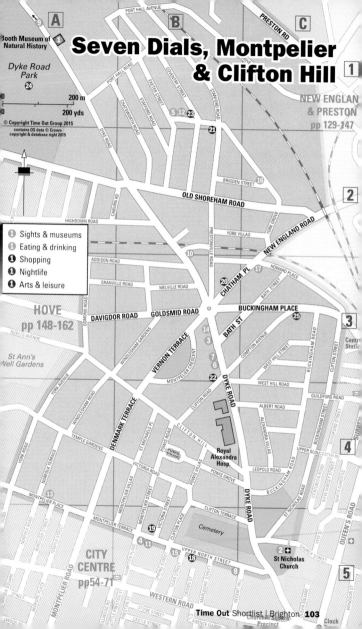

Seven Dials, Montpelier & Clifton Hill

A **B** **C** **1**

PORT HALL AVENUE

PRESTON RD

Booth Museum of
Natural History

Dyke Road
Park

200 m
200 yds

© Copyright Time Out Group 2015
contains OS data © Crown
copyright & database right 2015

NEW ENGLAND
& PRESTON
pp 129-147

PORT HALL ROAD

CHATSWORTH ROAD

DYKE ROAD

EXETER STREET

STAFFORD ROAD

COVENTRY STREET

STANFORD ROAD

BRIGDEN STREET **16**

CABURN RD

2

OLD SHOREHAM ROAD

HIGHDOWN ROAD

VINE GROVE

PRESTONVILLE ROAD

YORK VILLAS

NEW ENGLAND ROAD

1 Sights & museums
1 Eating & drinking
1 Shopping
1 Nightlife
1 Arts & leisure

ADDISON ROAD

10

GRANVILLE ROAD

MELVILLE ROAD

CHATHAM PL **20** **17** HOWARD PLACE

BATH STREET

HOVE
pp 148-162

OSMOND ROAD

DAVIGDOR ROAD

GOLDSMID ROAD

WINDLESHAM GARDENS

BUCKINGHAM PLACE

BATH ST

COMPTON AVENUE

25

WEST HILL STREET

BUCKINGHAM ROAD

CLIFTON STREET

Centre
Station

3

NICELLS AVENUE

St Ann's
Well Gardens

VERNON TERRACE

14
3
7 **6**
22

DYKE ROAD

WEST HILL ROAD

GUILDFORD ROAD

YORK AVENUE

MONTPELIER CRESCENT

ALBERT ROAD

ALEXANDRA VILLAS

UPPER GLOUCESTER RD

4

DENMARK TERRACE

TEMPLE GARDENS

ST MICHAELS PL

CLIFTON HILL

POWIS ROAD

POWIS
SQUARE

Royal
Alexandra
Hosp.

LEOPOLD ROAD

BUCKINGHAM ROAD

BUCKINGHAM STREET

CENTURION RD

NEW ENGLAND STREET

NORTH GARDENS

SURRE

NORFOLK TERRACE

VICTORIA ROAD

POWIS GROVE

BUCKINGHAM ROAD

ST NICHOLAS ROAD

QUEEN'S ROAD

13

MONTPELIER PLACE

MONTPELIER VILLAS

MONTPELIER STREET

VICTORIA STREET

CLIFTON PLACE

CLIFTON TERRACE

DYKE ROAD

Cemetery

19

CITY
CENTRE
pp54-71

MONTPELIER TERRACE

HAMPTON PLACE

11

15
18

UPPER NORTH STREET

8

2 St Nicholas
Church

WESTERN ROAD

Clock

Time Out Shortlist | Brighton **103**

left: Joe's Café; right: Mr Wolfe;
bottom: Nowhere Man.
All p106

After a refurb at the beginning of 2015, there's now more space to eat in.

Billie's Café

34 Hampton Place, BN1 3DD (01273 774386, www.billiescafe.co.uk). Bus 1, 2, 5, 6, 18, 21, 25, 46, 49. **Open** 9am-4pm daily. **£. Café. Map** p103 B5 ④

A cosy crush of blue-checked tablecloths, folding chairs and wasted clubbers, this corner café just back from Western Road is a hangover institution thanks to its extensive hash menu. A giant pile of fried potatoes and onions is topped with everything from guacamole, salsa, sour cream and cheese (the Mexican) to swede, cabbage and crispy bacon (the Irish).

Chimney House

28 Upper Hamilton Road, BN1 5DF (01273 556708, chimneyhousebrighton. co.uk). Bus 5, 14, 27, 56. **Open** noon-11pm Tue-Sat, noon-9pm Sun. **£££. Gastropub. Map** p103 B1 ⑤

When is a pub not really a pub? Arguably when it sells its own jams, chutneys and sourdough bread, hosts the local book group and employs a company called Forager to keep it supplied with wild native ingredients. Sussex-born Charlie Brookman cooks up an inventive storm at this chandelier-decked local. Here, you can start with breadcrumbed pig's head, major on venison neck and rape greens, and finish with sea buckthorn, meringue and barley malt. What it's less suited to is just sinking a pint.

Coggings & Co

NEW *87-93 Dyke Road, BN1 3JE (01273 220220, www.coggingsandco.com). Bus 22, 56.* **Open** noon-11pm Mon-Sat; noon-7pm Sun. **££. Burgers. Map** p103 B3 ⑥

Only Sussex beef goes into the burgers and only local beer goes into the glasses at this high-end burger restaurant in a gastropub-style setting. Burger toppings include mushroom tapenade and dry-cured honey-glazed streaky bacon; the buns come from Real Patisserie

(p118); there are soy cashews while you wait, and organic espresso ice-cream for dessert. Very Seven Dials.

Cow

95-97 Dyke Road, BN1 3JE (01273 772370, www.thecow.pub). Bus 22, 56, N7. **Open** 11am-midnight Mon-Thur; 11am-1.30pm Fri; 10am-1.30am Sat; 11am-10pm Sun. **Pub. Map** p103 B3 ⑦

There are over 30 craft beers (including limited-edition bottles from micro-breweries such as Flying Dog and Brooklyn) at this large bar and restaurant. Craft beer is also celebrated in the decor, while there are Persian rugs on the wooden floor, and a neon sign by Andy Doig in the corner. Food runs to posh burgers, fish and chips, pies and steaks.

Craft Beer Company

22-23 Upper North Street, BN1 3FG (01273 723736, www.thecraftbeerco. com/pubs/brighton). Bus 22, 56, N29. **Open** 4pm-12.30am Mon-Thur; 4pm-1.30am Fri; noon-1.30am Sat; noon-11pm Sun. **Pub. Map** p103 B5 ⑧

Since 2012, this airy and pleasantly arranged neighbourhood pub has been the only non-London branch of the Craft Beer Company, replete with 27 draught pumps and one bottle that costs £50 (most of their range is competitively priced). In 2014, it introduced a partnership with Forty Burger, which uses Aberdeen beef sourced only from royal warrant holders to the Queen.

Dyke

218 Dyke Road, BN1 5AA (01273 555672, www.dykepub.co.uk). Bus 14, 27, N7. **Open** noon-midnight Mon-Thur; noon-1am Fri, Sat; noon-11pm Sun. **££. Gastropub. Map** off p103 A1 ⑨

One of the most popular places for family dining in Brighton, Dyke has a pan-European menu sourced mainly from organic, GM-free and free-range suppliers, and there's also inventive pizzas and tapas. Children get toys, colouring books and half-size Sunday roasts.

Good Companions

132 Dyke Road, BN1 3TE (01273 204993, www.goodcompanions.pub). Bus 14, 27, 56, N7. **Open** 11am-noon Mon-Thur; 11am-1am Fri, Sat; noon-midnight Sun. **Pub**. Map p103 B2 ➓

Like the Dyke, the Goodies is a large, long-established Seven Dials boozer that's been rehabilitated as a family dining pub. Harry McGann, who's in charge of the menu, has a background working with Michelin-starred chefs, but hasn't turned his nose up at steak, sausage and mash, and burgers. There's a large decked courtyard, a choice of eight hand pumps with local selections, and an array of seating around the square central bar, with more upstairs.

Hampton Arms

57 Upper North Street, BN1 3FH (01273 731347). Bus 14, 18, 22, 37, N1, N2, N5. **Open** noon-midnight Mon-Thur, Sun; noon-1am Fri, Sat. **Pub**. Map p103 B5 ⓫

This grand yet cosy Montpelier pub next door to St Mary Magdalen's Church is both geographically near and psychologically far from the main shopping drag of Western Road. It promotes local cask-conditioned ales, and Heart & Soul Food are now running the kitchen (serving the likes of honey-bourbon glazed pork ribs and jumbo shrimps in chilli, garlic and coriander). There's a nice covered courtyard through french doors at the back.

Joe's Café

24 Upper Hamilton Road, BN1 5DF (01273 503917, www.joescafebrighton. com). Bus 5, 14, 27, 56. **Open** 9am-2pm Mon; 8am-4pm Tue-Fri; 9am-4pm Sat; 9am-3pm Sun. **£**. **Café**. Map p103 B1 ⓬

This used to be a greasy spoon serving users of the nearby launderette. Now it's taking on Billie's (p105) in the awesome breakfast hash department, with a hangover kill-or-cure called the Hashegeddon. It also serves three types of Full English ('big', 'bigger' and 'biggest') and veggie and vegan options. All ingredients are

Sussex-sourced. A word-of-mouth reputation is starting to draw out-of-town customers up the hill from the train station – it now takes reservations.

Mr Wolfe

5 Montpelier Place, BN1 3BF (07972 252787). Bus 18, 37. **Open** 8am-5pm Mon-Fri; 9am-5pm Sat; 10am-5pm Sun. **Café**. Map p103 A4 ⓭

This tiny but handsome café (dark grey exterior, low hanging bulbs, blackboard walls) is run by a couple from Melbourne. He sources Sussex produce from CanTina's empanadas to Magpie's pies, while she bakes cakes with an occasional Aussie influence (Lamingtons, or chocolate layer cake with orange-blossom ganache). There's Monmouth organic coffee, and a granita menu in the summer.

Murasaki

115 Dyke Road, BN1 3JB (01273 326231, www.murasakirestaurant.co.uk). Bus 22, 56. **Open** 12.30-2.30am, 6.30-11pm Tue-Fri; 12.30-3pm, 6.30-11pm Sat, Sun. **££**. **Japanese**. Map p103 B3 ⓮

This small Japanese restaurant just off Seven Dials is intimate and authentic, better suited to couples than big parties. Approach the large menu tapas-style and order small dishes such as spicy squid tempura, spinach in sweet tahini and saké sauce or chicken dipping dumplings, adding dishes as you go. There are also more substantial mains, including a seafood hotpot, and a separate lunch menu with dishes around £7, all served with miso soup.

Nowhere Man

NEW *53 Upper North Street, BN1 3FE (01273 660499).* Bus 22, 56. **Open** 8am-7pm Mon-Fri; 9am-7pm Sat, Sun. **Café**. Map p103 B5 ⓯

With a music-themed loyalty card, merch and band art in the corners, furniture from eBay and an old record player on which you're welcome to play your own LPs, this new café-cum-rehearsal space is studenty in the best of ways. Alongside coffee and cake, it serves the kinds of specials (mac 'n' cheese toastie, anyone?) that you crave after late-night drinking with noise-core bands. It also hosts the odd charity comedy gig and acoustic night.

Prestonville

64 Hamilton Road, BN1 5DN (01273 701007, www.prestonville-arms.co.uk). Bus 5, 14, 27, 37, 38, 56. **Open** 5-11pm Mon-Thur; noon-midnight Fri, Sat; noon-5pm Sun. **Pub. Map** p103 C2 ⑯
The antidote to the growing number of Seven Dials gastropubs: an old-fashioned neighbourhood boozer committed to real ale and real conversation, with a curry night every Wednesday. It has the very Brighton benefit of being both 'off the beaten track' and still only ten minutes' walk from the station.

Shakespeare's Head

1 Chatham Place, BN1 3TP (01273 329444). Bus 7, 14, 18, 27, 37, 56. **Open** 5-11.30pm Mon-Thur; 4pm-12.30am Fri; noon-12.30am Sat; noon-11.30pm Sun. **Pub. Map** p103 C3 ⑰
Seven Dials' best-loved pub, the Shakies has candlelit tables, Tudor-style paintings, board games and an atmospheric dearth of natural daylight in which to enjoy a pint of Badger or Tanglefoot. It's still known as 'the sausage and mash pub' (tipsy mathematicians reckon the menu affords 1,000 combinations). You'll fight for a table on the raised-decked front porch for Sunday roasts.

Shopping

Brand New Bag

47 Upper North Street, BN1 3FH (07971 176554, www.brandnewbagbrighton. com). Bus 22, 56. **Open** noon-5pm daily. **Map** p103 B5 ⑱
Having traded for years in Covent Garden via Lyme Regis, fabric expert Alistair McCready is now settled in a quiet row of Brighton shops. Here, he makes bespoke shoulder bags using textiles from around the world, sitting

with his sewing machine among the rugs from rural Iran and Afghanistan.

Four Candles

NEW *2 Victoria Street, BN1 3FP (01273 757258, www.fourcandlesshop.com). Bus 18, 22, 37, 56.* **Open** 10am-5.30pm Tue-Sat. **Map** p103 B5 ⑲
Behind grey stable doors on a residential road just off Upper North Street is this new studio co-run by the fashion designer daughter of Ronnie Corbett, of all people. Four Candles even takes its name from a *Two Ronnies* sketch. It sells men's and women's fashion, furniture and home furnishings, including a range of leather shoulder bags and cowhide rugs. Prices range from £4 to £1,200.

NHR Organic Oils

24 Chatham Place, BN1 3TN (01273 746 505/202729, www.nhrorganicoils.com). Bus 7, 14, 18, 27, 37, 56. **Open** 9am-5pm Mon-Sat. **Map** p103 B3 ⑳
Behind the turquoise doors of this small, exquisitely scented shop is one of the largest ranges of organic essential oils in the world. These are enticingly displayed in glass vials, alongside spritzable floral waters and boxed gift sets. The staff also run workshops in the distilling process and making creams.

Quilty Pleasures

1B Upper Hamilton Road, BN1 5DF (01273 563032, www.quilty-pleasures. co.uk). Bus 5, 14, 27, 56. **Open** noon-5pm Thur; or by appointment. **Map** p103 B1 ㉑
This little shop now has a successful online operation and runs an array of courses. The manager studied textiles at the London College of Fashion, and will help you to choose from a fabric range that includes vintage 1960s and '70s designs. Prices start from £65 for baby quilts.

Sixty Seven

67 Dyke Road, BN1 3JE (01273 735314, www.shopatsixtyseven.co.uk). Bus 22, 56. **Open** 10.30am-5.30pm Mon-Sat. **Map** p103 B3 ㉒

Outdoor arts

The city now has its first dedicated open-air theatre – thanks to one man and the friends who made his dying dream a reality.

Up at Dyke Road Park, an unusual legacy is taking root. It has a lawned stage, acoustic design, and raked seating wide enough for 425 people to stretch out with picnics. This is the **Brighton Open Air Theatre**, or BOAT.

Best known as the creator of anything-goes performance club Zincbar, Adrian Bunting was an artist and producer with a galvanising mantra of 'fuck it, book it'. Diagnosed with terminal cancer in 2013, he gathered five friends and told them of his final wish – to create a flexible performance space without literal walls or creative boundaries.

'I wouldn't have done it for anyone else,' says screenwriter James Payne, Bunting's friend of 25 years. 'I mean, it was a bit of an ask: an open air theatre? Are you not happy with a bloody bench?'

Bunting left detailed plans for the grassy auditorium, along with £18,000. He had a lifelong interest in bringing audience and performer closer together. 'That's why he designed it with a thrust stage,' says Payne. 'Open air theatre is also more informal. He liked that slightly rabbley feel.'

In May 2015, BOAT opened with the Globe's Brighton Festival performance of *Romeo & Juliet*. The broad ongoing programme, will include everything from comedy, musicals and circus to spoken word and film screenings.

'We've just been trying to realise our mate's dream,' says Payne. 'It's amazing to see it coming to life.'

As the vintage lip-sofa in the window suggests, Sixty Seven has more style than your average card and candle shop – including the odd piece of 1960s Ercol furniture. Think high-end gifts such as Chocoholly organic chocolate fish and crocheted octopus baby rattles, plus Rob Ryan prints and Ora Kiely gardening gear.

Wright & Co

16 Upper Hamilton Rd, BN1 5DF (01273 232335, 07850 485189, www.wrightandcobrighton.co.uk). Bus 5, 14, 27, 56. **Open** *10.30am-5.30pm Wed, Thur, Sat; 11.30am-5.30pm Fri.* **Map** p103 B1 ㉓

This vintage and antique interiors shop is all about the joy of one-off finds. You might pick up a 1960s Peter Hoyte armchair or limed oak desk, Turkish kilim rug or chesterfield ready for reupholstering. Smaller items include chopping boards, Hungarian sack-cloth bolsters, metal troughs and framed architectural drawings.

Arts & leisure

See also p106 **Nowhere Man**.

Brighton Open Air Theatre

NEW *Dyke Road Park, BN3 6EH (no phone, www.brightonopenairtheatre. co.uk). Bus 14, 27.* **Map** p103 A1 ㉔
See box left.

West Hill Hall

66 Compton Avenue, BN1 3PS (www. westhillwhistler.wordpress.com/1937-2/). Bus 7, 14, 18, 22, 27, 37. **Map** p103 C3 ㉕
This village-hall style space (the stage is lit by an old-fashioned standard lamp) is one of the more intriguing assets of Brighton's music scene. Mary Hampton recorded her stunning debut album here; John Peel's favourite UK songwriter, Liane Hall, is the venue's caretaker; and the Miserable Rich once held a mini residency. The gigs aren't particularly well publicised, so check community magazine and website for listings.

Sussex Square

Kemp Town & Hanover

With the long **St James's Street** and its characterful side-streets stretching centipede-like through the centre, **Kemp Town** is now defined as the area east of the Old Steine. It used to refer solely to the buildings designed and funded by early 19th-century property developer Thomas Read Kemp further to the east – luxury townhouses that attracted visitors such as Charles Dickens and Lewis Carroll. Two centuries on, Kemp Town is in need of the physical rejuvenation that is hoped will radiate outwards from the new Circus Street development (p110). But its spirit has showed no signs of tiring.

The district is, famously, home to Brighton's gay quarter (or the 'gay village'), where expressions of sexuality pulse from shops, restaurants and bars, and form the foundation of the nightlife. You'll find countless cafés and coffee shops, enticing delis, unabashed bars, welcoming pubs and stylish restaurants. On St James's Street, charity shops jostle companionably with sex shops, while New Steine Gardens has since 2009 been home to the *AIDS Memorial Sculpture* by local artist Romany Mark Bruce. Depicting two entwined figures whose shadows form the shape of the HIV/AIDS red ribbon, it's a striking invitation to sit and contemplate. Madieira Drive, by the seafront, is home to the larger gay nightspots, and there's a naturist beach hidden in the shingle.

This stretch of Kemp Town merges into the quieter Kemp Town Village to the east. From Upper St James's Street through to **St George's Road**, planted in between Victorian townhouses, there's a trail of interesting vintage shops. Further into the residential area, Thomas Read Kemp has been immortalised in the magnificent buildings of Sussex Square, Arundel Terrace and Lewes Crescent, the largest crescent in Britain.

Kemp Town is poised to get a new gateway. In autumn 2014, the old municipal market on Circus Street (recently host, in its derelict state, to big-name Brighton Festival exhibitions and other pop-up performances) will be demolished. In its place, work will begin on a £100 million development scheme to build a new housing, retail and cultural quarter, including a new studio for South East Dance and a public square.

North of Kemp Town is the residential district of **Hanover**, fondly called Muesli Mountain due to its perceived hippy vibe. The 15-acre Queen's Park is the focal point for the active Hanover community; Charles Barry, architect of the Houses of Parliament, designed the two entrance arches. The area is known for its excellent locals, and the 'Southover Shuffle' pub crawl up

steep Southover Street – stopping in at the **Greys** and the **Geese**, among others – is a classic route. The Metway Studios on Canning Street are home to Brighton's famous folk-rock exports the Levellers – Joe Strummer, Orbital and new Kemp Town resident Nick Cave have recorded here. Hanover's spine is Elm Grove – now home to a second branch of the artisan **Four Pot Bakery**, which has just opened in, of all things, a former brothel. Follow this steep road to the top and you reach the edge of the South Downs and **Brighton Racecourse**. It's a relatively small horse racing track, but with a cracking sea view.

Old Steine, Grand Parade and Lewes Road form the western boundary of this chapter, and Elm Grove the northern boundary. We have also included the seafront east of the Brighton Pier and along

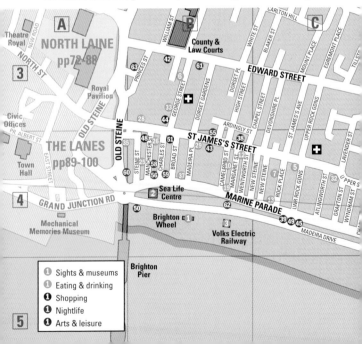

- ❶ Sights & museums
- ❶ Eating & drinking
- ❶ Shopping
- ❶ Nightlife
- ❶ Arts & leisure

Madeira Drive, which eventually brings you to Brighton Marina. This windswept road is all but pedestrianised, and often used for antiques fairs and car-boot sales. It throbs with vintage engines during the famous Brighton Speed Trials and Mods & Rockers-themed Brighton Burn-Up. Visit www.brightonrun. co.uk for a calendar of all the races.

Sights & museums

Brighton Wheel

Daltons Bastion, Madeira Drive, BN2 1TB (01273 722822, www.brighton wheel.com). Bus 12, 14, 27, 37, 47. **Open** 10am-9pm Mon-Thur, Sun; 10am-11pm Fri, Sat. Admission £8; £2-£6.50 reductions. **Map** p110 B4 ①

The Brighton Wheel is the city's attempt to 'do a London Eye', but with a rather incongruous commentary by

Alan Partridge creator and Brighton resident Steve Coogan. Understandably, he's not really sure how to pitch it. Adult tickets are £8, which buys you three revolutions at 160ft (50m) above sea level in one of 36 glass pods (for up to two adults and two children). Brighton, of course, has a lot less in the way of big historic buildings than London, and a lot more in the way of sea, so some find the 'panoramic views' slightly low on interest points. Then again, that hasn't deterred the makers of the i360 (p55), which will be two and a half times taller. The Wheel has planning permission to remain in place until May 2016, coming down just before the i360 opens.

Sea Life Centre

Marine Parade, BN2 1TB (01273 604234, www.visitsealife.com/brighton). Bus 12, 14, 16, 27, 37, 38, 47, 52. **Open** 10am-5pm Mon-Fri; 10am-6pm

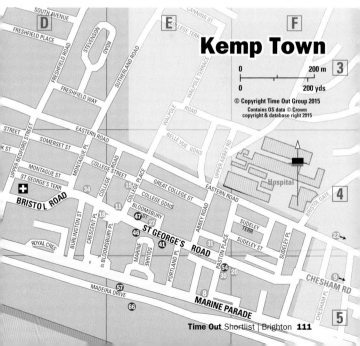

Sat, Sun. **Admission** £17.50; £14.50 reductions; online discounts available. **Map** p110 B4 ②

The world's oldest operating aquarium, the Sea Life Centre is now prized for its splendid Victorian columns as much as for its fishy inmates. Highlights include interactive rock pools for children, the new Rainforest Adventure trail featuring piranhas and poison dart frogs, an underwater tunnel with sharks and giant turtles, and a giant Pacific octopus that plays a mean game of hide-and-seek. Head up to the auditorium above the main tank to board a glass-bottom boat. There are tours throughout the day, with the ever-popular shark feedings on Tuesdays, Thursdays, Saturdays and Sundays.

Volk's Electric Railway

Aquarium Station, Madeira Drive (no phone, www.volkselectricrailway.co.uk). Bus 12, 14, 16, 27, 37, 38, 47, 52. **Open** Easter-Sept (trains run every 15mins) 11.15am-5pm Mon, Fri; 10.15am-5pm Tue, Wed, Thur; 10.15am-6pm Sat, Sun. Closed Sept-Easter. See website for dates of 'late running' evenings. **Tickets** (return) £3.60; £2.10 reductions. **Map** p110 B4 ③

Since 1883, Volk's Railway has trundled the one and a quarter miles between the pier-end of Madeira Drive to near what is now Brighton Marina. The world's oldest operating electric railway was designed by pioneering British engineer and Brighton resident Magnus Volk. It's a charming children's entertainment and an ironic rite of passage for students. It only stops at Halfway Station, near Yellowave (p128), en route.

Woodvale Cemetery

Lewes Road, BN2 4DU (www.brighton-hove.gov.uk). Bus 23, 24, 25, 29, 38, 48, 49, 78. **Open** Summer 9am-5.30pm Mon-Sat; 11am-5.30pm Sun. Winter 9am-4pm Mon-Sat; 11am-4pm Sun. **Admission** free. **Map** off p113 B1 ④

Nestled in a wooded valley off a particularly ugly stretch of Lewes Road, the 42-acre Woodvale Cemetery is worth

a detour. This is not your average cemetery: it features hundreds of specially planted trees and shrubs, landscaped lawns, rockeries, flowerbeds, a waterfall and stream, and impressive 19th-century twinned Gothic crematorium chapels. There is a circular way-marked trail and walker's guide.

Eating & drinking

See also p128 **Marlborough Pub & Theatre,** p126 **Patterns** and p126 **Verdict.** For some of Brighton's best pizza – takeaway only – try **Pizzaface** (35 St George's Road, 01273 699082, www.pizzaface pizza.co.uk). Artisan baker **Flour Pot** (p77) has a new outpost at 124 Elm Grove (01273 625854, www. flour-pot.co.uk).

Black Dove

74 St James's Street, BN2 1PA (01273 671119, www.blackdovebrighton.com). Bus 1, 2, 7, 16, 18, 21, 37, 38, N7. **Open** 4pm-midnight Mon-Thur; 4pm-1am Fri; noon-1am Sat; 4-11pm Sun. **Bar. Map** p110 C4 ⑤

A bog-standard boozer on the outside, an antiquarian's emporium with waist-coated mixologists within. Patrons lounge on chesterfields under candelabra, checking out the vintage curios and listening to Delta blues. The bespoke artwork includes a phenomenal urban canvas that's a mirror image of the bar in some crazy alternate reality. Surprisingly, there are over 50 beers too.

Bom-Bane's

24 George Street, BN2 1RH (01273 606400, www.bom-banes.com). Bus 1, 2, 7, 16, 18, 21, 37, 38. **Open** 5-11pm Tue, Thur; 12.30-11pm Wed; 5-11.30pm Fri; 12.30-11.30pm Sat. **££. Café/global. Map** p110 B3 ⑥

This bewitching café-restaurant takes its name and unique character from owner Jane Bom-Bane – hat-maker, harmonium player, Edinburgh Fringe hit and now hostess. The excellent

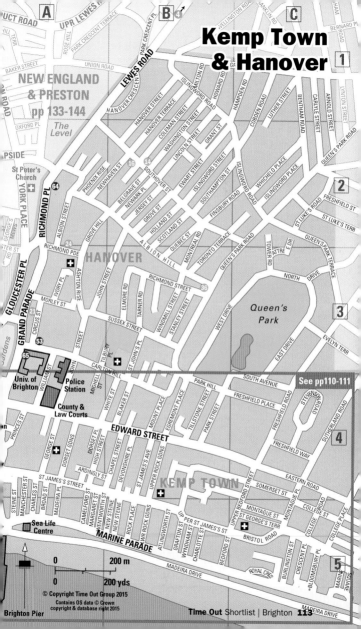

Kemp Town & Hanover

food ranges from Scandinavian-style venison to bresaola, but it inevitably plays second fiddle to the mechanical tables, including one that rotates slowly, eventually swapping your plate with your companion's, and another featuring a tiny working model of the pier. Jane's partner and co-host, Nick Pynn, plays the fiddle, and impromptu performances from Jane, Nick and friends (among them comedian Stewart Lee) are regular occurrences. Programmed gigs, films and puppet shows are held downstairs, and there's even a weekly homework club for secondary schoolers.

Brighton Rocks

6 Rock Place, BN2 1PF (01273 600550, www.brightonrocksbar.co.uk). Bus 1, 2, 7, 16, 18, 21, 37, 38, N7. **Open** 4-11pm Mon-Thur; 4pm-1am Fri-Sat; noon-11pm Sun. **Bar**. **Map** p110 C4 **7**
This intimate, retro-chic bar offers good cocktails, a growing list of craft beers and a sea view from its little heated terrace. The superior roast sells out every Sunday. Come August, the bar hosts one of the biggest Pride street parties in Brighton. It now offers cocktail masterclasses too.

Bristol Bar

Paston Place, BN2 1HA (01273 605687, www.thebristolbar.co.uk). Bus 12, 14, 27, N12, N14. **Open** 11.45am-10.30pm Mon-Wed, Fri-Sun; 11.45am-12.30am Thur. **Pub**. **Map** p111 E5 **8**
Always a good contender for an early evening drink thanks to its panoramic seafront view, this traditional boozer got a facelift and a fancier menu in 2014. Live jazz night on Thursdays is always rammed, and the landlord stays open late if people are still drinking.

Busby & Wilds

8-9 Rock Street, BN2 1NF (01273 696135, www.busbyandwilds.co.uk). Bus 37, 47. **Open** noon-10pm Tue-Sat; noon-8pm Sun. **Food served** noon-3pm, 6-10pm Tue-Sat; noon-6pm Sun. **££**. **Gastropub**. **Map** off p111 F5 **9**

Named after the architects who built nearby Sussex Square, this family-run gastropub opened in 2013 with the intention of offering residents of the eastern end of Kemp Town a top-notch local. But the sumptuous food, served beneath large latticed windows and duck-egg blue walls, beckons diners from much further afield. Tuesdays are Busby Burger night: £12 for a drink and a burger made with mince sourced from nearby Ashmore farm served in a brioche, with twists like smoked bacon jam.

Camelford Arms

30-31 Camelford Street, BN1 1TQ (01273 622386, www.camelford-arms. co.uk). Bus 1, 2, 7, 16, 18, 21, 37, 38, N7. **Open** noon-11pm Mon-Thur, Sun; noon-1am Fri, Sat. **Pub**. **Map** p110 B4 **10**
Popular with the LGBT community (with the 'B' also standing for 'bear' here), this is a cosy community pub with great Sunday lunches. The small decked 'Moroccan' garden is far from the usual smoking area by any other name. It's lovingly and rather sweetly decked out with draped fabrics and camel murals, and available to book.

Compass Point Eatery

NEW *19 St George's Road, BN2 1EB (01273 672672, www.cpeatery.com).* Bus 37, 47. **Open** 8am-6pm Mon, Tue, Thur, Fri; 8.30am-6.30pm Sat; 8.30am-5pm Sun. **££**. **American café/deli**. **Map** p111 E4 **11**
Run by a Londoner and a New Yorker who fell in love in Miami, this new kid on the block distinguishes itself with an American, Southern-inflected deli-style menu. Think po'boy sandwiches, NY subs and sides of mac 'n' cheese and sweet-potato mash. The biggest hitter so far is the meatloaf hoagie. The owners display and sell knick-knacks and collectibles too.

Diva

NEW *94 St James's Street, BN2 1TP (01273 660825, www.cafediva.co.uk).* Bus 1, 2, 7, 16, 18, 21, 37, 38.

Open 8am-5pm Mon-Sat. **£. Cypriot café/deli**. Map p110 B4 ⑫

Bringing Cypriot breakfasts to St James's Street, this small, quirky café and espresso bar opened at the close of 2014. Its smiley Cypriot owner used to run a café in London's Piccadilly. Sitting in her window seat with a Wake Up Brighton fruit cocktail, and eating grilled halloumi, garlic sausage and fresh herbs with your fry-up is an uplifting way to start your day.

Drakes

43-44 Marine Parade, BN2 1PE (01273 696934, www.therestaurantatdrakes. co.uk). Bus 12, 14, 27. **Open** 12.30-2pm, 7-9.45pm daily. **£££. Modern British**. Map p110 C4 ⑬

In one of Brighton's best boutique hotels, the restaurant at Drakes carries the quality of the residence into the intimate basement dining room. Chef Andrew Mackenzie conjures a mix of English seasonal food with French stylings, incorporating creative combinations such as scallops with chervil root purée and seaweed tuile. The cocktail bar has a great view of the sea and pier.

Geese

16 Southover Street, BN2 9UA (www. thegeese.co.uk). Bus 37. **Open** 4-11.30pm Mon-Thur; 4pm-12.30am Fri; noon-12.30am Sat; noon-11pm Sun. **Pub**. Map p113 B2 ⑭

This Hanover local has taken over from Shakespeare's Head in Seven Dials as *the* Brighton sausage-and-mash pub (which is hardly surprising since the team all decamped here in 2013). For £8.95, choose your sausage, your mash and your gravy from a mouthwatering list (including veggie options). The landlord's personal favourite? Wild boar sausage with colcannon and onion gravy. The Geese has come a long way since its days as a Guinness boozer called The Geese Have Gone Over The Water (named, depending on who you get talking to at the bar, in reference to either a Yeats poem or an IRA code phrase).

Ginger Dog

12-13 College Place, BN2 1HN (01273 620990, www.thegingerdog. com). Bus 1, 7, 14, 23, 37, 47, 52. **Open** noon-2pm, 6-10pm Mon-Thur; noon-3pm, 6-10pm Fri, Sat; 12.30-4pm, 6-10pm Sun. **££. Gastropub**. Map p111 E4 ⑮

One of the Gingerman's group of three gastropubs and one restaurant in and around Brighton, the Ginger Dog's menu reflects the gastronomic bent of its owners, with dishes such as roast Sussex pheasant, and fillet of seabass with polenta, crown prince squash, beet leaves and verjus. There's a popular two-course £12.50 lunch menu during the week.

Greys

105 Southover Street, BN2 9UA (01273 680734, www.greyspub.com). Bus 37. **Open** noon-11pm Mon-Wed, Sun; noon-11.30pm Thur; noon-12.30am Fri, Sat. **Pub**. Map p113 B2 ⑯

This little local pub has provided a stage for more folk and Americana veterans than will fit on its staircase of fame. The long-term owners left in 2012, leading to a period of uncertain programming. But the new landlords insist they're 'here to stay', and are booking gigs (plus the odd comedian too) in earnest. They've also introduced a new menu, including Mediterranean grazing plates and a lamb kleftiko option for Sunday lunch.

Hand in Hand

33 Upper St James's Street, BN2 1JN (01273 699595). Bus 1, 7, 14, 23, 37, 47, 52. **Open** noon-midnight Mon-Sat; noon-11pm Sun. **Pub**. Map p111 D4 ⑰

This tiny street-corner pub deep in Kemp Town strikes a winning balance between traditional and trendy. It offers an outstanding range of ales, plus live jazz, vintage slot machines and Victorian pin-ups. The most appropriate order would be the Kemp Town ale brewed on the premises in the microbrewery. Don't ask for a Foster's.

BRIGHTON BY AREA

top: Busby & Wilds p144;
middle left: Marmalade;
middle right: Metrodeco;
bottom: Plotting Parlour p183

Kemp Town Deli & Bistro

108 St George's Road, BN2 1EA (01273 603411). Bus 1, 7, 14, 23, 37, 47, 52. **Open** 8am-4pm Mon-Sat; 10am-2pm Sun. **££. Deli/bistro. Map** p111 D4 ⑱

On the crammed shelves of this delicatessen is a seductive selection of regional cheeses and fresh produce. There's not too much capacity in the cosy bistro with its spotty tablecloths, but people rotate in and out quickly and there's extra seating downstairs. Sandwiches and potato rösti come in several variations, and full English and eggs benedict consistently hit the mark. The kitchen shuts an hour before the deli.

Legends

31-34 Marine Parade, BN2 1TR (01273 624462, www.legendsbrighton.com). Bus 12, 14, 16, 27, 37, 38, 47, 52, N12, N14. **Open** 11am-5am daily. **Bar/club. Map** p110 B4 ⑲

As well as being 'Brighton's largest gay hotel', Legends is a popular gay club and bar, and a surprisingly solid option for a Sunday roast (noon-3pm, followed by cabaret at 3.30pm). The terrace bar has views over the sea and Brighton Pier, and serves homely staples and light bites. Cocktails replace coffees in the early evening. On Wednesdays, Fridays, Saturdays and Sundays, the Basement Club's dancefloor is in operation.

La Marinade

77 St George's Road, BN2 1EF (01273 600992). Bus 1, 7, 14, 23, 37, 47, 52. **Open** 6-11pm Tue, Wed; noon-3pm, 6-11pm Thur-Sat. **££. French. Map** p111 F5 ⑳

A petite, family-run French restaurant where the chef comes to your table to discuss the specials. The menu is concise, thoughtfully devised and reasonably priced, offering starters such as pan-fried baby squid with mixed herbs cooked in white wine. Mains include fillet of 28-day hung Scottish beef with sautéed wild mushrooms, crispy french fries and mixed leaves.

Market Diner

19-21 Circus Street, BN2 9QF (01273 608273, www.marketdinerbrighton. co.uk). Bus 23, 25, 28, 29, N5. **Open** all night 7.30pm-2pm daily. **£. Cafe. Map** p113 A3 ㉑

Hidden away on Circus Street behind the Old Steine, this all-night café (closed only between afternoon and early evening) has played a crucial role in many a classic Brighton bender. In contrast to the clientele, the fry-ups, pizzas and burritos are all very fresh, while cherry pie and spotted dick lay the comfort on thick. If you've been having it excessively large, try the famous gut-buster breakfast – with a cup of stewed tea, of course.

Marmalade

NEW *237 Eastern Road, BN2 5JJ (01273 606138, www.cafemarmalade.co.uk). Bus 1, 7, 14, 23, 37, 52.* **Open** 8am-6pm Mon-Sat; 9am-5pm Sun. **££. Café. Map** off p111 F4 ㉒

Since opening in 2013, this café has been so taken to Brighton's heart that it's expanding into hosting occasional supper clubs. It's perhaps not surprising: the owner co-founded Sussex food institution Bill's, and the light and airy Marmalade has some of its laidback foodie vibe. But here the passion feels more personal. Staff might bring dishes cooked at home, and pin favourite recipes to the counter. Their scrambled egg and salmon is the discerning Kemp Town resident's hangover cure.

Metrodeco

38 Upper St James's Street, BN2 1JN (01273 677243, www.metro-deco.com). Bus 1, 7, 14, 23, 37, 47, 52. **Open** 9.30am-6pm Mon-Sun; 9.30am-8pm Fri, Sat. **££. Café. Map** p110 C4 ㉓

The vintage iron dog bowls on the doorstep say it all: this eccentric 1930s-styled tearoom and basement antiques shop was one of the first dedicatedly dog-positive venues in the city. So much so that it offers an extensive doggy menu. People can shop for collectibles and furniture – largely 20th century – then relax with one of a wide choice of teas and infusions and slice of moist homemade cake. We've never seen so many beautifully dressed young men taking afternoon tea.

Planet India

4-5 Richmond Parade, BN2 9PH (01273 818149). Bus 23, 25, 28, 29. **Open** 6-10pm Tue-Sat; occasional Sun. **£**. **Indian**. **Map** p113 A3 ㉔

'Authentic homemade food made by authentic homemade Indians' reads the bright-pink frontage of this family-run vegetarian restaurant, just round the corner from Journeys hostel. A café-like space lined with family photos, it's beloved by anyone who appreciates healthy, authentic food at bargain prices. There are numerous gluten-free options, the water comes in up-cycled juice bottles and the hearty dhals and crisp samosas are often served barefoot. Hippy heaven.

Plotting Parlour

NEW *6 Steine Street, BN2 1TE (01273 621238). Bus 12, 14, 27, 37, 38, 16, 47, 52, N12, N14.* **Open** 3pm-midnight Mon-Thur, Sun; 3pm-1am Fri, Sat. **Cocktail bar**. **Map** p110 B4 ㉕

This intimate cocktail bar (which also serves great cake) arrived in a central yet tucked-away Kemp Town street in late 2014. The floor-length door curtains, Renaissance-style paintings and wood-burning stove conjure cosy old-English cheer. Cocktails come in around £7-£9 and include the Hemingway Daiquiri, served with a page from one of the great man's works, and a lip-tingling chilli and ginger margarita. Just be warned: once word gets round, the waiting time for your carefully constructed cocktail may soar.

Pomegranate

10 Manchester Street, BN2 1TF (01273 628386, www.pomegranatebrighton. co.uk). Bus 1, 2, 7, 12, 14, 16, 18, 21, 27, 37, 38, 16, 47, 52. **Open** noon-3pm, 6-11pm daily. **££**. **Contemporary Middle Eastern**. **Map** p110 B4 ㉖

An excellent modern Middle Eastern restaurant run by a Kurdish husband and wife who honour their national fruit in both their restaurant's name and their cooking. It's set over two floors, with wooden floors, brick fireplaces and colourful paintings by the husband (a successful artist as well as the head chef). Lebanese favourite tabouleh comes with a twist in the form of dried apricots; traditional mains such as shish kebabs are joined by European-influenced dishes like salmon fillets with goat's cheese, dill and pomegranate sauce. Sprinklings of the ruby-red seeds are added to many dishes.

Real Pâtisserie

34 St George's Road, BN2 1ED (01273 609655, www.realpatisserie.co.uk). Bus 1, 7, 14, 23, 37, 47, 52. **Open** 7am-5.30pm Mon-Sat. **Bakery**. **Map** p111 E4 ㉗

One of five outlets operated by local specialists in artisanal bread and French pâtisserie, whose founder trained in France. The Kemp Town shop and café was set up as an 'open bakery', where you can see how simply and honestly the food is being prepared, and has a real community feel. Staff mix, prove and bake everything from beautifully decorated chocolate mousse logs and glistening raspberry tarts to spiced lentil sausage rolls and goat's cheese quiches on the premises. You can even take bread-baking classes.

Redroaster

1D St James's Street, BN2 1RE (01273 686668, www.redroaster.co.uk). Bus 1, 2, 7, 16, 18, 21, 37, 38. **Open** 7am-7pm Mon-Sat; 8am-6.30pm Sun. **£**. **Café**. **Map** p110 B3 ㉘

This independent coffee house has been providing sanctuary for shoppers, dreamers, natterers and the chronically hungover for the best part of two decades. Because of its popularity, it expanded in 2008, with a new local roastery to fulfill demand from neighbouring hotels, restaurants and cafés. Frequently busy, it offers coffees in a wide variety of beans, styles and blends. Drink in, take away or purchase beans by the bag. For lunch, try the organic sandwiches. It also holds literary and musical events; see the café's Facebook page for details.

Saint James Tavern

16 Madeira Place, BN2 1TN (01273 626696). Bus 1, 2, 7, 16, 18, 21, 37, 38. **Open** noon-11pm Mon-Thur, Sun; noon-midnight Fri, Sat. **Pub. Map** p110 B4 ㉙

A rum pub, plain and simple. It stocks more than 70 varieties, from all four corners of the world, to make your insides feel as rich and warm as the mahogany surroundings – and the bar staff are happy to educate you on the merits of the different varieties too. The food is one of the better Thai options in Kemp Town.

Sam's of Brighton

1 Paston Place, BN2 1HA (01273 676222, www.samsofbrighton.co.uk). Bus 1, 7, 14, 23, 37, 47, 52. **Open** noon-3pm, 6-10pm Thur; noon-3pm, 6-10.30pm Fri, Sat; noon-4pm, 6-9pm Sun. £££. **Modern British. Map** p111 E5 ㉚

The eponymous owner of Sam's worked in top London restaurants before returning to his native south coast, where he runs this casual contemporary British bistro. At the time of writing, he'd just gone into long-term partnership with Ollie Couillaud, a big name on the London gastronomic scene, who'll be heading up the kitchen for a while. The menu shouldn't stray too far from Sam's modern British fare, but expect innovation. Watch out for new Brighton ventures from the pair, too.

Seven Bees Café

St George's Church, BN2 1ED (01273 279448, www.stgeorgesbrighton.org). Bus 37, 47. **Open** 9.30am-3pm Mon-Fri. **Café. Map** p111 E4 ㉛

For one of the best cooked breakfasts in Brighton (with sausages and bacon from local outdoor-reared pigs), get yourself to church. Seven Bees has migrated from the Lanes to the north aisle of St George's, Kemp Town's neoclassical parish church, where it now functions as a not-for-profit community café on weekdays. (St George's hosts some great gigs courtesy of local promoters Melting Vinyl, too.)

Sidewinder

65 St James's Street BN2 1PJ (01273 679927). Bus 1, 2, 7, 16, 18, 21, 37, 38, N7. **Open** noon-1am Mon-Thur, Sun; noon-2am Fri, Sat. **Pub. Map** p110 C4 ㉜

Located towards Kemp Town village, this large pub with two well-furnished beer gardens is a popular and vaguely bohemian hang-out, with various quiz, DJ and open-mic nights. The new management brought in popular independent Mexican kitchen Smokin' Gringos Mexican in 2014. On Sundays there's a 'build your own Bloody Mary' bar.

Tea Cosy

3 George Street, BN2 1RH (no phone, www.theteacosy.co.uk). Bus 1, 2, 7, 16, 18, 21, 37, 38. **Open** noon-5pm Wed-Fri, Sun; noon-5.30pm Sat. ££. **Café. Map** p110 B3 ㉝

The eccentric individual who set up this tearoom, decked it out in commemorative Royal Family china and established its etiquette (no clanking of teaspoons or biscuit-dunking, please) sold on in 2010. His sharp-tongued snootiness is much missed. But while the whole experience now feels more tongue-in-cheek, where else can you have a Wills and Kate High Tea, Charles and Camilla Elevenses or a Prince Harry (a boiled egg and soldiers, naturally) for breakfast?

Thomas Kemp

8 St George's Road, BN2 1EB (01273 683334). Bus 1, 2, 7, 14, 23, 37, 47, 52, N7, N12, N14. **Open** noon-midnight Mon-Thur, Sun; noon-1am Fri, Sat. **Pub. Map** p111 D4 ㉞

BRIGHTON BY AREA

Scene of the crime

Thrillers with a Brighton backdrop.

The villain had been on the run for two years when the detective spotted him in Brighton city centre. Jumping out of his car, he gave chase. They threaded through the Lanes, the detective closing in on the suspect. By the Clock Tower, in the heart of town, the officer rugby-tackled his target and arrested him. 'It's just like a Peter James novel,' exclaimed the criminal. The detective emailed Peter James to tell him about the incident.

Give or take a murder or two, the fictional Brighton of Peter James is painstakingly accurate to the Brighton of fact. The ten best-selling Roy Grace crime novels are set in the city, detailing the parks and the pubs, the courts and the criminals, with uncanny detail. Even the protagonist is based on a real, high-profile policeman, who reads the drafts.

'I go out, on average, once a week with the police,' says James. 'Whether on a drugs raid, with the dive teams or just to the briefing in the morning. I'm closely involved with Sussex Police and its detectives.'

In the preface to his first book, *Dead Simple*, he explains: 'Writing is always regarded as a solitary occupation, but for me it is a team effort.' Following a personal request, the 11th Roy Grace book, *You Are Dead*, due out in 2015, features a skeleton being dug up near superstar DJ Norman Cook's Big Beach Café (p149) in Hove. His wife, Zoe Ball, is a fan.

James was born and brought up in Brighton. 'I'm steeped in its criminal culture,' he says. 'It's become a hip, cool city, but it was quite edgy. Brighton started as a smuggling village. And then the railway came in 1841, and all the villains came down, bringing cockfighting, prostitution, loan-sharking and gangs. By the 1930s, Brighton was the murder capital of Europe.'

He reels off a list of reasons why Brighton is the perfect place for criminals: a major seaport, an airport in Shoreham, miles of unguarded coastline, Brighton Marina, the Eurotunnel, and Gatwick Airport '25 minutes away in a fast car'.

The local tourist board doesn't seem to mind James highlighting the city's dark underbelly: the official Peter James Walking Dead Tour has been doing great business since 2013, and is set to be extended.

'There are so many good deposition sites for a body in Brighton,' says James. 'I'm always finding new secret tunnels. Did you know you can go down a manhole cover and come out on Hove Lagoon?'

City Books (p159) usually has signed copies of his latest books.

The Thomas Kemp, named after Kemp Town's founder, is a large and inviting rustic bar with a good beer garden for summer drinking. At the weekend, it livens up (and shuts down conversations) with loud and eclectic DJ sets. The decked outdoor seating area is heated, but if it's really cold, it's more comfortable to huddle around the log fires. A broad menu of sandwiches and bigger mains is served from noon until 9.30pm daily.

VIP Pizza

NEW *19 Old Steine, BN1 1EL (01273 677377, www.pizzavip.co.uk). Bus 1, 2, 7, 16, 18, 21, 33, 37, 38, 52.* **Open** noon-10.30pm daily. **£. Italian. Map** p110 A4 ㉟
Authentic Italian pizzas are served by authentically gorgeous young Italian waiters at tables so close that your knees and conversations brush with those of your neighbours. Opened in 2014, this family business with roots in 19th-century Naples has turned around a previously uninviting site with big and tasty wood-fired pizzas and deli options, and an interior with cheerful red metal chairs. The name stands for 'Very Italian Pizza'. It sells Italian cheese, wines and salami too, and coffee is served from 10am.

Wild Cherry

91 Queen's Park Road, BN2 0GJ (01273 691494, www.wildcherrybrighton.co.uk). Bus 18, 23, 37. **Open** 9.30am-7pm Mon, Tue, Thur, Fri; 10.30am-6pm Sat; 11.30am-5pm Sun. **££. Café/deli. Map** p113 B3 ㊱
The beauty of natural produce is all the decoration needed at this organic neighbourhood deli and café, where the counters are lined with colourful seeds, spices and seasonal veg. Locals deliberately keep quiet about this family business, which has been here since 2005, and was one of the first to take gluten- and wheat-free options seriously. Grab a slice of moussaka and a helping of sticky superfood pudding for a picnic at nearby Queen's Park (kids are also well catered for with organic snacks and baby food). Or sip a cup of coffee on the suntrap porch.

WitchEZ

NEW *16 Marine Parade, BN2 1TL (01273 673652, www.thewitchez-cafe. co.uk). Bus 12, 14, 16, 27, 37, 38, 47, 52.* **Open** 2.30-9.30pm Tue-Fri. Times vary Mon, Sat, Sun; phone to check. **££. Eastern European. Map** p110 B4 ㊲
Everything is a little out of the ordinary (or should we simply say English?) at this fantastic new café-restaurant near Brighton Pier, run by three Polish women, with help from their dog and their model witch, Greta. They call themselves the UK's first Photo Design Café Bar, offering passport, pet photography and other photo services while you eat, and they also screen old black and white films at the back. But their real selling point is the food: beautifully presented stews, dumplings, sausages and rösti. Sweet Little Hooves is a dessert of potato dumplings with sugar, cinnamon and cream.

Shopping

Acoustic Music Company

39 St James's Street, BN2 1RG (01273 671841, www.theacousticmusicco.co.uk). Bus 1, 2, 7, 16, 18, 21, 37, 38. **Open** 11am-4pm Tue-Sat. **Map** p110 B4 ㊳
This vendor represents more than 40 guitar and mandolin makers. Picking the right instrument, we're told, can take hours, if not days, especially when you can choose from new and used guitars and mandolins – or pick a bargain from 'the dusty corner', the place for long-forgotten instruments in need of a loving home.

Andy Doig Fishtail Neon Studio

282 Madeira Drive, BN2 1PT (01273 694662, www.andydoig.com). Bus

12, 14, 16, 27, 37, 38, 47, 52. **Open** 10am-6pm Mon-Fri; by appointment Sat, Sun. **Map** p110 C4 ㊴

In one of several little gallery workshops housed in the Madeira Drive Arches, Andy Doig has been making neon artworks for more than 20 years. Having learnt his craft on West End musicals, he has had his work shown at venues including Tate Modern and Brighton Town Hall (on to which he projected neon ravens taking flight). His signs and fairground-style crosses are especially popular – though a bright pink question mark will set you back £700.

Brighton Flea Market

31A Upper St James's Street, BN2 1JN (01273 624006, www.flea-markets. co.uk). Bus 1, 2, 7, 14, 23, 37, 47, 52. **Open** 10am-5.30pm Mon-Sat; 10:30am-5pm Sun. **Map** p111 D4 ㊵

A bright pink hub filled with curious collectibles, antiques and furniture, this sister to Lewes Flea Market opened in 1990 and should be your fixed point on any trundle through Kemp Town's vintage scene. The numerous stalls, filled with globally hunted-down treasures, are spread over two floors. You might come away with a set of plates, a piece of taxidermy or a Bakelite telephone, regardless of what you went in for.

Butlers Wine Cellar

88 St George's Road, BN2 1EE (01273 621638, www.butlers-winecellar.co.uk) Bus 1, 7, 14, 23, 37, 47, 52. **Open** 11am-7pm Tue-Sat; noon-3pm Sun. **Map** p111 E4 ㊶

One of Brighton's favourite wine shops – or, rather, two. The charismatic Henry Butler, who inherited the wine merchants from his parents, opened this Kemp Town branch in 2011. The broad and eclectic range is opened up to you through the knowledgeable service, and staff have close relationships with producers of local sparkling wines such as Lewes's Breaky Bottom. Butlers stocks over 2,000 wines, including two-bottle-only rarities and everyday tipples for under a tenner. The original Hanover Butlers is at 247 Queen's Park Road (01273 698724).

Dig For Victory

175 Edward Street, BN2 0JB (01273 676402, www.digforvictoryclothing.com). Bus 1, 2, 7, 14, 52. **Open** 10am-6pm Thur-Sat; by appointment Mon-Wed. **Map** p110 B3 ㊷

MIA and Bat For Lashes have been among the customers at this fantastic shop specialising in handmade retro-inspired dresses. You can browse the vast array of vintage and end-of-roll fabrics before having a prom, swing, tea or even wedding dress custom made. Owner Eleanor Callaghan started the business on Etsy and made such a success of it that she's had to teach her boyfriend to sew too. Both moonlight, as do many of Callaghan's quirkier creations, in Brighton twee-pop band the Bobby McGees.

Doggy Fashion

98 St James's Street, BN2 1TP (01273 695631, www.doggyfashion.co.uk). Bus 1, 2, 7, 16, 18, 21, 37, 38. **Open** 9am-5pm Mon-Sat. **Map** p110 B4 ㊸

How on earth did Kemp Town's fashion-conscious mutts manage before these guys came along? Whether your pup needs a spritz of perfume, a rainbow lead or a hand-beaded collar, this is the place. It's recently doubled in size and has diversified into more general pet products (including an open-plan multi-species grooming parlour). But canines – especially the really, really tiny ones – are still top dog.

Gef Tom Son

2 George Street, BN2 1RH (01273 945317, www.gef-tom-son.co.uk). Bus 1, 2, 7, 16, 18, 21, 37, 38. **Open** 10am-5.30pm Mon-Sat. **Map** p110 B3 ㊹

Geoff Thompson's necklaces, bracelets and earrings use over 70 varieties of

Dig For Victory

forvictoryclothing.com

VICTORY

stone, from rubies to freshwater pearls, and are handmade in his Kemp Town shop (he has another in Eastbourne). Good old-fashioned glamour is his game, but he's not sniffy about small budgets. He'll advise you attentively (and, if you desire it, bitchily), whether you're a famous actress spending £3,000 on a dramatic necklace or a teenager buying a £10 amethyst pendant.

JAG Gallery

283A Madeira Drive, BN2 1PT (07810 523984, www.jagartgallery.co.uk). Bus 12, 14, 16, 27, 37, 38, 47, 52. **Open** 10am-5pm Sat, Sun; by appointment Mon-Fri. **Map** p110 C4 **45**
Former England cricketer Phil Tufnell is (in his spare time) among the 22 artists who work at this studio-gallery. They include illustrators, ceramicists and photographers. Another is Julie Anne Gilbert, who painted the cover for local boy Fat Boy Slim's greatest hits album. It's a friendly, idiosyncratic and very Brighton place.

Kemptown Bookshop

91 St George's Road, BN2 1EE (01273 682110, www.kemptownbookshop.co.uk). Bus 1, 7, 14, 23, 37, 47, 52. **Open** 9am-5.30pm Mon-Sat. **Map** p111 E4 **46**
Now regularly listed as one of the best independent bookstores in the UK, this shop owes its success – and its three storeys – to customer-turned-owner Darion Goodwin. He expanded the building upwards and downwards and also runs the successful Bookroom Art Press. The weeny upstairs café is the sort of place poets might go for an illicit rendezvous. But pride of place is given, of course, to the carefully chosen 10,000 or so titles.

Kemptown Trading Post & Coffee Shop

28 St George's Road, BN2 1ED (01273 698873). Bus 1, 7, 14, 23, 37, 47, 52. **Open** 9am-5pm Tue-Fri; 10am-5pm Sat; 10am-2pm Sun. No credit cards under £10. **Map** p111 E4 **47**

A mini community in itself, this large showroom of ever-changing retro furniture and collectibles rents out cabinets and units to local sellers. It also operates a café, where you can contemplate purchases over coffee and cake. You'll find lovingly selected and eclectic items from 1950s Coca-Cola machines and rare Scorsese film posters to vintage pearls and gnomes.

Merlin & Ellis

NEW *9 Manchester Street, BN2 1TF (01273 623560, www.merlinandellis. net). Bus 1, 2, 7, 12, 14, 16, 18, 21, 27, 37, 38, 47, 52.* **Open** 10am-6pm Tue-Sat; noon-5pm Sun. **Map** p110 B4 **48**
Many Kemp Town shops function partly as an overspill for their owner's personality, but careful thought has gone into this artfully cluttered boutique. Owner Ellis (Merlin was his late Labrador) sells vegan grooming products and high-end vintage pieces while hosting artist-led ceramics workshops and lino printing classes on the first floor. The plan is to grow the shop as an LGBT hub with regular author events.

Modern World Gallery

283 Madeira Drive, BN2 1PT (01273 567168, www.modernworldgallery.com). Bus 12, 14, 27, 37, 38, 16, 47, 52. **Open** 10am-5pm Sat-Sun. Varies Mon-Fri; phone to check. **Map** p110 C4 **49**
Brighton was a fairly safe bet for the UK's only mod art gallery, specialising in 'art and collectibles inspired, created, and signed by mods', and situated not far from where *Quadrophenia*'s famous beach battle was filmed. It also puts on the odd gig and scooter rally. Red, white and blue predominate.

Oh So Swedish

Unit 4, Lower Promenade, BN2 1ET (07913 226245, www.ohsoswedish.net). Bus 12, 14, 27, 37, 47. **Open** 1-5pm daily. **Map** p110 B4 **50**
Buy hand-painted baskets, cheese-shaped pencil holders, elk placemats, screen-printed Lapland notebooks, bags

made from recycled Swedish coffee packaging and even crocheted kettle holders at this studio and workshop selling handmade gifts and homewares from Sweden. All except the driftwood garlands, that is, which come from Brighton beach.

Prowler

112-113 St James's Street, BN2 1TH (01273 683680, www.prowler.co.uk). Bus 1, 2, 7, 16, 18, 21, 37, 38. **Open** 10.30am-6.30pm Mon-Sat; noon-6pm Sun. **Map** p110 B4 ⑤
This gay lifestyle shop offers a wide variety of sexually encouraging toys, enhancements and bondage accessories, plus aromas, clothing, magazines and books.

Room Service

34 Upper St James's Street, BN2 1JN (01273 628428, www.roomservice brighton.com). Bus 1, 2, 7, 14, 23, 37, 47, 52. **Open** 10am-5pm Mon-Sat; noon-4pm Sun. **Map** p110 C4 ⑤
Formerly Brick-a-Brack, this long-established vintage furniture and lighting store is one of the classiest and friendliest shops in Kemp Town. It sources pieces to suit every clean-line fetish, from coffee tables and swivel chairs to anglepoises, clocks and old shop signs. Don't see what you're after? The owners are happy to go hunting.

Wood Store

16 Circus Street, BN2 9QF (01273 570500, www.woodrecycling.org.uk). Bus 23, 25, 28, 29. **Open** 9am-5.30pm Mon-Sat. **Map** p113 A3 ⑤
This not-for-profit community carpentry workshop and store was the first of its kind in the country. Staff collect and recycle waste timber, turning it into bespoke tables, bookshelves and benches. They also sell reclaimed wood such as floorboards in their raw state – a lifestyle market that's rocketed since the Wood Store opened in 1998. The large gallery shop features work in wood by handpicked local artists. From September 2015, they will be relocating to make way for the new Circus Street development – keep an eye on the website for details.

Nightlife

See also p115 **Greys**, a pub set to resume hosting gigs and comedy; p117 **Legends**, a gay bar with basement club; and p112 **Bom-Bane's**, a unique restaurant with impromptu musical performances, films and gigs.

Brighton Ballroom

83 St George's Road, BN2 1EF (01273 605789, www.brightonballroom.com). Bus 1, 7, 14, 23, 37, 47, 52, N7, N12, N14. **Open** varies. **Map** p111 E5 ⑤
This unusual green-domed building was once a mausoleum – the family grave of 19th-century British Indian Sir Albert Sassoon – and has been through many guises since. Finally, in 2010, the owners of Proud Camden reopened it as a cabaret and supper club with an eye to the ever-growing market for 'vintage glamour': think speakeasy nights, masquerade balls and lots of burlesque. Local Dynamite Boogaloo star (and David Bailey model) Dolly Rocket is a quality regular.

Bulldog

31 St James's Street, BN2 1RF (01273 696996, www.bulldogbrighton.com). Bus 1, 2, 7, 16, 18, 21, 37, 38, N7. **Open** 11am-2am Mon-Wed; 11am-4am Thur; 11am-7am Fri; 11am-8am Sat; noon-3am Sun. **Map** p110 B4 ⑤
Brighton's longest-established gay pub (it's been open more than 35 years) also operates some of the longest opening hours in the city, with a 24-hour licence at weekends. Like its canine namesake, it isn't the prettiest of drinking dens, and can be slightly intimidating from the outside. But inside it's as friendly as it is boozy, and though gay men make up the large majority, all are welcome. It now has a restricted door policy in the early hours, with a £5 fee (that includes your first drink) on weekends.

BRIGHTON BY AREA

Charles Street

8 Marine Parade, BN2 1TA (01273 624091, www.charles-street.com). Bus 12, 14, 16, 27, 37, 38, 47, 52, N12, N14. **Open** noon-2am Mon, Fri; noon-1am Tue, Wed, Sun; noon-3am Thur, Sat. **Map** p110 B4 ❺❻

This bar and club is owned by a chain that knows how to create an enticing gay-friendly atmosphere. With two floors, the bar can hold a good crowd and offers a simple pub menu. There's an outdoor terrace on the ground floor, and club nights and cabarets are held at Club Envy on the second.

Concorde 2

Madeira Shelter Hall, Madeira Drive, BN2 1EN (01273 673311, www.concorde2.co.uk). Bus 12, 14, 27, N12, N14. **Open** varies. **Map** p111 E5 ❺❼

Perhaps Brighton's best-known music venue, Concorde 2 was the birthplace of Norman Cook's famous mid '90s club night Big Beat Boutique, and for years an essential stop-off for big UK touring bands. These days, exciting bookings are fewer and further between, while that long windswept walk from the station to the seafront venue can put visiting fans off. But the place certainly has a distinctive atmosphere, and the new sound system may change things again.

Latest Music Bar

14-17 Manchester Street, BN2 1TF (01273 687171, www.thelatest.co.uk/musicbar). Bus 1, 2, 7, 12, 14, 16, 18, 21, 27, 37, 38, 16, 47, 52, N7. **Open** from 6pm daily. Closing times vary. **Map** p110 B4 ❺❽

The magic city stage-set mural isn't the only thing to linger since this venue's days as the Joogleberry Playhouse. It has also meandered on with an eclectic policy that includes popular local bands, fringe theatre and literary nights. The brilliant monthly Catalyst Club has been providing weird and wonderful lectures for over ten years. Above the basement performance space is a spacious and flexible bar, giving the whole venue a laid-back if rather changeable vibe.

Patterns

NEW *10 Marine Parade, BN2 1TL. (01273 606906, www.patternsbrighton.co.uk). Bus 12, 14, 27, 37, 38, 16, 47, 52, N12, N14.* **Open** *May-Sept* noon-3pm Mon-Thur, Sun; noon-4am Fri, Sat. *Oct-Apr* 5pm-3am Mon-Thur, Sun; 5pm-4am Fri, Sat. **Map** p110 B4 ❺❾

Audio is no more. But its well-earned rep as a real clubber's club should linger on in the site's new guise as Patterns – even if the ground floor has undergone a total redesign ('art deco with a touch of Bauhaus', apparently). New owners Mothership Group operate several hip East London venues, and confirmed promoters both local and national include Mute, Rhythm Junction, Disco Deviant, Bugged Out and old favourites Bastard Pop, with live bands performing in both the downstairs club and upstairs bar. Watch out for local pop-ups at the new food kiosk on the terrace.

Revenge

32-34 Old Steine, BN1 1EL (01273 606064, www.revenge.co.uk). Bus 1, 2, 7, 16, 18, 21, 33, 37, 38, 52, N5, N7, N12, N14. **Open** 11pm-3am Tue; 10.30pm-4am Thur; 10.30pm-5am Fri, Sat. **Map** p110 A4 ❻⓿

The biggest gay club on the south coast, spread over three floors with a roof terrace and an LED-lined box bar, and some great drinks deals. Established back in 1991, with the later addition of Bar Revenge (formerly R-Bar) on Marine Parade, it holds a crucial place in the city's LGBT scene. But these days, you'll find as many straight revellers dancing to cheese (or, on X-Factor Fridays, the latest talent show evictee).

The Verdict

159 Edward Street, BN2 0JB (01273 674847, www.verdictjazz.co.uk). Bus 1, 2, 7, 18, 23, 52. **Open** *Café* 8am-4pm Mon-Fri. *Venue* from 7pm Wed, Fri, some Sats. **Map** p110 B3 ❻❶

BRIGHTON BY AREA

Sets in the city

Overcoming the pebbles problem for beach volleyball.

Playing beach volleyball on Brighton's lumpy pebbles used to be more of an exercise in masochism than a sport. But **Yellowave Beachsports** (p128), Britain's first dedicated beach sports venue, has solved the problem – with the help of a whole lot of sand.

On sunny summer days, the centre's six sand-filled courts are crowded with Brightonians bouncing volleyballs, keeping up footballs, throwing Frisbees and hurling rugby balls. It's not exactly quiet when it's cloudy, either. Yellowave attracts sturdy types and, such is the addictive quality of beach volleyball, fanatics have been known to play in the snow.

Yellowave was opened in 2007 by Brighton-born Katie Mintram and her family. Katie was one of the top ten beach volleyball players in the country, and wanted to recreate the beach lifestyle she had experienced in California.

Beach volleyball has soared in popularity since the 2012 Olympics, but it's not the only thing that draws people to this stretch of Madeira Drive, just past Concorde 2. The Barefoot Café, with its decked area looking towards Brighton Pier, is a popular spot for a smoothie, sandwich or glass of wine. There are also monthly barbecues from May to August, a free sandy play area, and acoustic gigs in the summer. In 2014, Yellowave added a wood-clad clubhouse, which hosts weekly yoga, pilates and children's classes.

'We've created a community,' Katie says. 'People just come down and hang out, meet friends and have a drink here.' Whatever the activity, soft landings are guaranteed.

Court hire is £21 per hour. Lessons, tasters and league memberships are also available.

You don't expect to find a jazz joint opposite the AmEx building, which may be why even some residents aren't aware of the Verdict's existence. By day it's a great little licensed café with a garden. On Wednesday, Friday and some Saturdays the 60-capacity cabaret-style basement hosts the odd folk and comedy gig alongside local, top Brit and the occasional American jazz bookings. Kit Downes, Gilad Atzmon and the late Stan Tracey have all played here.

Volks Bar & Club

3 The Colonnade, Madeira Drive, BN2 1PS (01273 682828, www.volksclub. co.uk). Bus 12, 14, 16, 27, 37, 38, 47, 52, N12, N14. **Open** *varies.* **Map** p110 B4 **62**
A pretence-free seafront club with two grimy rooms and an enduring commitment to drum 'n' bass. Outside promoters put on psy-trance, hip hop and breaks nights too, but never a hint of cheesy techno. The Monday reggae fixture endures, and on Thursdays, bass night Roll Through will keep your organs judering till 5am. The terrace is a popular summer drinking spot.

Arts & leisure

Marlborough Pub & Theatre

4 Prince's Street, BN2 1RD (01273 570028, www.marlboroughtheatre. org.uk). Bus 5, 21, 22, 24, 25, 28, 48, 56, N5. **Map** p110 B3 **63**
Housed above a queer pub that's been intrinsic to Brighton counterculture since the 1970s is this tiny 60-seat theatre with a miniature proscenium arch. It runs Pink Fringe, an ambitious annual February-to-July programme of LGBT performance and heritage, as well as hosting alternative theatre, comedy and cabaret. Jonny Woo, Le Gateau Chocolat and Bette Bourne have all performed here, while the bi-monthly steampunk events have been a fixture since 2008. The theatre and bar have now fused, with performances spilling downstairs and the creative and party atmospheres mingling gorgeously.

Phoenix Brighton

10-14 Waterloo Place, BN2 9NB (01273 603700, www.phoenixarts.org). Bus 23, 25, 28, 29, 37. **Open** 11am-5pm daily *during exhibitions.* **Map** p113 A2 **64**
You wouldn't guess it at a glance, but working away behind the 1970s concrete façade of this huge building are more than 100 visual artists, from painters to potters and sculptors to printers. Phoenix Brighton is a not-for-profit organisation which, in addition to providing workshop space and art courses, stages around six exhibitions a year. In 2014, it got a facelift (with a heritage paint scheme inspired by Bauhaus colourist Johannes Itten, since you asked), and renovation of the gallery and foyer is scheduled for completion by the end of 2015.

Sallis Benney Theatre & University of Brighton Gallery

58-67 Grand Parade, BN2 0JY (01273 643010, www.arts.brighton.ac.uk/ whats-on). Bus 18, 23, 25, 28, 29. **Map** p113 A3 **65**
This theatre and gallery complex with a long glass frontage belongs to the University of Brighton. It hosts a huge range of events, from major artist retrospectives to indie gigs, comedy to free public lectures. It's busiest come the annual spring graduate degree shows, and when hosting Brighton Festival productions and screenings as part of Brighton film festival Cine-City. For evening and weekend performances, the theatre entrance is located at the north end, on the corner of Kingswood Street.

Yellowave Beachsports

299 Madeira Drive, BN2 1EN (01273 672222, www.yellowave.co.uk). Bus 12, 14, 27. **Open** *Mar-Oct* 10am-10pm Mon-Fri; 10am-8pm Sat, Sun. *Nov-Feb* 11am-9pm Tue-Thur; 11am-7pm Fri; 10am-5pm Sat, Sun. *Times vary according to the weather and demand.* **Map** p111 E5 **66**
See box p127.

Open Market p145

New England Quarter & Preston

Although the name 'New England Quarter' – after New England Road, upon which it is centred – is a relatively new term, it's a moniker that has been readily accepted by Brightonians. In this chapter, we have also included the area up to Lewes Road to the north-east, and Preston Circus, with Preston Park and Preston Manor, to the north-west.

Since construction work began in 2004, the redevelopment of the New England Quarter has drastically altered the landscape of the centre of Brighton. This narrow strip of hillside immediately east of Brighton station had housed locomotive and goods yards. After they closed in 1964, the land remained derelict apart from some high-density housing developments, small businesses and car parks. Brighton & Hove City Council finally gave planning permission for the development of what was the city's largest

brownfield site in 2002, and any visitor who has been away from the city in the intervening years will be amazed at the number of new buildings.

Once the butt of lazy local comedians' jokes, the adjacent London Road (the southerly end of the A23) and adjoining York Place have undergone a more exciting and recent transformation. The regeneration hinges around three big developments. The old Co-Op building, once a four-storey department store, has been turned into student housing, with shop space underneath, preserving the curving 1930s façade.

Add to this the complete renovation of **the Level** park and recreation ground and rebirth of the **Open Market**, and it's no wonder independent local businesses have been emboldened to take a punt on previously deserted shop spaces.

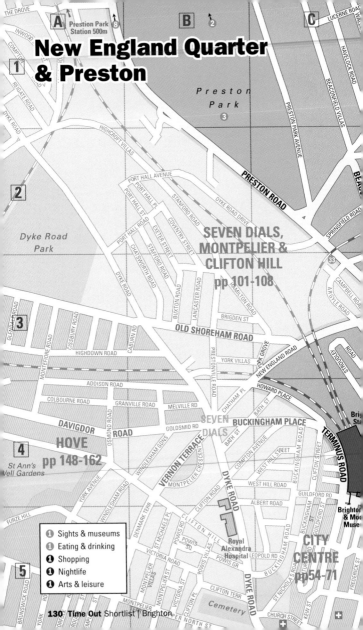

New England Quarter & Preston

A Preston Park Station 500m **B** **C** LUCERNE ROAD

THE DROVE
INWOOD
COMPTON ROAD

REGATE ROAD
DYKE ROAD

Preston
Park
3

HIGHCROFT VILLAS

Dyke Road
Park

PORT HALL AVENUE
PORT HALL PL
PORT HALL ST
PORT HALL ROAD
CHATSWORTH ROAD
DYKE ROAD
STANFORD ROAD
COVENTRY STREET
EXETER STREET
STAFFORD ROAD

DYKE ROAD DRIVE

PRESTON ROAD

PRESTON PARK AVENUE

BEACONSFIELD VILLAS
HAVELOCK ROAD

BEA

SPRINGFIELD ROAD

CAMPBELL ROAD
ARGYLE ROAD

**SEVEN DIALS,
MONTPELIER &
CLIFTON HILL
pp 101-108**

HAMILTON ROAD
BUXTON ROAD
LANCASTER ROAD
BRIGDEN ST

OLD SHOREHAM ROAD

GLENDALE ROAD
MONTEFIORE ROAD
FISSBURY ROAD
HIGHDOWN ROAD
CABURN RD

PRESTONVILLE ROAD
YORK VILLAS

NEW ENGLAND ROAD

ROAD
STANLEY

ADDISON ROAD
COLBOURNE ROAD

GRANVILLE ROAD
MELVILLE RD
GOLDSMID RD

CHATHAM PL
BATH ST

HOWARD PLACE

DAVIGDOR ROAD

**HOVE
pp 148-162**

St Ann's
Well Gardens

OSMOND ROAD
WINDLESHAM GDNS
VERNON TERRACE
MONTPELIER CRESCENT

**SEVEN
DIALS**

BUCKINGHAM PLACE

BATH ST
COMPTON AVENUE
WEST HILL STREET
WEST HILL ROAD
ALBERT ROAD

CLIFTON STREET
CLIFTON PLACE

BUCKINGHAM ROAD

TERMINUS ROAD

Brig
Sta

Brighton
& Mo
Muse

FURZE HILL
YORK AVENUE

DENMARK TERR
ST MICHAELS PL
POWIS RD
POWIS SQ

CLIFTON HILL

VICTORIA ROAD

POWIS VILLAS

CLIFTON STREET

DYKE ROAD

Royal
Alexandra
Hospital
LEOPOLD RD
POWIS GR

COMPTON AVENUE

GUILDFORD RD
GUILDFORD ST
BUCKINGHAM ST

**CITY
CENTRE
pp54-71**

BRUNSWICK ROAD
MONTPELIER VILLAS
MONTPELIER ROAD
VICTORIA ROAD
VICTORIA PL
CLIFTON TERR
CLIFTON RD

MONTPELIER
PLACE
CLIFTON
TERRACE
NORTH ST

ST NICHOLAS RD
FREDERICK'S

KEW ST

Cemetery
CHURCH STREET

- **1** Sights & museums
- **1** Eating & drinking
- **1** Shopping
- **1** Nightlife
- **1** Arts & leisure

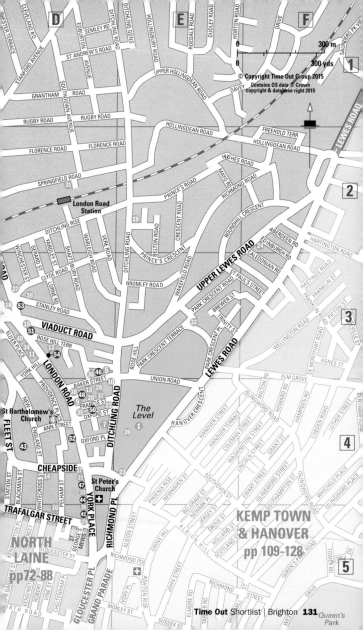

© Copyright Time Out Group 2015

Contains OS data © Crown
copyright & database right 2015

300 m

300 yds

D   **E**   **F**

1

2

3

4

5

CLEVELAND RD
HESTER TERRACE
SEMLEY RD
EDBURTON AVENUE
DITCHLING RISE
HOLLINGBURY ROAD
ROEDALE ROAD
DUDLEY ROAD
HORTON ROAD
DRIVE
SAUNDERS PK VW
LEWES ROAD

STANFORD AVENUE
ST ANDREW'S ROAD

GRANTHAM ROAD
SOUTHDOWN AVENUE

RUGBY ROAD
RUGBY ROAD

FLORENCE ROAD
FLORENCE ROAD

SPRINGFIELD ROAD

DAVEY DRIVE

UPPER HOLLINGDEAN ROAD

HOLLINGDEAN ROAD

FREEHOLD TERR
HOLLINGDEAN ROAD

31

London Road
Station

19

DITCHLING RISE

WINCHESTER ST
GERARD ST
YARDLEY ST
SHAFTESBURY ROAD
WARLEIGH ROAD
VERE ROAD

DITCHLING ROAD

HUGHES ROAD

MAYO RD
RICHMOND ROAD

PRINCE'S ROAD

CRESCENT ROAD

BELTON ROAD

ROUNDHILL CRESCENT

ABERDEEN RD
EDINBURGH RD
CALEDONIAN RD
HARTINGTON ROAD
HASTINGS ST
FRANKLIN ST
PICTON ST
FRANKLIN ROAD
STILLES CT

27
26

CLYDE ROAD
LORNE RD

BROMLEY ROAD

CRESCENT ROAD

PRINCE'S CRESCENT

WAKEFIELD ROAD

UPPER LEWES ROAD

ST PAUL'S STREET

PARK CRESCENT ROAD
BREWER ST

WELLINGTON ROAD
DE MONTFORT ROAD
AGNES ST

18
53

STANLEY ROAD

VIADUCT ROAD

15
51

40
34
14

EDEN PLACE

ROSE HILL TERR
54

YORK HILL

LONDON ROAD
PROVIDENCE PLACE

ROSE HILL
PARK CRESCENT TERRACE

PARK CRESCENT PL
TRINITY ST

32

LEWES ROAD

ELM GROVE
MILTON RD
LUTHER ROAD
BEN HAM ST

36 46 5
13 28
48 20 37
FRANCIS ST
35 50 22
OXFORD ST

BAKER STREET

DITCHLING ROAD

UNION ROAD

HANOVER CRESCENT

HANOVER STREET
HANOVER TERRACE
COLEMAN STREET
WASHINGTON STREET
LINCOLN STREET
GRANT ST
EWART STREET

SINGWOOD STREET
SOUTHAMPTON STREET
SINGWOOD ROAD
COBDEN ROAD
HOWARD RD
HAMPDEN RD
WHITECROSS PLACE
SINGWOOD ROAD

St Bartholomew's
Church

52
OXFORD ST

The
Level

1
39

HANOVER CRESCENT

ANN STREET
NEW ENGLAND ST

43

FLEET ST

CHEAPSIDE

17
47

STATION ST
BLACKMAN ST
WHITECROSS ST
PELHAM ST

YORK PLACE
RICHMOND PL

St Peter's
Church

25
29
44
41

TRAFALGAR STREET

GLOUCESTER ST
ST GEORGE'S MEWS
KENSINGTON ST
KENSINGTON PLACE
ROBERT ST
VINE ST
JOHN ST

GLOUCESTER PL

GRAND PARADE

**NORTH
LAINE**
pp72-88

RICHMOND PDE

CHEATHAM PL

ALBION HILL
PHOENIX RISE
NEWHAVEN ST
BELGRAVE ST
NEWMARK PL
JERSEY ST
GROVE ST
HOLLAND ST
SCOTLAND ST

ALBION STREET
GROVE HILL

QUEEN'S ROAD
ELMORE ROAD

IVORY PL
ASHTON RISE

RICHMOND
STREET

TOWER RD
QUEEN'S PARK ROAD

**KEMP TOWN
& HANOVER**
pp 109-128

MORLEY ST

SUSSEX ST

On York Place, opposite St Peter's Church, an interesting cluster now includes **Nordic Coffee Collective**, **Hisbe** ethical supermarket, **One Eyed Jack's** photography gallery and London import **MEATliquor**. On London Road itself, **Presuming Ed Coffeehouse** has taken over the old HSBC building opposite KFC, and **Emporium Brighton** theatre and café bar has opened under the patronage of Alan Rickman in a gorgeous old church. Many more quirky little shops and restaurants are springing up on the narrow adjoining roads connecting through to the Level. Longstanding local pubs such as the **Druid's Arms**, **Hare & Hounds**, the **Hobgoblin** and the rechristened **Joker** are also experiencing new leases of life.

The key to the success of this redevelopment is that, despite its pound-shop image, this area of Brighton has always had much to offer – including two whopping great historical landmarks: the pre-Victorian Gothic **St Peter's** church in York Place and **St Bartholomew's**.

The ugly eight-storey tower block New England House has actually been home for years to hundreds of artists, craftspeople and digital creatives, whose studios are a highlight of the Artists' Open Houses festival (p37). The renowned **Duke of York's Picturehouse** sits, as it has done for more than a century, at the top end of London Road overlooking Preston Circus.

Further north, beyond the huge Grade II-listed London Road viaduct (colourfully illuminated in the evenings), is Brighton's largest urban park, the beautiful **Preston Park**, with **Preston Manor**, open to the public as an Edwardian museum, in the north-west corner.

With the regeneration continuing apace, it's unlikely any derelict space will remain empty for long. The site of the old Harlequin and Brighton Arts Clubs, in the shadow of St Bart's on Providence Place, has become the latest acquisition by the city's luxury holiday house rental company, Beatnik Breaks (see box p179).

Sights & museums

The Level
St Peter's Place, BN1 4SA (www. brighton-hove.gov.uk). Bus 18, 21, 22, 23, 24, 25, 26, 28, 29, 37, 46, 49, 50. **Map** p131 E4 ❶
Completely transformed in 2013, this great flat triangle of ground to the north of St Peter's Church is once again an attractive and thrumming recreational space, as it was in the 18th century. The centrepiece is the polished concrete skate park next to the Velo café (p143). In the landscaped scented garden you can play pétanque, boccia and chess (the latter at art-worked picnic tables), with free balls and chess sets available from the on-site gardener on weekdays. The play park is now one of the best and biggest in the city, with seagull ride-ons, miniature beach-huts and a grassy picnic area complete with grazing model sheep. In summer, there are fountains for children to play in. The northern side, bordered by 19th-century elms along Union Road, is now spruced up and street lit, but still popular with street drinkers and crusties. Funfairs come here regularly, and it's also the site of community arts fairs, t'ai chi and Brazilian dance displays.

Preston Manor
Preston Drove, BN1 6SD (03000 290900, www.virtualmuseum.info). Bus 5. **Open** *Apr-Sept* 10am-5pm Tue-Fri; 2-5pm Sun. Closed Oct-Mar. **Admission** £6.40; £3.40-£5.20 reductions. **Map** off p130 B1 ❷
Said to be one of Britain's most haunted houses, the green-shuttered Preston Manor has been preserved as an example of Edwardian life, with an *Upstairs, Downstairs* mix of elegant

clockwise from top left:
Preston Manor; the Level (2);
Preston Park p135; St
Bartholomew's Church p135

top: Café Rust; bottom: Caroline of Brunswick p136

reception rooms and bedrooms contrasting with kitchens and servants' quarters. During the summer, visitors are escorted around the manor during daylight hours. The nights are left to the spooks and spectres: regular late-night ghost tours can be booked throughout the year.

Preston Park

Preston Road, BN1 6HL (www.brighton-hove.gov.uk). Bus 5. **Map** p130 B1 ❸

An expanse of peace amid the bustle of Brighton – especially since the introduction of a wild flower meadow (take the winding path through the poppies, marigolds and lupins from May to November). Also here are tennis courts, football pitches, bowling greens, cricket pitches, a softball pitch, a velodrome, a children's playpark, a community vegetable garden and the Preston Twins, the largest and oldest English elms in the country. The Rotunda Café, purchased from the 1924 Wembley Exhibition, overlooks a stepping-stone pond and large rose garden, with two wonderfully camp gold statues. It's also hard to miss the Grade II-listed, red-brick clock tower. Explore the outskirts to find the sweet walled garden next to Preston Manor. Cross over the London Road to find the steep pathways of Rookery Rockery, the country's largest municipal rock garden.

St Bartholomew's

Ann Street, BN1 4GP (01273 620491, www.stbartholomewsbrighton.org.uk). Bus 5, 56. **Open** 10am-1pm, 2-4.30pm Mon-Sat. **Admission** free. **Map** p131 D4 ❹

Local legend has it that this huge red-brick church, with its steep roof and round window visible for miles around, was built by local architect Edmund Scott to the exact dimensions of Noah's Ark. You can see why the story persists – St Bart's, opened in 1874, towers over the nearby shops and houses at a curious angle, as if it really had just run aground behind London Road. The

incongruousness of its location is part of the appeal. But its interior also offers opulent surprises – including a baldacchin over the altar in red and green marble. Not everyone's a fan, but Sir John Betjeman was. 'In the noise and glitter of cheerful Brighton,' he wrote, 'this great church is a tall sanctuary of peace. Its interior awes beholders to silence.' St Bartholomew's hosts major concerts of classical and choral music.

Eating & drinking

For some of the best curry in Brighton – takeaway only – try **Desi** (7 Oxford Street, 01273 608885, www.desi-brighton.co.uk). See also p146 **Cowley Club**.

Bardsley's

22-23A Baker Street, BN1 4JN (01273 681256, www.bardsleys-fishandchips. co.uk). Bus 5, 18, 21, 22, 37, 38, 48, 50, 56. **Open** noon-3pm, 4.30-9.30pm Tue-Sat. **££. Fish & chips. Map** p131 D4 ❺

A fish-and-chips institution, Bardsley's has passed through four generations of the same family since it was founded in 1926. The restaurant is fully licensed. A back room houses the Max Miller Appreciation Society's official collection (with one of the comedian's florid suits in a glass case), while on hot days the glass front can be folded back. Owner Roy takes care to use fish from sustainable sources.

Café Rust

NEW *50 Preston Road, BN1 4QF (01273 684206, www.caferust.com). Bus 5.* **Open** 9am-5pm daily (may close later in summer). **Café. Map** p130 C3 ❻

This industrial-rustic-styled café opened in early 2015, and will soon be expanding into pop-up suppers. Slices of orange polenta cake sit under bell-jars, serving platters are beautifully presented with strawberry slices and mint sprigs, and there's a great lunch deal: £4 for a chunky sandwich such as parma ham, sun-blushed tomato and pesto, served with green salad and home-made vegetable crisps. Take out or eat in at wooden tables with jars of hyacinths and thistles.

Caroline of Brunswick

39 Ditchling Road, BN1 4SB (01273 624434, www.carolineofbrunswick. wordpress.com). Bus 18, 21, 24, 26, 37, 38, 46, 50. **Open** noon-midnight Mon-Thur, Sun; noon-2am Fri, Sat. **Pub. Map** p131 D4 ❼

One of the great alternative Brighton pubs (and the only one with a mythical three-headed dog slathering down over the bar), Caroline of Brunswick hosts both Brighton's only classic rock karaoke night and sci-fi quiz the Geekest Link. The function room attracts notable alternative musicians (punk, electronica) and its Edinburgh Fringe comedy preview season punches well above its weight. The walls of the bar are covered in bizarre artwork and cult album covers; rock usually blasts out from the sound system. There's a menu of home-made burgers and pies.

Crown & Anchor

213 Preston Road, BN1 6SA (01273 559494). Bus 5. **Open** 5-10pm Mon; noon-10pm Tue; noon-11pm Wed, Thur; noon-midnight Fri; 10am-11pm Sat; 10am-9pm Sun. **Pub. Map** off p130 A1 ❽

A spacious pub in the old Preston village, the Crown & Anchor is convenient if you're visiting Preston Park and the manor – and hence popular with families. The menu is good value and includes gluten-free options and a popular weekend breakfast. The three house ales come from the South Downs' award-winning Long Man Brewery.

Da Vinci

NEW *113 London Road, BN1 4JG (01273 933594). Bus 18, 21, 26, 37, 38, 46, 48, 49, 50.* **Open** 8am-11pm daily. **£. Italian. Map** p131 D4 ❾

The folks behind Bella Napoli at Brighton Marina are trying something new with this Italian (and wholly Italian-staffed) café, with restaurant-style table service from around 8pm. Pizza, pasta and steaks are all to be found on the flexible menu, and freshly squeezed juices are another focus. By day you can grab hot and cold plates from the long, colourful counter.

Druid's Arms

79-81 Ditchling Road, BN1 4SD (01273 680596). Bus 18, 21, 26, 37, 38, 46, 50. **Open** noon-1am Mon-Thur; noon-3am Fri, Sat. **££. Pub/American. Map** p131 D4 ❿

Gone is the weird snorkelling mural and the Thai menu. In has come the Big Eats Co – turning the pub into a smokehouse serving pork, chicken, beef, lamb and vegetables stacked into burgers, shredded into crispy mounds or soaked in the likes of Somerset cider, along with chunky chips and dipping pots. The pub itself seats a nicely varied crowd (including, it has been known, the odd famous rapper) at its wooden benches, with late drinking at weekends.

Eastern Eye

58 London Road, BN1 4JE (01273 685151, www.easterneyerestaurant. co.uk). Bus 5, 22, 48, 49, 56. **Open** 6-11pm Mon, Sun; noon-2.30pm, 6-11pm Tue-Thur; noon-2.30pm, 6-11.30pm Fri, Sat. **££. Indian. Map** p131 D3 ⓫

One of the better Indian restaurants in Brighton, the light and airy Eastern Eye specialises in well-presented south Indian dishes. Try the chef's favourite, spicy swordfish *achari* cooked in pickling spices, or seawater crab masala. The dosas make good lunch options.

Emporium Brighton

88 London Road, BN1 4JF (no phone, www.emporiumbrighton.com). Bus 5, 22, 48, 49, 56. **Open** 9am-late daily. **£. Café/bar. Map** p131 D3 ⓬

Spilling on to the street, the Emporium Brighton's café-bar is a big, cosily theatrical space with high wooden beams, thick curtains, booths, sofas and tables lit by candles and standing lamps. Light meals, snacks and drinks are served from the bar. It recently became the UK's first 'happiness café' – with books, leaflets and talks about human connection and positive psychology courtesy of the local branch of Action for Happiness. For the theatre here, see p146.

Flying Saucer

Unit 5, The Open Market, Marshalls Row, BN1 4JU (no phone). Bus 18, 21, 26, 37, 38, 46, 48, 50. **Open** 9am-5pm Mon-Sat; 10am-4pm Sun. **£**. **Café**. **Map** p131 D4 ⑬
The best place to sit watching the bustle of the new Open Market, this open-fronted organic café has a range of retro seating, artisanal coffee (with foam shaped into a teddy bear on request) and an arty, laid-back vibe. Food ranges from gourmet sandwiches to scotch eggs.

Gallery Restaurant

City College Brighton & Hove, Whitecross Street, BN1 4UP (01273 557711, www. ccb.ac.uk/public/college/life-the-gallery). Bus 37, 38. **Open** varies; phone or email sp3@ccb.ac.uk for reservations. **££**. **Modern British**. **Map** p131 D4 ⑭
Staffed by students from the catering and hospitality courses at City College Brighton & Hove – where former students include Ben McKellar, founder of the local Gingerman restaurants group – the Gallery is great value for money. The menu is modern British, the service extremely attentive, the venue – well, pretty institutional, but it's always a novel experience.

Hare & Hounds

🆕 *75 London Road, BN1 4JF (01273 682839, www.hareandhoundsbrighton. com). Bus 5, 56.* **Open** noon-midnight Mon-Thur, Sun; noon-1am Fri, Sat. *Food served* 5-9pm Mon; noon-3pm, 5-10pm Tue-Fri; noon-9pm Sat; 3-9pm Sun. **££**. **Pub/Mexican**. **Map** p131 D3 ⑮
The first Brighton pub to serve Meantime Brewery Fresh tank beer (crisp, unfiltered and un-pasteurised, straight from the vats), with a build-your-own Mexican menu courtesy of North Laine's La Choza (p78). A £700,000 redesign has brought in exposed brickwork, steel, red light-lined booths and murals by street artist Arrow. The large, heated garden area is a popular hangout.

Helm Ston

🆕 *1B Pelham Street, BN1 4FA (no phone). Bus 37, 38.* **Open** 8am-4pm Tue-Sat. **£**. No credit cards. **Vegetarian café**. **Map** p131 D5 ⑯
Pineapple and coconut-cream pies spotted with pomegranate seeds, and chocolate-orange cakes decorated with fresh clementine halves, entice you in as you peer into this tiny vegetarian café just off Trafalgar Street. Inside, you'll find a large menu with Indonesian and Indian influences: breakfasts include gado gado and apple pancakes with lime, palm toffee and cinnamon. For lunch, you can take away a bhaji or 'supernatural noodle' box. The soup comes with spelt soldiers, and the bread's from Flint Owl (p166). Helm Ston calls what it does 'friendly folk food', and it hasn't sprung from nowhere: the owner used to be head chef at Bill's (p74).

Hobgoblin

31 York Place, BN1 4GU (01273 682933, www.hobgoblinbrighton.co.uk). Bus 5, 22, 48, 56. **Open** noon-midnight Mon-Thur; noon-2am Fri, Sat. *Food served* noon-3pm Mon-Thur; noon-9pm Fri, Sat; noon-6pm Sun. **££**. **Pub/burgers**. **Map** p131 D4 ⑰
Squatting on the ugliest corner of London Road, the Hobgoblin has an enticing interior of exposed brick walls, candles in wax-laden bottles and junk-shop seating – plus a huge decked garden that's humming in summer. Formerly a favourite with goths and grungesters, it still has a venue hosting gigs and occasional comedy nights upstairs. But these days, the bigger draw is the Troll's Pantry, birthplace of the Brighton burger revolution.

BRIGHTON BY AREA

Joker

NEW *2 Preston Road, BN1 4QF (01273 675769, www.thejokerbrighton.com). Bus 5, 37, 38, 56.* **Open** 4pm-midnight Mon; noon-midnight Tue-Thur, Sun; noon-2am Fri-Sat. **££.** **Pub/barbecue**. **Map** p135 D1 🔞

The Joker promises many playful twists on the usual pub experience. It features a train-carriage snug separated by glass doors, and an upstairs bar and venue called the Devil's Disco replete with giant skull and flickering neon lights. The kitchen is run by Shoreditch's award-winning chicken-wing purveyor, the Orange Buffalo, in its first permanent home. For £7, you can play 'Snake in a Basket': essentially Russian roulette but with chicken wings spiced from medium through to 'viper'.

Jolly Poacher

100 Ditchling Road, BN1 4SG (01273 683967, www.thejollypoacher.com). Bus 26, 46, 50. **Open** 9am-11pm Tue-Sat; 10am-10pm Sun. **££.** **Gastropub**. **Map** p131 E2 🔞

A good place for a classy but laid-back date, this gastropub is the only joint within a two-mile radius likely to be found truffling a cabbage. Despite the shabby-chic turquoise panelling, the dark furniture and low lighting can make it a little gloomy; but with the fire roaring, it's perfect for colder months. On warmer days, sit out on the pretty terrace instead. The local and seasonal menu includes creative vegetarian mains such as a confit of wild mushroom arancini, artichoke hearts, spinach and portobello mushroom with smoked aubergine dressing.

Kouzina

NEW *Unit 40, The Open Market, Marshalls Row, BN1 4JU (07939 022531). Bus 18, 21, 26, 37, 38, 46, 48, 50.* **Open** 8.30am-6pm daily (occasional early closing). **£.** **Greek**. **Map** p131 D4 🔞

A 'modern rustic' Greek café tucked in the corner of the refurbished Open Market, offering hearty mains such as briam, veggie moussaka and meatballs in lemon sauce, or lighter options such as spanakopita and meze plates. For a quid, you can add your choice of two Mediterranean salads. It's all local, organic, and very fresh.

LangeLee's Cafe Lounge

30 York Place, BN1 4GU (01273 684840, www.langelees.com). Bus 5, 22, 49, 56. **Open** 8am-5pm Mon-Fri; 9am-5pm Sat, Sun. **£.** **Café**. **Map** p131 D4 🔞

It's easy to miss this café on a corner opposite St Peter's Church. You certainly don't expect the large courtyard garden, or the champagne breakfast menu (well, prosecco really). But that's why locals have such a soft spot for LangeLee's. The 13 cooked breakfast options include the South African, with Boerewors beef sausage and chakalaka relish.

Lix Café

59-61 Ditchling Road, BN1 4SD (01273 609407). Bus 18, 23, 25, 28, 29, 37, 38. **Open** 8am-4.30pm Mon-Fri; 9am-4.30pm Sat. **£.** **Café**. **Map** p131 D4 🔞

There's been a lot of hyperbole about the full-English breakfasts at this small café and takeaway sandwich joint. We reckon this has something to do with the schadenfreude of watching joggers circle the park while you dig in, though it's true they're generous with their wedges of toast, and never mess up a poached egg.

Loving Hut

The Level, St Peter's Place, BN1 4SA (www.brighton.lovinghut.co.uk, 01273 689532). Bus 23, 25, 28, 29. **Open** 11am-7pm Mon, Tue, Thur-Sat; 11am-6pm Sun. **£.** **Vegan café**. **Map** p131 E4 🔞

Though it's big news in Asia, there are only four branches in the UK of this organic vegan restaurant informed by the compassionate teachings of Supreme Master Ching Hai. Brighton's branch is perched on a corner of the Level opposite St Peter's Church in a little hut with a bright yellow awning.

top left: Hare & Hounds p137;
top right: Emporium Brighton
136; bottom: MEATliquor p140

It serves bean burgers, noodles, 'not-dogs', satay sticks and hot soybean drinks. A fifth Loving Hut is planned for North Laine.

Martha Gunn

100 Upper Lewes Road, BN2 3FE (01273 681671, www.marthagunn brighton.co.uk). Bus 23, 24, 25, 28, 29, 48, 49, 50. **Open** 2pm-midnight Mon-Thur; noon-2am Fri, Sat; noon-midnight Sun. **Pub. Map** p131 F2 ㉔
Formerly the sort of backstreet boozer even students scurried past, in late 2014 the Martha Gunn was transformed with stag heads, a heated garden, a good selection of craft beers, and Mexican street food courtesy of award-winning locals the Dead Good Burrito Co. It's named after the famed Brighton 'dipper', who hauled bathing machines into the sea during the height of the Regency sea-swimming craze.

MEATliquor

22-23 York Place BN1 4GU (01273 917710, www.meatliquor.com/brighton). Bus 5, 22, 49, 56. **Open** noon-11pm Mon-Thur; noon-11.30pm Fri, Sat; noon-10.30pm Sun. **££. American. Map** p131 D4 ㉕
No recent Brighton restaurant opening has generated a buzz on a par with MEATliquor, a London export serving juicy junk food American-style – the likes of burgers, chilli cheese fries and bourbon Coke floats – in club-like premises. Decor is certainly dramatic: imagine a dark space, neon-lit with a purplish hue, decorated by a tripping graffiti artist; then throw in distorting funhouse mirrors.

Mediterraneo

2A Stanley Road, BN1 4NJ (01273 674350, www.mediterraneodeli.co.uk). Bus 5, 56. **Open** Fri, Sat evenings (reservations only). **££. Italian. Map** p131 D3 ㉖
Mediterraneo is a tiny Sicilian restaurant, well off the beaten track but handy for the Duke of York's Picturehouse. A husband-and-wife team serve authentic arancini, *parmigiana di melanzane* and limoncello cake just two nights a week – and to booking customers only. You'll need to plan ahead (around three months ahead to be really sure) but it's worth it for the flavours they can bring out with just a drizzle of olive oil and sprinkle of salt.

Moe's @ the Circus

1 Clyde Road, BN1 4NN. (01273 686662). Bus 5, 56. **Open** 7am-10pm Mon-Fri; 9am-4pm Sat, Sun. **£. Café/ wine bar. Map** p131 D3 ㉗
With its weekday late opening and its alcohol licence, this café has been thriving since opening on a corner opposite Duke of York's Picturehouse in late 2013. The Wi-Fi, power points and chilled-out music make it a popular point for club get-togethers, solitary book-reading or informal business meetings. There's great coffee, wine, bottled beers and Italian draught lager, and snacks including iced cronuts.

Mohammed Spice of Life

Unit 19, the Open Market, Marshalls Row, BN1 4JU (07985 176812). Bus 18, 21, 26, 37, 38, 46, 48, 50. **Open** 8am-6pm Mon-Sat; 10am-4pm Sun. **£.** No credit cards. **Indian/Goan. Map** p131 D4 ㉘
Chef Mohammed has closed his popular restaurant Goa Spice of Life and opened this new café and takeaway in the Open Market. His speciality is Bangladeshi, Indian and Goan dishes made with hand-ground spices – baltis, dansaks and a variety of crispy vegetable snacks, as well as less well-known offerings. He also sells bangla sweets and pastries. Just follow your nose.

Moksha Caffe

4-5 York Place, BN1 4GU (01273 248890, www.mokshacaffe.com). Bus 5, 17, 40. **Open** 7am-7pm Mon-Fri; 8am-7pm Sat; 8am-6.30pm Sun. **£. Café. Map** p131 D5 ㉙
This modern café serves own-blend coffees, smoothies, home-made cakes,

sandwiches and toasties, and has wines for an early-evening tipple. Moksha is a popular exhibition space for contemporary Brighton artists, and also hosts regular spoken-word events, open-mic evenings and the odd bit of stand-up comedy. They've just opened a second location on Trafalgar Street.

Nordic Coffee Collective

16 York Place, BN1 4GU (01273 673070). Bus 5, 17, 40. **Open** 8am-5.30pm Mon-Fri; 9am-5pm Sat; 10am-4pm Sun. **£**. **Café**. **Map** p131 D5 ③⓪
Fancy something different with your coffee? This Icelandic-run café has swirly *lussekatter* saffron buns, liquorice and chocolate-flavoured meringues, rum balls, *kanelbullar* (cinnamon rolls) and small dipping doughnuts known as *kleina*. The packets of dried haddock pieces are a slightly harder sell. The minimalist Scandinavian interior is decorated only with china plates depicting hunters and huskies.

Open House

146 Springfield Road, BN1 6BZ (01273 880102). Bus 5, 26, 46, 50, 56. **Open** noon-midnight Mon-Thur, Sun; noon-1am Fri, Sat. **Pub**. **Map** p131 D2 ③①
A spacious and stylish pub, the Open House is a popular location for family meals, with superior burgers, sandwiches and veggie casseroles all available in children's portions. Paintings by the local Fiveways Artists Group adorn the walls, and jazz and folk evenings are top-notch. There's also a huge decked beer garden with ceilings and cushioned booths.

Park Crescent

39 Park Crescent Terrace, BN2 3HE (01273 604993, www.theparkcrescent. co.uk). Bus 18, 21, 22, 26, 37, 38, 46, 48, 50. **Open** 3pm-midnight Mon-Thur; noon-1am Fri, Sat; noon-11pm Sun. **Pub**. **Map** p131 E3 ③②
This local pub just north of the Level takes its name and much of its business from the neighbouring crescent

of houses circling their own private park. A new menu has steered tasty mains above the £10 mark, but the candlelit window seats are a lovely place for a pint of Badger First Call or Tanglefoot – all ales are brewed by Hall & Woodhouse in Dorset.

Pizza 500

83 Preston Road, BN1 4QG (01273 911933, www.pizza500.co.uk). Bus 5, 56. **Open** 6-11pm Tue-Sat; 6-10pm Sun. **£**. **Pizza**. **Map** p130 C3 ③③
Some of Brighton's best pizza comes from this uninviting-looking place in the shadow of the railway viaduct. Inside (mind the step!) you'll find a proper restaurant with distinctive wooden tables provided by the wood workshop next door. There are 24 pizzas to choose from, or you can build your own. Scoop the crusts into a side order of southern Italian *peperonata* (stir-fried potatoes and peppers), and finish with a scoop of house-made gelato or a slice of *torta della nonna* (made with *pasta frolla*, custard cream and pine nuts).

Poppy's Sandwich Bar

58 London Road, BN1 4JE (01273 672235). Bus 5, 22, 48, 49, 56. **Open** 8am-6pm Mon-Fri; 9am-6pm Sat. **£**. No credit cards. **Café**. **Map** p131 D3 ③④
There's seating in the tiny upstairs room and a table at the downstairs window for anyone who wants to linger over their lunch here. A daily specials board turns up giant panini stuffed with tofu, mushrooms and chilli jam or oozing with brie and bacon, or a freshly grilled salad of halloumi and potato with artichokes and lemon. Be prepared to wait at busy times.

Presuming Ed Coffeehouse

NEW *114-115 London Road, BN1 1JL (01273 911991). Bus 18, 21, 26, 37, 38, 46, 48, 49, 50.* **Open** 8am-7pm Mon-Sat; 9am-6pm Sun. **£**. **Café**. **Map** p131 D4 ③⑤
If you know your cult films you'll twig that the name of this trendy, multi-space coffeehouse is a *Withnail & I*

top: Nordic Collective p141;
bottom: Semolina

reference, and might correctly guess at a link to the Marwood (p96) in the Lanes. Like the Marwood, Presuming Ed serves excellent coffee, with regular guest blends, and lush hunks of cake. But the look is entirely its own: little lace curtains on runners, huge stacks of pulp fiction, and the odd broken doll staring blank-eyed from a corner. Until very recently, this was an HSBC, and there's still a pen attached to the counter. The safe, meanwhile, has been turned into a bookable private room replete with a table built on (fake) £5 notes and stacks of *The Rich Man's Ready Reckoner*. The welcoming staff and jars of help-yourself Marmite ward off any hint of archness. There'a a recording studio and workshop space upstairs.

Semolina

NEW *15 Baker Street, BN1 4JN (01273 697259, www.semolinabrighton.co.uk).* Bus 5, 18, 21, 22, 37, 38, 48, 50, 56. **Open** noon-10.30pm Wed-Fri; 11am-10pm Sat; noon-6pm Sun. **££**. **Café/bistro**. **Map** p131 D3 ❸

A husband-and-wife team run this café/bistro tucked just off London Road. The ingredients come from Sussex suppliers, the coffee from a micro-roaster in Horsham, the loose teas from Portsmouth, and the sculpted paintings on the walls from a local artist. Simple but inventive mains include roasted duck breast with spiced red cabbage and parsnip gratin, with blood-orange polenta cake for dessert.

Smorl's Houmous Falafel & Salad Bar

NEW *Unit 30, The Open Market, Marshalls Row, BN1 4JU (no phone).* Bus 18, 21, 26, 37, 38, 46, 48, 50. **Open** 9am-5.30pm daily. **£**. **Middle Eastern**. **Map** p131 D4 ❸

Smorl's made its name selling homemade houmous at local farmers' markets, and has now spread into freshly fried falafel. For under a fiver they'll assemble a giant pitta or a salad box,

with a choice of houmous according to your tolerance for garlic. Most people take away but you can eat at two small tables outside the stall.

Sunbirds Deli

NEW *108 London Road, BN1 4JG (07427 695119).* Bus 18, 21, 26, 37, 38, 46, 48, 49, 50. **Open** 8am-6.30pm Mon-Fri; 9am-7pm Sat. **£**. **Middle Eastern**. **Map** p131 D4 ❸

This lime-green Middle Eastern café and deli is one of Brighton's best lunch places: a meze box crammed with dolmades, spanakopita, falafel, stuffed sweet peppers, tabbouleh and spiced chicken. The beautiful display counter has rows of tiny pastries such as baklava, while the wall is lined with boxes of loose-leaf teas.

Velo Café

Rose Walk, The Level, BN1 4ZN (01273 270707, www.velo-café.co.uk). Bus 18, 21, 22, 23, 25, 26, 28, 29, 37, 38, 46, 48, 49, 50. **Open** 8am-6pm daily. **£**. **Café**. **Map** p131 E4 ❸

Brighton's first cycling café, Velo is smack bang in the middle of the rehabilitated Level, with plenty of outdoor seating, and duly popular with parents and kids. There's Small Batch coffee, a pizza menu, and a counter selection of chunky sandwiches, tasty salads, arancini and pastries. As a hub of Brighton's cycling scene, Velo organises several ride-outs a week, with the promise of mac 'n' cheese and a beer at the end. The café's healthy outdoor theme is reflected in the lawn-covered and solar-panelled roof. The on-site cycle repair service unites its clientele: those pumps are handy for buggy tyres too.

World's End

60-61 London Road, BN1 4JE (01273 692311). Bus 5, 22, 48, 49, 56. **Open** 11am-midnight Mon-Thur, Sun; 11am-1am Fri, Sat. *Food served* noon-10pm daily. **££**. **Pub/Tex Mex**. **Map** p131 D3 ❹

Open Market

A trading place reborn.

It wasn't until the flashy sign that changes colours arrived on Ditchling Road that Brighton finally started to believe in the rebirth of the Open Market.

A market has stood on the site between the London and Ditchling roads for over half a century. Following closure for redevelopment, an all-new market reopened in 2014. Now, trendy makers rub shoulders with old-school traders – like fruit and veg sellers Victor Charles Patrick Mears, whose family have had a stall here for more than three decades – around a central covered square. It's not the prettiest piece of architecture, but the community feel is very real.

On the ground floor are 45 permanent open-fronted units, home to vendors including Foodshed, Brighton Apothecary (for natural, environmentally sustainable products), Studio 45 (local artworks and giftcards) and Eco-makers Emporium (for up-cycled clothes and furniture). There's also a ramshackle second-hand bookshop. Real Patisserie and the Chilli Shop have outposts here too.

On a balcony above are 12 glass-fronted arts and crafts studios, trading in everything from jewellery to electronics. Temporary stalls in the covered square host individual pop-up sellers during the week; there are themed clusters of stalls for regular vintage, craft and healthy-living fairs at weekends. There's often a band, circus skills workshop or lindy hop demo going on here, too.

There's one crucial reason to stop in at this big black pub: it's the Bar-B-Q Shack, a pop-up burger and Tex-Mex restaurant. Most mains are big, Southern, sticky and tender (sides include candied sweet potatoes, gratin potatoes and green rice with black beans). Sports screenings, bar billiards, table tennis and regular live music and DJ sets will keep you here past the last bite.

Shopping

Baker Street Bikes

7-8 York Place, BN1 4GU (01273 675754, www.bakerstbikes.co.uk). Bus 5, 22, 48, 56. **Open** 9am-6pm Mon-Sat; 10am-4pm Sun. **Map** p131 D5 ⓵

This excellent local bike shop is co-owned by a former racing cyclist and an engineer who built Harrier jets for British Aerospace. Their knowledge and passion shine through in their shop. They run a repairs service, and sell folding bikes, electric bikes and children's Frog cycles, plus bells, water bottles, chains and other accessories. One of the owners arrives for work on a bright green 'tall bike' built from two connected frames. Ask him how he gets on.

EatonNott

26 Preston Road, BN1 4QF (01273 911634, www.eatonnott.co.uk). Bus 5. **Open** 10am-5pm Mon-Sat; or by appointment. **Map** p131 D3 ⓶

This interior design store with a difference sells 'roadkill couture', human skulls, Victorian post-mortem instruments and other outlandish conversation-starting pieces. If you're after something antique and odd, off-putting to some but beautiful to others, look no further. The co-owners are local conceptual artist and fashion designer Jess Eaton, best known for her wearable taxidermy, and tattooist and bone collector John Nott. They love a special request – dead pet commissions included.

E-Kagen Shop

5 Fenchurch Walk, BN1 4GX (01273 819850, www.ekagen.mitsu-hide.com/ shop). Bus 37, 38. **Open** 10am-6pm Mon-Sat; noon-5pm Sun. **Map** p131 D4 ㊸

The Japanese restaurant on Sydney Street (p77) is so popular that it has opened this food and takeaway lunchbox shop just a few streets away. The shelves of dried and frozen Japanese ingredients and chiller cabinets with bento boxes offer a pleasing alternative to the Sainsbury's opposite.

Hisbe

20 York Place, BN1 4GU (01273 608028, www.hisbe.co.uk). Bus 5, 22, 48, 56. **Map** p131 D4 ㊹ 9am-8pm daily.

The name of this independent supermarket is an acronym for 'how it should be': it puts people before profit, selling healthy, fresh, seasonal and – where possible – local produce, while keeping an eye on prices, wastage and animal welfare. The bread is baked in Brighton, the meat reared on family farms in Sussex, the grocery shelves filled with small, responsible brands. A small café-bar serves Cafédirect coffee. This is the pilot store for a proposed chain – good luck to it.

Jilted Dog Gallery

46 New England Road, BN1 4GG (07963 554757, www.jilteddogart.com). Bus 5, 37, 38, 56. **Open** noon-4pm Fri-Sun. **Map** p130 C3 ㊺

A lovely little independent gallery just off Preston Circus, with a mission to 'support artists who struggle to find a platform'. Recent exhibitions have included classic gig posters remixed as book covers by local pop artist the Stereotypist – all framed and signed for £35.

Monkey Music Emporium

43 Baker Street, BN1 4JN (07814 955217). Bus 5, 18, 21, 22, 37, 38, 48, 50, 56. **Open** 10am-6pm Mon-Sat. **Map** p131 D3 ㊻

Brighton may be famed for its second-hand record shops, but too few vinyl-hunters stumble upon this great little place just off London Road. It's run by a hairy dude who also has a penchant for prog and old-school hi-fi equipment (housed in a back room). You can also buy an old turntable on which to play your new Orange Juice seven-inch or James Brown collectible. It's impossible to leave without a new-old LP under your arm.

One Eyed Jacks Gallery

28 York Place, BN1 4GU (07743 098530, www.oneeyedjacksgallery.com). Bus 5, 22, 48, 56. **Open** 11.30am-6.30pm Wed-Fri; 10am-5.30pm Sat, Sun. **Map** p131 D4 ㊼

A small, limited-edition photography gallery on the corner of London Road, founded by local photographer and writer Matt Henry. Many of the exhibitions reflect his interests in narrative work and small-town America.

Open Market

NEW *London Road, BN1 4JU (01273 234047, www.brightonopenmarket. co.uk).* Bus 5, 17, 18, 21, 26, 37, 38, 40, 46, 48, 50. **Open** 9am-5pm Mon-Fri; 10am-5pm Sat-Sun (some traders closed Sun). **Map** p131 D4 ㊽

See box p144.

South Coast Costumes

NEW *9-10 Circus Parade, BN1 4GW (01273 696999, www.southcoast costumes.co.uk).* Bus 5, 37, 38, 56. **Open** noon-6pm Mon, Tue; 10am-6pm Thur-Sat; Wed by appointment. **Map** p130 C3 ㊾

It's great fun just to snoop around this costume shop, packed to the rafters with rails of vintage, retro and theatrical costumes. If you happen to be looking for a fur coat or a military jacket, a Santa suit or a Regency gown, the staff (a choreographer, a cabaret artiste, a costume supervisor and a film and theatre designer) are well placed to help. There's always a selection of ex-hire garments for sale.

Woody's Music

12 Oxford Street, BN1 4LA (01273 272271, www.woodys-music.co.uk). Bus 5, 18, 21, 22, 37, 38, 48, 50, 56. **Open** 10am-6pm Tue-Sat. **Map** p131 D4 🔟

Local luthier David Hardwick builds, repairs and recycles instruments in this music shop just one road along from his old premises. He sells most stringed instruments from electric and acoustic guitars to violins, mandolins and banjos – and makes them by hand on site to commission.

Nightlife

The **Caroline of Brunswick** (p136), **Hobgoblin** (p137), **Joker** (p138) and **World's End** (p143) all host regular entertainment. The **Cowley Club** (below) is also a club and gig venue by night.

Bleach

NEW *above the Hare & Hounds, 75 London Road, BN1 4JF. (01273 682839, www.bleachbrighton.com). Bus 5, 56.* **Map** p131 D3 🔟

Hoping to establish itself as a right-of-passage for rising bands, this 150-capacity live music venue above the Hare & Hounds has already played host to the likes of Dels, the Wytches and recent Rough Trade signing Girl Band. They're working with some great promoters including Southampton's Club Psychedelia and, on the Americana and folk front, Brighthelmstone. The most you'll pay is £12, and many gigs are free.

Arts & leisure

Cowley Club

12 London Road, BN1 4JA (01273 696104, www.cowleyclub.org.uk). Bus 5, 22, 48, 49, 56. **Open** noon-6pm Wed-Fri. No credit cards. **Map** p131 D4 🔟

This volunteer-run social club incorporating a radical bookshop and vegan café is named after Brighton resident and social activist Harry Cowley, who was a key figure in opposing Oswald

Mosley's British Union of Fascists and also helped establish the original Open Market (see box p144). You can chat about feminism or libertarianism over organic hot drinks and food; buy new political texts or borrow films from the library out back. After 7pm, it becomes a private members' bar, so you'll need a member to sign you in for the busy programme of open-mic nights, alternative club events and film screenings.

Duke of York's Picturehouse

Preston Circus, BN1 4NA (0871 902 5728, www.picturehouses.co.uk). Bus 5, 37, 38, 56. **Map** p131 D3 🔟

See box p147.

Emporium Brighton

88 London Road, BN1 4JF (www. emporiumbrighton.com). Bus 5, 18, 21, 22, 37, 38, 48, 50, 56. **Map** p131 D3 🔟

Two large statues of eagles guard the entrance to this characterful theatre housed in a former Methodist church, at the back of the popular café/bar of the same name (p136). The jewel in the rejuvenated London Road's crown and a hub for the area's cultural life, Emporium is a professional producing theatre with a classic repertory programme, quality original annual pantomime, and regular comedy and children's shows.

SAMA Factory

7-8 Circus Parade, BN1 4GW (01273 605335, www.samafunfactory.co.uk). Bus 5, 37, 38, 56. **Open** 9.30am-5pm Mon-Fri; 9am-3pm Sat; 10am-3pm Sun. No credit cards. **Map** p130 C3 🔟

If you don't have young children, this compact, independently run indoor playground may seem like a lesser circle of hell. If you do, and it's raining, it's a godsend. There's a two-level soft play area, a mini ball pit, a chill-out space with books and crayons and, crucially, a café space serving Small Batch coffee. It also runs weekly themed film nights with food and a large drop-down screen.

The grand old Duke of York

A very special cinema.

There's no better emblem for Brighton's slight fantasy feel than the 20-foot pair of can-can dancer's legs protruding from this cinema's roof. The **Duke of York's Picturehouse** (p146) is, as you'll surmise, no ordinary cinema.

Referred to locally as the Duke's, the single-screen venue opened over a century ago, on 22 September 1910, and has remained open in this capacity ever since – giving it a strong claim to the title of Britain's oldest cinema. The listed building has changed little over the years, barring the addition, in 1991, of those black-and-white-striped stockinged pins.

The rear of the auditorium, formed by the walls of the old Amber Ale Brewery, predates the cinema itself. Today, the Duke's has a café-bar on the first floor, leading on to a movie-heaven balcony where film fans can stretch out on sofas, armchairs and plush cinema seats to enjoy the action over a slice of cake, cup of coffee or (why not, it's Tuesday lunchtime) a bottle of wine.

The first film shown here was *Byways of Byron*, by local filmmaker George Albert Smith, and the cinema retains close connections with the local creative community – not least with its lively part-time staff of students, actors and musicians. Music festival the Great Escape and local promoters Melting Vinyl use the venue for gig and live soundtrack performances, and it has a tight relationship with the annual Brighton film festival, Cinecity. Among the cinema's local patrons are actor Steve Coogan, musician Nick Cave

and director John Hillcoat. When Cave and Hillcoat released their last film, *Lawless*, they rolled out the (miniature) red carpet for its première here.

Now part of the nationwide Picturehouse chain, the Duke's remains a respected arthouse cinema. It doesn't shy away from mainstream features, but focuses on international films and curios. Regular special screenings include Late Nights (on Fridays), Silver Screen (for seniors), Big Scream (for parents and babies), Kids' Club, and autism-friendly and access screenings. It also hosts live satellite links to other arts venues, and Q&A sessions. General manager Felicity Beckett keeps a video blog, Flick's Flicks (www.picturehouseblog.co.uk), where she discusses the latest releases.

Since 2012, the Duke's splits a larger programme between these original premises and a new two-screen cinema at Komedia (p86) in the North Laine: replete, of course, with a pair of can-can legs, this time in red and white.

BRIGHTON BY AREA

Hove

A walk along the seafront quickly reveals the difference in atmosphere between Brighton and Hove. As soon as you pass the peace statue (a winged angel holding an orb and an olive branch, marking the Brighton–Hove border), the number of tourists and rock shops thins and the promenade widens, relaxing into rows of multi-coloured beach huts and the serene backdrop of Hove Lawns.

Hove is the home of celebrities and ladies who lunch, Regency terraces and Victorian villas, chichi showrooms and shabby-chic cafés. But for every upmarket restaurant there's a down-to-earth boozer, and for each polished boutique there's a historic family-run store.

Hove developed at the same time as Brighton, and has always been inextricably linked to its brasher eastern neighbour. But when the town of Hove was merged with Brighton to form the Brighton & Hove unitary authority in 1997,

residents began to complain. According to lore, when asked by outsiders where they live, Hovians will distinguish themselves from their neighbours with, 'Brighton… well, Hove, actually', a maxim said to have originated from one-time Hove resident Sir Laurence Olivier.

The truth is that, despite their apparent haughtiness, Hovians are more likely to venture into Brighton – with all its amenities and attractions – than vice versa. But that has left many areas of Hove with a strong community feel. Brunswick Town, in particular, framed by the creamy yellow Regency buildings of the Brunswick Estate, is a distinctive pocket off Western Road, with its own arts festival in **Brunswick Square** every August. Here, you'll find brilliant reborn arts venue the **Old Market**, bijou seafood restaurant the **Little Fish Market**, and **City Books**. As a general rule, wander off Western Road in this stretch close to the Brighton border, and you'll discover a great pub or eaterie. And to the north are the winding leaf-canopied paths of **St Ann's Well Gardens**.

Further west, where Western Road becomes **Church Road**, cafés and restaurants begin to dominate the main street. This is the point where many tourists, looking seawards and seeing nothing but wide avenues of flats, turn back for Brighton. If you know where to dig, you'll unearth huge beer gardens, galleries, bookshops and cult restaurants.

Pedestrian-friendly **George Street** is largely a bland row of high-street shops but is the busiest part of Hove. To the north, **Blatchington Road** and **Portland Road** are dotted with interesting independents. Far to the west, **Richardson Road** is its own shopping village.

Another of Hove's hidden assets is the **British Engineerium** (www.britishengineerium.org), a museum of historic mechanical objects set to reopen as the World of Engineering in 2016. It's housed in a striking high Victorian Gothic building on the Droveway near the north side of Hove Park. North Hove is also the unexpected site of a historic windmill, **West Blatchington Mill** (www.sussexmillsgroup.org.uk/blatchington.htm). Painted by Constable in 1825, it was restored in 2011, and is open on Sundays from May to September for corn-grinding and ladder climbing.

Follow the Kingsway coastal road just off our map and you'll reach **Hove Lagoon**, home to a watersports centre and Norman Cook's **Big Beach Café** (01273 911080, www.bigbeachcafe.com). The DJ lives a stone's throw away in Western Esplanade, a seafront cul de sac with its own private beach. Cook bought the café from Paul McCartney's ex wife Heather Mills, whose vegan VBites restaurant has now moved to East Street.

For this guide, we have taken Boundary Passage (an alleyway parallel to York Road), Norfolk Square and Western Street to the sea as the Brighton-Hove border, with these roads belonging to the City Centre chapter. To the north, we have followed York Avenue up Osmond Road to connect with Old Shoreham Road just short of Dyke Road Park.

Sights & museums

Hove Museum & Art Gallery

19 New Church Road, BN3 4AB (03002 290900, www.brighton-hove-rpml.org. uk). Bus 1, 6. **Open** 10am-5pm Mon, Tue, Thur-Sat; 2-5pm Sun. **Admission** free. Map p150 B3 **1**

Hove's own small museum features a Wizard's Attic filled with 18th-century toys and little hidden cupboards and crawl spaces for children to explore. Other galleries are dedicated to 19th-century movie-making, Hove history and contemporary crafts. The museum is housed in an Italianate Victorian villa with an unusual Indian gateway.

Hove Park Miniature Railway

Hove Park, BN3 7BF (www.hovepark railway.co.uk). Bus 14, 56. **Open** *Apr-Oct* 2-5pm Sat, some Mon. Usually closed Nov-Mar. **Tickets** £1; £0.50 reductions. Map p150 C1 **2**

This miniature steam railway at the north end of Hove Park is one of the city's most charming – and least trumpeted – attractions. You don't so much board the train as straddle it, and there are miniature tunnels and traffic lights.

Eating & drinking

See also p162 the **Brunswick**, p161 the **Three Angels** and p151 **I Gigi**. There are two branches of Brighton chain **Small Batch Coffee** (see box p155), at 70 Goldstone Villas (01273 734590) and 67C Church Road (01273 710627).

Hove

WEST BLATCHINGTON

A B C

Hove Park

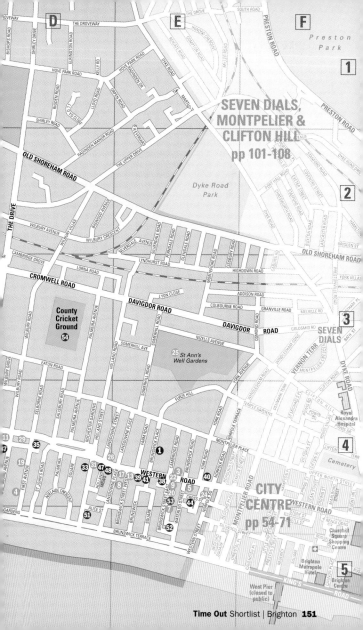

SOUTH ROAD
THE DRIVE
PRESTON ROAD

F

Preston Park

1

D THE DROVEWAY

DROVEWAY
B BISHOPS ROAD
SHIRLEY DRIVE

E

HOVE PARK ROAD
RIGDEN ROAD
LLOYD CLOSE
LLOYD ROAD
KELLY RD
HOVE PARK ROAD
DYKE ROAD
MATLOCK

PRESTON ROAD
STANFORD AVENUE
DYKE ROAD

SHIRLEY ROAD
BADMINTON MANOR ROAD
THE UPPER DRIVE
UPPER DRIVE

PORT HALL ROAD
EXETER STREET
COVENTRY STREET

2

OLD SHOREHAM ROAD

Dyke Road Park

CHATSWORTH ROAD
PORT HALL STREET
STAFFORD ROAD
TRAFALGAR STREET
LANCASTER STREET

THE DRIVE
WILBURY AVENUE
WILBURY VILLAS
BORWOOD AVENUE
WILBURY CRESCENT

SILVERDALE AVENUE
SILVERDALE ROAD
FONDDALE ROAD
GLENDALE ROAD

DYKE ROAD
OLD SHOREHAM ROAD
BRIGHTON ST

CAMBRIDGE GROVE
WILBURY GARDENS
LORNA ROAD
LYNDHURST ROAD
CISSBURY ROAD
MONTEFIORE ROAD
HIGHDOWN ROAD

YORK VILLAS

CROMWELL ROAD

DAVIGDOR ROAD
LYON CLOSE
ADDISON ROAD
COLBOURNE ROAD
GRANVILLE ROAD
MELVILLE RD

3

County Cricket Ground 54

WILBURY GROVE
PALMEIRA AVENUE
HOLLAND ROAD
SOMERHILL ROAD
SOMERHILL AVE
NIZELLS AVENUE
DAVIGDOR ROAD
OSMOND ROAD
GOLDSMID ROAD

SEVEN DIALS

VERNON TERR
MONTPELIER VILLAS

SEVEN DIALS, MONTPELIER & CLIFTON HILL pp 101-108

EATON ROAD
25 **St Ann's Well Gardens**

BACK ST

WILBURY ROAD
SELBORNE ROAD
SALISBURY ROAD
PALMEIRA AVENUE
ROCHESTER GARDENS
HOLLAND STREET
LANSDOWNE STREET
FURZE HILL
YORK AVENUE
CLIFTON HILL

TEMPLE GARDENS
ST STEPHENS
VERNON TERRACE

11
29
35

LANSDOWNE PLACE
FARM ROAD
BRUNSWICK PLACE
1
CAMBRIDGE ROAD
BRUNSWICK ROAD
TOR ROAD
MONTPELIER PLACE

YORK ROAD
NORFOLK TERRACE
Royal Alexandra Hospital

BUS TO

4

19
FIRST AVENUE
ST JOHN'S ROAD
PALMEIRA
33 31
47
48
26
17 13
8
22
39 41
20
3
38
WESTERN ROAD
5
40
UPPER NORTH STREET

CLIFTON ROAD
Cemetery

4
ALICE ST
BRUNSWICK STREET WEST
BRUNSWICK STREET EAST
53
44
CROSS ST
2
WESTERN ROAD
STONE ST

CITY CENTRE pp 54-71

51
BRUNSWICK SQUARE
WATERLOO STREET
52

MONTPELIER ROAD
PRESTON STREET
CLARENCE ST
DEAN ST
BEDFORD ST

FRENCH GARDENS

Churchill Square Shopping Centre

5

GARDENS
BRUNSWICK TERRACE
WESTERN TERRACE

ADELAIDE CRESCENT

Brighton Metropole Hotel

KING'S

RUSSELL SQ

Brighton Centre

West Pier (closed to public)

KING'S ROAD

Archipelagos

121 Western Road, BN3 1DB (01273 779474, www.archipelagosbrighton. co.uk). Bus 1, 2, 5, 6, 21, 25, 46, 49. **Open** 5-11pm Mon-Thur; noon-3pm, 5-11pm Fri; 11am-11pm Sat, Sun. **££**. **Greek**. Map p151 E4 **3**

The space is small, the helpings large and the service warm at this classic Greek taverna. Lamb kleftiko, beef *stifado* and pork *souvlakia* are fresh and succulent, while the meze and *mezedakia* dishes encourage you to experiment a little.

Bali Brasserie

Kingsway Court, First Avenue, BN3 2LR (01273 323810, www.balibrasserie. co.uk). **Open** noon-2pm, 6.30-11pm Tue-Sun. **££**. **Malaysian/ Indonesian**. Map p151 D4 **4**

In the basement of a concrete block of flats, this Malaysian and Indonesian restaurant is preserving the 1970s in all their carpeted glory. It's a time warp well worth visiting. For £17, you can feast on four courses at the Indonesian *rijsttafel* (rice table) – or just grab a snack at the Tropical Bar, a snaking space with a pool table, regular live entertainment and plenty of bamboo.

Bee's Mouth

10 Western Road, BN3 1AE (01273 770083). Bus 1, 2, 5, 6, 21, 25, 46, 49, N1, N2, N25. **Open** 4.30pm-12.30am Mon-Thur, Sun; 4.30pm-1.30am Fri; 3.30pm-1.30am Sat. **Bar**. Map p151 E4 **5**

If any bar deserves the adjective 'Lynchian', it's this dark, narrow, red-lit and musky drinking den. The bar boasts both unusual bottled beers and a revolving mannequin's head, and the mirrored basement hosts free cinema, live music and life-drawing classes.

Black Radish

NEW *149 Portland Road, BN3 5QJ (01273 723392). Bus 2, 46, 49.* **£**. **Café**. **Open** 8.30am-4.30pm Mon-Sat. Map p150 A3 **6**

Try the salad bar and sausage rolls at this specialist organic greengrocer and mini café. Yellow courgettes and green tomatoes are stacked in wooden crates, spices and herbs come from Hove's own Pinch Seasonings, and they're just branching out into sushi.

Bottom's Rest

NEW *16 Lower Market Street, BN3 1AT (01273 733513). Bus 1, 2, 5, 6, 21, 25, 46, 49.* **Open** 11am-11.30pm Mon-Wed, Sun; noon-12.30am Thur-Sat. **Pub**. Map p151 E5 **7**

Buried in the mews on the sea-side of the Old Market venue, this is the kind of pub you stumble on and lose again. It has low-hanging bulbs, ultra-friendly staff, a good Sunday roast and a donkey's head above the bar.

Burger Off

52 Brunswick Street West, BN3 1EL. (01273 326655). Bus 1, 2, 5, 6, 21, 25, 46, 49. **Open** noon-10pm Tue, Thur, Fri, Sat. **£**. **Burgers**. Map p151 E4 **8**

This burger restaurant is famed for serving a burger so spicy you have to be over 18 and sign a disclaimer (the XXX Hot Burger contains chilli 18,000 times hotter than the blandest peppers, and recently hospitalised two local reporters after a single bite). But it doesn't need the gimmick: the regular burgers – juicy, chargrilled and stacked high with extras such as onion rings and black pudding – are some of the city's favourites.

Caribou Rooms Café

NEW *51-55 Brunswick Street, BN3 1AU (01273 723911, www.caribourooms.com). Bus 1, 2, 5, 6, 21, 25, 46, 49.* **Open** 9am-5.30pm Mon-Sat; 9am-5pm Sun. **£**. **Café**. Map p151 E4 **9**

This private-hire venue now operates a public café on its ground floor. It's a great place for breakfast: pull up a wooden chair by one of the large windows, and order a champagne and orange juice with your homemade granola. You can also book afternoon tea (£15 per head). Look out for flyers for the odd ticketed event in the basement.

top: Caribou Rooms Café;
bottom: Wick Inn p158

Connaught

48 Hove Street, BN3 2DH (01273 206578, www.connaughtpub.co.uk). Bus 1, 6, 49. **Open** noon-midnight Mon-Thur; noon-12.30am Fri, Sat; noon-10.30pm Sun. **Pub. Map** p150 B4 ⑩

Sister to the Dyke (p105) in Seven Dials, this pub is similarly popular for family dining, with its spacious bar, lovely lawned garden, boxes of toys and books for children, and classy twists on pub classics. Mains might include scrumpy and maple-baked ham steak with marmite chips, poached eggs and truffle hollandaise (£14.50).

Crafty Chooks

NEW *10 Victoria Grove, Second Avenue, BN3 2LJ (01273 722846, www.crafty chooks.co.uk). Bus 1, 2, 5, 6, 21, 25, 46, 49.* **Open** 10.30am-11pm Mon-Thur; 10.30am-midnight Fri, Sat; 11.30am-10.30pm Sun. **££. Rotisserie. Map** p151 D4 ⑪

This rotisserie chicken restaurant, where the birds are all free range and from local butchers, is the latest addition to the Golden Lion Group (which also owns Hove Place; p156). Pride of place on the menu is the spit roast chicken with house seasoning and a choice of three sauces. Craft ales make a good accompaniment.

Foragers

3 Stirling Place, BN3 3YU (01273 733134, www.theforagerspub.co.uk). Bus 2, 5, 46, 49. **Open** noon-11.30pm Mon-Thur; noon-midnight Fri, Sat; noon-11pm Sun. *Food served* noon-3pm Mon-Fri; noon-4pm Sat; noon-6pm Sun. **££. Gastropub. Map** p150 B3 ⑫

Hidden in a side street, this gastropub has been a trailblazer for sustainable, seasonal and responsibly sourced produce since 2006. Meat comes from nearby Clayton Farm, game from Uckfield, seafood from the Sussex coast, and lots of the herbs and greens from foraging. Other places have followed suit, but for truly local modern British dishes, and a vibe that's about relaxing

diners without relaxing principles, the Foragers is hard to beat. It occasionally closes early on Monday and Tuesday.

Freemasons

38-39 Western Road, BN3 1AF (01273 732043). Bus 1, 2, 5, 6, 21, 25, 46, 49, N1, N2, N25. **Open** noon-1am Mon-Thur; noon-2am Fri, Sat; noon-midnight Sun. **Pub. Map** p151 E4 ⑬

With its art deco portico decorated with masonic symbols, you're unlikely to miss this large pub on Western Road. In 2013, InnBrighton took the place over, ripping out some of the more garish fittings (though the interior remains incongruously modern). As befits the place that gave DJ duo the Freemasons their name, it hosts weekly live music and has an app-based secret DJ system for punters to control the soundtrack.

George Payne

18 Payne Avenue, BN3 5HB (01273 329563, www.thegeorgepayne.co.uk). Bus 2, 46, 49. **Open** noon-11pm Mon-Thur; noon-1am Fri, Sat; noon-11pm Sun. **Pub. Map** p150 A2 ⑭

Former dive the Kendall Arms has been transformed into a community hub with one of the nicest beer gardens in the city (the astro-turfed children's play area even has a TARDIS). There's a changing selection of guest ales.

Giggling Squid

129 Church Road, BN3 2AE (01273 737373, www.gigglingsquid.com). Bus 1, 6, 49. **Open** noon-4pm, 6-10.45pm Mon-Sat; 6-9.45pm Sun. **££. Thai. Map** p150 C4 ⑮

There are now ten of these rustic Thai restaurants across the south, a testament to the quality, range and chattily informative menu. Glorious Morning, a speedy ong choi, chilli and garlic wok fry, was inspired by a roadside encounter in Bangkok's Chinatown. There's a whole section for local catch, a lunchtime menu of tapas sets, and you'll want a side of the deep-fried salt and pepper squid.

BRIGHTON BY AREA

Small Batch Coffee

The DIY baristas behind Brighton's roasting revolution.

For a party town, Brighton was once weirdly incapable of producing a decent cup of coffee. These days, though, the city is obsessed with the stuff and quality coffee houses are booming.

At the centre of this coffee revolution is **Small Batch** (www.smallbatchcoffee.co.uk), a company started in 2007 by two young local baristas. They now have six of their own cafés across Brighton and Hove (the latest in the new Cycle Hub at Brighton station), and distribute their beans to numerous others. In their own stores alone, they sell two million cups of coffee a year. Key to Small Batch's success is ethical, sustainable and traceable sourcing – plus passion and perfectionism in the process. As the name suggests, they only roast small amounts of no more than 12 kilogrammes at a time, so batches can be scrapped if they don't come up to scratch.

At the Goldstone Villas espresso bar and roastery (no. 70, 01273 734590), just down from Hove train station, you can hear the beans cascading into the gas-fired vintage Diedrich roaster and smell them cooking while you sip. At the Seven Dials branch (108A Dyke Road, 01273 711912), housed in a converted bank, you can take a barista workshop in the steel-lined downstairs vault. The Lab, as they call it, teaches everything from agronomy and processing to milk steaming and latte art, and trains a constant flow of café workers alongside interested amateurs (the beginner's Home Brew course is £35 for 90 minutes).

'The average customer is now more clued up about coffee, and after a smaller and more balanced drink,' says co-owner Alan Tomlins. 'If you roast the bean for longer, the flavour is sweeter and more complex.' When not travelling around South America and Africa sourcing and blogging about beans, he still puts on an apron to muck in at the roastery.

It's no coincidence, for the success of Small Batch, that Brighton has one of the highest rates of self-employment in the country. At the busiest branch, on Jubilee Street in North Laine (no. 17, 01273 697597), the shared tables and high stools accommodate a crush of creatives busily thinking outside the box.

'The future for Small Batch is expanding our wholesale market,' says Tomlins. 'We've talked about spreading the cafés to other cities but decided we just didn't fancy it. We're Brighton people.' Likewise, Brighton's love affair with the Small Batch flat white shows no signs of abating.

Ginger Pig

3 Hove Street, BN3 2TR (01273 736123, www.gingermanrestaurants.com). Bus 1, 6, 49. **Open** *11.30am-midnight Mon-Sat; noon-midnight Sun.* **£££. Modern British. Map** p150 B4 ⑯

This elegant and airy gastropub is – along with its sister restaurants the Ginger Dog (p115) and the Gingerman (p62) – a cornerstone of Brighton's foodie revolution. The cooking continues to improve without accompanying price hikes. Mains might include tandoori-crusted seabass or venison haunch with rosemary and date meatloaf.

Graze

42 Western Road, BN3 1JD (01273 823707, www.graze-restaurant.co.uk). Bus 1, 2, 5, 6, 21, 25, 46, 49. **Open** *6-10pm Fri; noon-2pm, 6-10pm Sat; 12.30-2pm, 6-9pm Sun.* **££££. Modern British. Map** p151 E4 ⑰

Two seven-course taster menus – one meat, one veggie – are at the heart of this restaurant's 'urban grazing' concept. Start with rosemary smoked goat's curd, beetroot, black treacle bread and Pedro Ximenez reduction, and finish with artichoke chiboust and vanilla ice-cream. The decor has certainly dated, but the place still offers a distinctive dining experience.

Hidden Pantry

59 Blatchington Road, BN3 3YJ (01273 203204, www.thehiddenpantry.co.uk). Bus 2, 5, 46. **Open** *8.30am-5pm Mon-Sat; 9am-5pm Sun.* **£. No credit cards. Café. Map** p150 B3 ⑱

Formerly named Ethel's Kitchen after the owner's grandmother, this vintage café aims to recreate the excitement of sneaking into an old-fashioned pantry for home-cooked treats. You'll find cream teas served in flowery china and kitsch figurine salt and pepper shakers.

Hove Place

35-37 First Avenue, BN3 2FH (01273 738266, www.hoveplace.co.uk). Bus 1, 2, 5, 6, 21, 25, 46, 49, N1, N5. **Open** *11am-11pm Mon-Wed; 11am-midnight Thur; 11am-1am Fri, Sat; noon-11pm Sun.* **Pub. Map** p151 D4 ⑲

The key draw to this pub and bistro, set down some steps, is the huge courtyard with trees and Italianate marble statues (among the rather less elegant patio furniture). Inside, the Golden Lion Group overdid it with clashing woods when they refurbished in 2012. There's a traditional bistro menu, and a very popular Sunday roast.

Little Fish Market

10 Upper Market Street, BN3 1AS (01273 722213, www.thelittlefish market.co.uk). Bus 1, 2, 5, 6, 21, 25, 46, 49. **Open** *7-9.30pm Tue-Fri; noon-2pm, 7-9.30pm Sat.* **££. No credit cards. Seafood. Map** p151 E4 ⑳

Duncan Ray, formerly of Heston Blumenthal's Fat Duck, serves just 20 diners a night at this cash-only seafood restaurant in a former fishmongers, opposite the Old Market. Since it opened in 2011, several flashier fish specialists have arrived on the scene. But for skill executed with simplicity and charm, the smallest is still the best.

Marrocco's

8 Kings Esplanade BN3 2WS (01273 203764, www.marroccos.co.uk). Bus 700. **Open** *9am-late daily.* **££. Italian/ ice-cream. Map** p150 B5 ㉑

Marrocco's has been serving ice-cream to seafront promenaders since 1969. In the '90s, they turned into a full-blown restaurant, with rather disappointing results. The queues snaking out of its door at the first sign of sunshine are there for one thing only: 24 flavours of home-made Italian ice-cream.

Paris House

21 Western Road, BN3 1AF (01273 724195, www.the-paris-house.co.uk). Bus 1, 2, 5, 6, 21, 25, 46, 49, N1, N2, N25. **Open** *noon-11pm Mon-Thur, Sun; noon-2am Fri, Sat.* **Bar. Map** p151 E4 ㉒

This Parisian-themed bar attempts to introduce an air of refinement hitherto entirely foreign to this stretch of Western Road. The wine list is exclusively French, there are cheese and charcuterie platters to accompany, and live gypsy jazz every Saturday.

Pizzaface

1 Coleridge Street, BN3 5AB (01273 965651, www.pizzafacepizza.co.uk). Bus 5. **Open** 4-10pm Mon-Thur, Sun; 4-11pm Fri; 1-11pm Sat. **££**. **Pizza**. **Map** p150 B2 ㉓

Pizzaface is primarily a takeaway (the Kemp Town branch, p112, exclusively so), but in Hove there is a table for customers who just can't wait. The Silverio includes pancetta marinated in red wine, blue cheese, rocket and avocado sauce. Extra toppings include truffle oil, rosemary, pine kernels and oyster mushrooms, and there are wholegrain spelt and gluten- and wheat-free base options too.

Robin Hood

3 Norfolk Place, BN1 2PF (01273 325645, www.peoplespubs.com). Bus 1, 2, 5, 6, 21, 25, 46, 49, N1, N2, N25. **Open** noon-11pm Mon-Thur, Sun; noon-1am Fri, Sat. **Pub**. **Map** p151 E4 ㉔

Britain's only charity pub, the Robin Hood pays its staff and its bills, then gives all its profits to charity. If that doesn't give you a warm glow, the red walls, worn banquettes and chesterfields, and the house-made pizzas will. Good board game stash, too.

St Ann's Well Gardens Café

St Ann's Well Gardens, BN3 1RP (01273 735187, www.thegardencafehove.co.uk). Bus 7, 21. **Open** 8.30am-4pm daily. **£**. **Café**. **Map** p151 E3 ㉕

It may be in the heart of St Ann's Well Gardens but this isn't your average park café. It serves booze, for one, and stays open late with a Spanish tapas menu on summer evenings. Daytime menu standards include halloumi pittas, fresh pasta and a full English breakfast. Just be prepared to dodge the squirts from organic baby food pouches.

Salvage Café

84 Western Road, BN3 1JB (01273 323884, www.cafeandsalvage.com). Bus 1, 2, 5, 6, 21, 25, 46, 49. **Open** 8.30am-6pm Mon-Fri; 9am-6pm Fri, Sat; 11am-varies Sun. **£**. **Café**. **Map** p151 D4 ㉖

One of the few cafés getting the popular combination of food and vintage finds just right. The mustachioed owner was once in the building trade: he hammered out the old French copper sink himself. Now he serves loose-leaf teas and homemade cakes to the ring of an old-fashioned till, while customers lounge on reclaimed sofas or retro cinema seats, admiring the mishmash of bookshelves, stools and antique typewriters for sale.

Sugardough Bakery

5 Victoria Terrace, BN3 2WB (01273 771218). Bus 77. **Open** 7.30am-5.30pm Mon-Fri; 8am-5.30pm, Sat, Sun. **£**. **Café/bakery**. **Map** p150 C4 ㉗

On a stretch of seafront road between Hove Lawns and the King Alfred's leisure centre, this café-bakery with vintage fittings is one of the prides of Hove. It's ideal if you're feeling stranded and windswept: order a beautifully crimped organic beef, red wine and garlic pie, and grab a loaf of seeded sourdough on your way out.

Treacle & Co

164 Church Road, BN3 2DJ (01273 933695, www.treacleandco.co.uk). Bus 1, 6, 49. **Open** 8.30am-5.30pm Mon-Fri; 9am-5.30pm Sat; noon-5pm Sun. **£**. **Café**. **Map** p150 B4 ㉘

Pear and walnut crumble cake, blood-orange upside-down cake and damp lemon, almond and polenta loaf are all recipes in the toolbox of this established local cake-maker. A long wooden counter is stacked high for browsing. You can also order savoury lunch (noon-3pm Mon-Sat) and it runs a takeaway summer picnic service.

Unithai Oriental Market

10 Church Road, BN3 2FL (01273 733246). Bus 1, 2, 5, 6, 21, 25, 46, 49.

Open noon-2.30pm Mon-Thur, Sun; noon-6pm Fri, Sat. **£. Thai. Map** p151 D4 ㉙

The best place for a cheap Thai lunch is a cluster of tables at the back of a South East Asian supermarket. Zingy tom yum soup, gloop-free pad thai and creamy duck curry are all cooked fresh to order by one Thai woman. So be prepared to wait to be seated, and wait some more to be served. Opening times can vary.

Urchin
ᴺᴱᵂ *15-17 Belfast Street, BN3 3YS (01273 241881, www.urchinpub.co.uk). Bus 2, 5, 46.* **Open** 11am-11pm daily. *Food served* noon-3pm, 5-10pm Wed-Fri, Sun; noon-10pm Sat. **££. Pub/ seafood. Map** p160 C3 ㉚

A neighbourhood pub specialising in shellfish and craft beer, from the people behind Small Batch Coffee. Prawns, lobster, crab and scallops are cooked and served for sharing in copper Portuguese *catapalanas*, and there are 100 craft beers to choose from. The pub was formerly the Bell, and its interior has been won over to the new fishy theme with reclaimed ship timber.

Wick Inn
63 Western Road, BN3 1JD (01273 736436, www.wickinnbrighton.co.uk). Bus 1, 2, 5, 6, 21, 25, 46, 49, N1, N2, N25. **Open** noon-midnight Mon-Thur, Sun; noon-2am Fri, Sat. **Pub. Map** p151 D4 ㉛

Climb the spiral stair at this emerald boozer on the corner of Palmeira Square and you'll find yourself in the Speakeasy, a Prohibition-themed bar that started life as a temporary pop-up and now serves cocktails to Hove's more bohemian elements every Friday and Saturday night from 8pm. The downstairs pub, with its island bar, is one of Western Road's more traditional establishments.

Wolfies of Hove
ᴺᴱᵂ *90 Goldstone Villas, BN3 3RU (01273 962395, www.wolfiesofhove. co.uk). Bus 7, 21.* **Open** noon-3pm, 4.30-10pm Mon-Fri; noon-10pm Sat; noon-8pm Sun. **£. Fish & chips. Map** p150 C2 ㉜

Wolfies arrived in late 2014 and quickly established itself as a traditional chippy with 21st-century considerations: it's the only place in the city with a dedicated gluten-free fryer. There are also guest pies from Piglets Pantry, and fish specials such as Caribbean red snapper, and there's limited seating inside and out. Look out for their even newer café, Rudy's Kitchen, opening a few doors along at 98 Goldstone Villas.

Shopping

There is also a branch of **Bert's Homestore** (p69) at 33 George Street, BN3 3YB (01273 732770).

Audrey's Chocolates
28 Holland Road, BN3 1JJ (01273 735561, www.audreyschocolates.co.uk). Bus 1, 2, 5, 6, 21, 25, 46, 49. **Open** 9am-5pm Mon-Sat. **Map** p151 D4 ㉝

The sort of chocolate shop where rich grandmothers go to spoil their grandsons, Audrey's has been going for over 60 years and always has a handsome chocolate teddy in its window. Firmly established as a top-rank chocolatier, it even makes its own drinking chocolate. Other beautifully wrapped treats include sugar mice and hand-dipped mints.

Bobby & Dandy
18 Blatchington Road, BN3 3YN (01273 776841 www.bobbyanddandy.co.uk). Bus 2, 5, 46. **Open** 10.30am-5.30pm Tue-Sat. **Map** p150 B3 ㉞

If you're on the vintage clothing trail, it's worth going the distance for this attractive boutique specialising in midcentury men's and women's clothing. The owner is a sometime showgirl, pattern-cutter and cover model for bimonthly gentlemen's bible *The Chap*, and is genuinely passionate about her stock.

Book Nook
1 St John's Place, BN3 2FJ (01273 911988, www.booknookuk.com). Bus 1, 2, 5, 6, 21, 46, 49. **Open** 9am-5.30pm Mon-Fri; 9.30am-5.30pm Sat. **Map** p151 D4 ㉟

A brilliant children's bookshop with a small café where children can read in the bow of a little wooden ship. It sells books for babies through to teenagers, including dual-language and curriculum-specific literature. There's storytime at 4pm on weekdays, and 11am and 3pm on Saturdays, plus regular themed events and author visits.

Brass Monkeys

109 Portland Road, BN3 5DP (01273 725170, www.brassmonkeys.org.uk). Bus 2, 46, 49. **Open** 10am-5pm Mon-Sat. **Map** p150 A3 ③⑥

Forty-five established and emerging jewellers sell in this showroom with a workshop at the rear. And it's not all metalwork: Lesley Strickland's colourful knot rings use cellulose acetate derived from cotton oil, while Marie Canning's porcelain brooches are thrown on a potter's wheel.

Cameron Contemporary Art

1 Victoria Grove, Second Avenue, BN3 2LJ (01273 727234, www.cameron contemporaryart.com). Bus 1, 2, 5, 6, 21, 25, 46, 49. **Open** 10.30am-6pm Mon-Sat; noon-5pm Sun. **Map** p151 D4 ③⑦

This classy contemporary painting and sculpture gallery has roughly eight exhibitions a year, featuring figurative and abstract work, supporting local artists and selling ceramics and jewellery alongside.

City Books

23 Western Road, BN3 1AF (01273 725306, www.city-books.co.uk) Bus 1, 2, 5, 6, 21, 25, 46, 49. **Open** 9.30am-6pm Mon-Sat; 11am-4.30pm Sun. **Map** p151 E4 ③⑧

City Books, which turns 30 in 2016, is much more than an independent bookshop. It stocks an enticing and intelligent range of titles. Service is friendly and knowledgeable. And yes, it's the sort of place where you can really smell the books (rather than coffee). But it also orchestrates a programme of around 30 literary events a year, whether it be Will Self interviewing Nick Cave in-store,

Johnny Rotten speaking at the De La Warr in Bexhill (p168), or Peter James (see box p120) launching his latest crime thriller at the end of Brighton Pier. Sussex's literary landscape wouldn't be quite the same without it.

La Cave à Fromage

W 34-35 Western Road, BN3 1AF (01273 725500, www.la-cave.co.uk) Bus 1, 2, 5, 6, 21, 25, 46, 49. **Open** 10am-7pm Mon-Thur; 10am-9pm Fri, Sat; 11am-8pm Sun. **Map** p151 E4 ③⑨

A posh cheese shop stocking farmhouse cheeses from Britain and Europe (including several exclusives), as well as charcuterie, condiments and artisan breads. Perch on a high stool to sample the wares, with a perfectly matched glass of vino.

Dowse

133 Western Road, BN3 1DA (01273 730091, www.dowsedesign.co.uk). Bus 1, 2, 5, 6, 21, 25, 46, 49. **Open** 11.30am-4pm Mon, Sun; 10.30am-5.30pm Tue-Sat. **Map** p151 E4 ④⓪

This British and European design shop is the sort of place you'd expect to find in the Lanes. It sells beautiful gifts, jewellery, art prints and homewares, from classic Futura mobiles to hand-illustrated Brighton bone-china mugs. It also has a specially commissioned collection at the London Design Museum.

I Gigi

31A Western Road, BN3 1AF (01273 775257, www.igigigeneralstore.com). Bus 1, 2, 5, 6, 21, 25, 46, 49. **Open** 10am-6pm Mon-Sat; 11am-4.30pm Sun. **Map** p151 E4 ④①

I Gigi has two locations. The General Store is on the ground floor at 31A, a showroom full of high-end shabby chic furniture in earthy colours. Upstairs is a country kitchen-style café. A couple of doors down, at no.37, you'll find the women's boutique, dedicated to carefully selected women's labels (Nygårds Anna, Blank, Privatsachen) and its own cashmere range.

BRIGHTON BY AREA

INFOLK

frankie

We go to
the gallery

top: Dowse p159;
bottom: Sage & Relish

JUGs

44 Blatchington Road, BN3 3YH (01273 719899, www.jugsfurniture.co.uk). Bus 2, 5, 46. **Open** 9.30am-5pm Mon-Sat; noon-2pm Sun. **Map** p150 C3 ㊷

Just Unusual Gifts stocks well-priced, authentic Thai and Indian furniture. The understated entrance is deceptive; inside, the shop teems with hand-carved coffee tables, painted trunks and animal ornaments collected on biannual rummaging trips abroad.

Mrs Canuticacq's Emporium

28 Stirling Place, BN3 3YU (07958 949486). Bus 2, 5, 46, 49. **Open** noon-5pm Thur-Sat, or by appointment. **Map** p150 B3 ㊸

The spirit of Ebay-age eclecticism manifests itself here as a titchy backstreet shop opposite the Foragers, selling everything from cocktail trolleys to toy cars, plus a very random vinyl selection stacked in vintage port crates. Its tagline: 'Furniture, frippery and fine vinyl'.

Oliver's Clock Shop

15 Cross Street, BN3 1AJ (01273 736542). Bus 1, 2, 5, 6, 21, 25, 46, 49. **Open** 10am-5pm Tue-Sat. **Map** p151 E4 ㊹

The oldest clock shop in Hove is all you'd want from that sobriquet: an old-fashioned, father-and-son run premises crammed with timepieces. They sell, and restore, everything from ornate mantelpiece clocks and pocket watches to towering grandfather clocks. Opening times can vary.

Poppets

50 Blatchington Road, BN3 3YH (01273 770449, www.poppets.biz). Bus 2, 5, 46. **Open** 9am-5pm Mon-Fri; 9.30am-5pm Sat. **Map** p150 C3 ㊺

This children's shop sells both new and second-hand clothing and toys, as well as ex-chain store labels such as Mini Boden, at bargain prices. Poppets is how Hove's little ones stay kitted out in the latest Hatley rainwear and bandana bibs. Nice gift cards, too.

Quaff

139-141 Portland Road, BN3 5QJ (01273 820320, www.quaffit.com). Bus 2, 46, 49. **Open** 9am-9pm Mon-Sat; 10am-8pm Sun. **Map** p150 A3 ㊻

One of two shops in the city (the other is on Ditchling Road) for this independent wine merchants. Quaff stocks over 500 wines (starting at a few quid a bottle and going up to the mid hundreds) from boutique wineries around the world, including English wines made in Sussex.

Rume

54 Western Road, BN3 1JD (01273 777810, www.rume.co.uk). Bus 1, 2, 5, 6, 21, 25, 46, 49. **Open** 9.30am-5.30pm Mon-Sat; 11am-3pm Sun. **Map** p151 D4 ㊼

A family-run contemporary furniture and furnishings shop for anyone with a taste for modern twists on quintessentially English styles – and a good whack of disposable income. Their own lines include the Chofa, a bold update on the chaise longue.

Sage & Relish

NEW *41 Western Road, BN3 1JD. (no phone, www.sageandrelish.co.uk). Bus 1, 2, 5, 6, 21, 25, 46, 49.* **Open** 10am-6pm Tue-Fri; 10am-4pm Sat. **Map** p151 D4 ㊽

An excellent deli run by a Greek couple who source herbs and spices, oils and olives, charcuterie, octopus and fresh truffles from all over the Mediterranean. They also make their own baklava, and sell recipe books and wicker hampers. A godsend for Yotam Ottolenghi recipes.

Three Angels

5 Hove Street, BN3 2TR (01273 958975, www.threeangels.co.uk). Bus 1, 6, 49. **Open** 10am-6pm Mon-Sat; 11am-4pm Sun. **Map** p150 B4 ㊾

Zinc baths, rusted garden chairs and planted pots spill on to the pavement outside this large-fronted store. Inside is old and new furniture sourced directly from France, and there's a tiny café papered with pages from a French dictionary. If your budget fails you here, try shabby chic emporium Velvet (66-68 Church Road, BN3 2FP).

Arts & leisure

Brighton Body Casting

Goldstone Gallery, 76 Goldstone Villas, BN3 3RU (01273 227153). Bus 7, 21.
Open 10am-6pm Tue-Fri; 11am-4pm Sat; Mon, Sun by appointment.
Map p150 C2 ⓹⓪
Brighton artist Jamie McCartney is best known for his *Great Wall of Vagina*, created from plaster casts of 400 different vulvas. At 30ft, it's too big for the showroom, but you can see a broad range of his body casts, as well as sculptures and photographs here. At his studio, just a minute's walk away at 88 Ethel Street (07961 338045), you can get your own body cast made, in materials from plaster to glass and gold. He's a travelling artist so you're advised to book well in advance. Prices start from around £200.

Brunswick

1 Holland Road, BN3 1JF (01273 733984, www.brunswickpub.co.uk). Bus 1, 2, 5, 6, 21, 25, 46, 49, N1, N2, N25.
Open noon-midnight Mon-Thur; noon-2am Fri; 10am-2am Sat; 10am-midnight Sun. **Map** p151 D5 ⓹①
This 1930s pub is the hub of the Brunswick Town community. It doesn't just serve classy grub and a daily local real ale selection (with a tasting club every Wednesday). It is also, and ever increasingly, a live venue, with bands, comedians and theatre companies performing in a wood-panelled room. There's a free jazz jam every Tuesday.

Duke Box Theatre

The Iron Duke, 3 Waterloo Street, BN3 1AQ (01273 734806, www.ironduke brighton.co.uk). Bus 1, 2, 5, 6, 21, 25, 46, 49. **Map** p151 E5 ⓹②
Catch intimate sketch shows, new plays, puppetry, cabaret and Edinburgh comedy previews at this lovely 40-seat theatre operating within the Iron Duke pub and guesthouse. It has recently

started programming at the beautiful St Andrew's Church across the street, too.

The Old Market (TOM)

11A Upper Market Street, BN3 1AS (01273 201801, www.theoldmarket. com). Bus 1, 2, 5, 6, 21, 25, 46, 49.
Map p151 E4 ⓹③
This grade II-listed venue was saved in 2010 by two local residents who happen to be the creators of international smash-hit *STOMP*. It's now one of the best (and best value) arts venues in the city, with an unbeatable acoustic, popular with mid-scale touring bands, an increasing forte for visual theatre and brilliant regular events such as life-drawing drop-in the Drawing Circus.

Sussex County Cricket Ground

Eaton Road, BN3 3AN (0844 264 0202, www.sussexcricket.co.uk). Bus 7, 21.
Map p151 D3 ⓹④
Sussex is England's oldest county cricket club, and has played most of its home matches at this Hove ground – where you can still watch from the comfort of a blue and white deckchair. Now hemmed in by high-rise flats, it feels rather beleaguered by modern life, but that's part of the appeal. In 2011, it got a new 1,700-seater stand. This is also the site of the biggest annual fireworks display in the city, and is occasionally used for big pop concerts by the likes of Madness and Elton John. Matches are held here from April to September and adult tickets start from £15.

Uniquely Organic Eco Spa

40 Church Road, BN3 2FN (726973, www. uoecospa.com). Bus 1, 5, 6. Open 10am-6pm Mon, Tue, Fri, Sat; 10am-7pm Wed-Thur; 11am-4pm Sun. Map p151 D4 ⓹⑤
Everything is organic, from the products to the towels, at this well-respected eco spa promising 'indulgence with a conscience'. The owners have also originated something called Chakrosanct: a treatment system targeting the seven chakras of the body.

Brighton Marina

Days Out

Brighton Marina

Brighton Marina, just a ten-minute bus ride from the city centre, is the setting for restaurants, bars and a curious range of shops. Mermaid Walk is an appealing pedestrian walkway with yachts on one side and shops the other. There are opportunities for water sports, plus a cinema, bowling alley and casino. Large chain restaurants cater to the many visiting families.

Opened in 1978, the marina has continued to grow. Its eastern edge now contains a plush residential area of balconied flats and houses, sandwiched between white cliffs and the outer harbour; many residents have boats bobbing outside.

There are more than 20 eating and drinking venues, the majority lining the upper-level boardwalk of the Waterfront, with gorgeous harbour views. The best placed for a scenic cocktail or meal is the Seattle

Restaurant at the **Alias Hotel Seattle** (p182), and you'll find the independent **Brasserie Fish & Grill** (3A The Waterfront, Marina Way, 01273 698989, www.brasserie fish-marina.co.uk) among the chains.

Every Saturday and Sunday, the **Mermaid Market** takes place in Marina Square between 11am and 4pm, with arts and crafts, jewellery and fresh local produce. High-street chains are increasingly squeezing out quaint local establishments such as **Pebble Beech** (Unit 45, the Waterfront, 07594 229747), which imports a range of ethical, global handmade crafts. Still going strong is **Laughing Dog Gifts & Gallery** (Unit 31, The Octagon, 01273 626886, www.laughing dogbrighton.com, open daily), incorporating a café and gallery.

Brighton Dive Centre (37 the Waterfront, 01273 606068, www. thebrightondivecentre.co.uk) offers PADI training courses, children's

top: Lewes;
bottom: Charleston
House p167

diving lessons and equipment hire. If you'd rather go on the water than in it, **Ross Boat Trips** (Pontoon 5, West Jetty, 07958 246414, www. watertours.co.uk) can give you a powerboat-style soaking, pier cruises, harbour tours, stag and hen trips and even sprinkle ashes at sea. Mackerel fishing trips can also be organised on two of its boats, holding 12 and 18 people.

Also of note, though more for its oddity than anything else, is the **Brighton Walk of Fame**. The first official Walk outside Hollywood, it consists of 100 plaques bearing names with local associations, from Sir Winston Churchill to Katie Price.

If it's atmosphere you're after, take a walk on the wilder side with a half-hour stroll along the **Undercliff Walk** from Brighton Marina to **Rottingdean**. The broad concrete path is actually a sea wall, built in the 1930s. White chalk cliffs tower to your left, rockpools alternate with shingle beach to your right. At the other end, Rottingdean is a worthy destination. Mentioned in the Domesday book, this pretty seaside village was both a home to Rudyard Kipling, and the 'local shop for local people' that inspired *The League of Gentlemen's* Royston Vasey.

Shoreham-by-Sea

The Wild Life Festival has unexpectedly put Shoreham-by-Sea (a 15-minute train journey to the west of Brighton) on the national music map. The biggest music festival in Sussex was held at Shoreham Airport in June 2015, bringing Disclosure, Sam Smith and Wu Tang Klan to this compact art deco curio. It's the oldest airport in the UK and hosts the Shoreham Airshow every August.

This historic former fishing village has its own rich, homegrown arts scene, too, palpable everywhere from the pub folk singalongs to the artists staking out their easels on

the shoreline, and bolstered by various community festivals and the excellent Ropetackle Arts Centre (Little High Street, 01273 464440, www.ropetacklecentre.co.uk).

Since 2013, an impressive glass and steel swing footbridge has taken pedestrians over the River Adur from the High Street to Lower Beach Road. It affords a striking view of the boats stretching out across the tidal waters towards the spires of Lancing College. On the other side are the Shoreham houseboats, a community of around 60 barges, tugs and sailing vessels, many home to artists and decorated and adapted in ingenious ways.

Back over the bridge, have a drink or a cream tea on the riverside balcony at the **Crown & Anchor** (33 High Street, 01273 463500, www. crownandanchor-shoreham.co.uk).

Lewes

A 15-minute train ride from Brighton, Lewes is a postcard-perfect South Downs county town with a surprising intellectual and artistic underbelly. The centrepiece is the Norman **Lewes Castle** (169 High Street, 01273 486290, www.sussexpast. co.uk, open daily). Its striking presence ensures you never quite get lost exploring the town's steep hills and narrow twittens, full of conspiratorial pubs, right-on artist co-operatives and bookshops dedicated to the town's distinctive and anarchic local history. Lewes is so independently minded that in September 2008 retailers introduced their own currency, the 'Lewes pound', with the aim of encouraging people to spend locally. Appropriately, 18th-century revolutionary Thomas Paine, who lodged over a tobacco shop here during several formative years, is the figurehead on the notes. There's a feeling here that locals would happily embrace a Republic of Lewes

– this is very much the vibe from the annual Lewes Bonfire, an infamous and bacchanalian Guy Fawkes Day celebration that draws thousands.

Emerging out of the attractive station, you'll spot the old **Harvey's Depot** in Pinwell Road. Harveys is the home of Sussex's most famous real ale, and a Lewes institution.

From the station, turn left along Priory Street for the historic Southover area of Lewes, including the timber-framed 15th-century **Anne of Cleves House** (52 Southover High Street, 01273 474610, www.sussex past.co.uk). On a warm day, picnic in **Southover Grange Gardens** (Southover House, Southover Road, open daily). Split in two by the Winterbourne stream, this colourful walled garden surrounds the 16th-century home of diarist John Evelyn, and is full of sculptural and horticultural surprises including England's oldest tulip tree. Another atmospheric spot is **Priory Park** (Cockshut Road) with its monastic ruins (thanks, Henry VIII) and historical herb garden.

For hustle, bustle and the best independent shops, instead turn right out of the station and up Station Street, past upmarket chocolatiers **Bruditz** (16 Station Street, 01273 480734). You'll emerge on to Lewes High Street. Take a left for history: the entrance to the castle, the low-ceilinged **Fifteenth Century Bookshop** (99-100 High Street, 01273 474160, www.oldenyoung books.co.uk, closed occasional Sun) at the top of the steeply cobbled Keere Street (leading back down to Southover Grange), and the **Tom Paine Printing Press** (151 High Street, 07956 821971, www.tompaine printingpress.com, closed Mon, Sun). The brainchild of local printmaker Peter Chasseaud, this is a working replica of an 18th-century wooden press of the sort that made it possible for Paine's revolutionary ideas to

spread. It prints writings, artworks and gift cards inspired by the great man himself. A detour up the tiny **Pipe Passage** brings you to a popular bijou bookshop (1 Pipe Passage, 01273 480744). The nearby **Round House**, a former windmill, was once owned by Virginia Woolf.

Turn right along the high street instead and you'll pass specialist fromagerie **Cheese Please** (46 High Street, BN7 2DD, 01273 481048, www.cheesepleaseonline.co.uk, closed Sun) on your way to the war memorial. The walk down the stretch of high street known as School Hill affords the quintessential Lewes view over Malling Down, and the perfect spot for lunch courtesy of **Flint Owl Bakery** (209 High Street, 01273 472769, www.flintowl bakery.com, closed Sun) with its lovely courtyard garden. Opened in 2013, it serves some of the best loaves in Sussex.

Continue downhill, through the pedestrianised area with its superior buskers and over the River Ouse, to reach **Harvey's Brewery and Shop** (6 Cliffe High Street, 01273 480217, www.harveys.org.uk). Testifying to the brew's growing popularity, there is now a whopping two-year waiting list for tours, and they've suspended advance bookings. Instead, check out the range of merchandise in the shop, or simply have a pint of the stuff at miniscule nearby boozer the **Gardeners Arms** (46 Cliffe High Street, 01273 474808).

Cliffe High Street is home to two other fundamental Lewes fixtures, the first being antiques shops. One of the largest and most fun to explore (along with Lewes Flea Market, in a converted church in Market Street) is the four-floor **Lewes Antiques Centre** (42 Cliffe High Street, 01273 486866). The other essential stop is **Bill's Produce Store & Café** (56 Cliffe High Street, 01273 476918, www.billsproducestore.co.uk), the first branch of a now-nationwide chain of café-restaurants inspired by old-fashioned grocers. This original is stacked with colourful fruit and veg displays and rows of own-made condiments.

Cliffe High Street leads on to South Street, from where you can take a steep walk up Chapel Hill for a charming view of the town and river. South Street is also worth exploring for its excellent children's bookshop, **Bags of Books** (1 South Street, 01273 479320, www.bags-of-books. co.uk, closed Sun) and the **Snowdrop Inn** (119 South Street, 01273 471018). This cosy local was the site of Britain's deadliest avalanche, which killed eight people in 1836.

Heading north of the high street, you can lunch on a ploughman's in the town's favourite pub, the **Lewes Arms** (1 Mount Place, 01273 473152, www.lewesarms.co.uk). Also in this area, the **Hop Gallery** (Castle Ditch Lane, 01273 487744, www.hopgallery. com, usually open Tue-Sun) and artist-run **Chalk Gallery** collective (4 North Street, 01273 474477, www. chalkgallerylewes.co.uk) deserve further exploration for their local art. One of many bespoke guitar-makers resident in Lewes, local luthier **Richard Osborne** specialises in mandolins and bouzoukis (Studio 14, Star Gallery, Castle Ditch Lane, 01273 473883, www.osborneguitars.co.uk).

This whole area, which is sometimes known as the North Street Cultural Quarter, is likely to change considerably in coming years, especially if local workshop owners based in the Phoenix Estate lose their ongoing battle against housing developers.

If you are planning to spend the night in Lewes, **Pelham House** (St Andrew's Lane, 01273 488600, www. pelhamhouse.com) is a converted 16th-century manor house that's now a 31-bedroom hotel. Stop here too for afternoon tea on the terrace.

Lewes holds one final treat for summer visitors in the form of **Pells Pool** (Brook Street, 01273 472334, www.pellspool.org.uk, closed mid Sept-mid May). The oldest freshwater pool in the country is over 150 years old, and sunbathing on its tree-lined lawn or splashing in the gin-clear water is a truly timeless pleasure.

If you're a fan of outdoor swimming, keep an eye on **Saltdean Lido** (www.saltdeanlido.co.uk). The grade II-listed 1930s swimming pool is currently being restored to its art deco glory by Terence Conran's design firm.

Charleston House

Five miles east of Lewes is **Charleston House** (Firle, East Sussex, 01323 811265, www. charleston.org.uk, closed Mon, Tue, autumn to spring; see website for exact dates). The Bloomsbury set's country retreat is a worthwhile excursion, though a bit of a trek from Glynde, the nearest train station. The Countryliner bus no.125 runs from Lewes from Wednesday to Friday, but a car makes it an easier option from Brighton. Guided tours are available Wednesday to Saturday. On Sundays and bank holidays, visitors are free to roam.

Artist Vanessa Bell set up house in East Sussex in 1916 – with her lover Duncan Grant, his lover, David Garnett, and her three children, by Grant and her husband Clive Bell. Vanessa revelled in the rural freedom, as her sister Virginia Woolf noted: 'Nessa seems to have slipped civilisation off her back, and splashes about entirely nude, without shame, and enormous spirit. Indeed, Clive now takes up the line that she has ceased to be a presentable lady – I think it all works admirably.'

Bell and Grant daubed every available surface with murals, and filled the farmhouse with textiles, ceramics and pieces of art – including works by Picasso and Sickert. The house looks as fantastical today as it did 90 years ago: a gloriously uninhibited explosion of colour and creativity.

The annual Charleston Festival in May keeps its history alive: past speakers have included Grayson Perry, Alan Bennett and Patti Smith, and there's a great short-story festival, Small Wonder, every September, too. The house and gardens close for the winter, but the café and superior gift shop open throughout the year.

Bexhill

Taking the 50-minute direct train from Brighton to Bexhill is like travelling back in time. The south-coast town where Eddie Izzard spent his childhood, Spike Milligan spent the early years of World War II and Fanny Craddock her final days is known as God's Waiting Room, and not without good reason. Richly stocked charity shops crowd the town centre.

Yet turn right when you reach the coast promenade from the station and you'll find the **De La Warr Pavilion** (Marina, 01424 229111, www.dlwp.com, open daily), the modernist icon whose clean white curves have been pepping up spirits since 1935. Reopened in 2005 after an £8 million refurb, the light-flooded building is reason enough to visit Bexhill. But the De La Warr is also well on its way to becoming a sort of Southbank Centre-by-Sea. Aside from comedy – including regular pop-up gigs from Izzard – and concerts, it's a top space for contemporary art: sculptor Antony Gormley once even exhibited on its roof.

Music fans should also pay a visit to **Music's Not Dead** (71 Devonshire Road, 01424 552435).

A minor miracle given its location, this independent record shop hosts its own gigs (with posters screenprinted on site) and opens late on days when the De La Warr has a band on. Local boys Keane played a secret gig here in 2013. Speaking of which, you can now trace the band's numerous lyrical references to the town via the actually-very-popular **Keane Trail** (www.keanetrail. co.uk). The seafront meeting point that inspired their song 'The Sovereign Light Café' sits on the newly modernised West Parade, next to the pristine pebble beach.

The recently launched **Coastal Culture Trail** connects the De La Warr with two other award-winning galleries, the Jerwood in Hastings and Towner in Eastbourne, and is becoming a popular weekend break. The handy 20-mile coastal path can also be covered in a day by bike. But don't push yourself. There's something rare and wonderfully relaxing about sitting in the De La Warr's excellent and informal restaurant, with its uninterrupted view of lawn, sea and sky, and knowing there isn't really anywhere else you should be.

If you want to stay in Bexhill, **Coast** (58 Sea Road, 01424 225260, www. coastbexhill.co.uk) is the town's first boutique B&B, and due to the town's increasing musical connections it's now just as likely to take bookings from indie kids as from retirees.

Ditchling Beacon

From the vantage point of Ditchling Beacon (reached by the 79 bus from the Old Steine in Brighton), the undulating contours of what Rudyard Kipling called the 'blunt, bow-headed, whale-backed Downs' stretch as far as the eye can see. To the west, the **South Downs Way** (www.nationaltrail.co.uk) dips and climbs the chalk escarpment

top: De La Warr Pavilion;
bottom: South Downs Way

for some 50 miles, heading into Hampshire; eastwards on the horizon lies the hazy blue-grey outline of the cliffs at the Seven Sisters, where the Downs finally reach the sea.

The Beacon, rising steeply above the villages and farmland of the Weald on one side, then sloping gently southwards towards the sea, has its own quiet charms. Once an Iron Age hillfort, it was first lit as one of a chain of fires to warn of the Spanish Armada's invasion. Just be warned – winding up it by car can involve a good deal of first gear and patience as you stare at cyclists' straining behinds. Scaling Ditchling Beacon, with its 16 per cent gradient spike, is a point of pride for cyclists – especially since the Tour of Britain passed here for the first time in 2014.

This is a landscape shaped by centuries of sheep grazing – the most profitable use for these precipitous inclines and shallow, chalky soils. Seen at ground level – as you stretch out at full length on the soft, springy turf – the seemingly bare hillside is actually teeming with life.

The most exhilarating thing about the climb is the sudden steep ascents on paths that are little more than a series of chalky foot-holds hewn into the sheer slope. And at the top? No café, no toilets, and certainly no cable car: just the spirit-lifting sweep of the Sussex Weald and the white ribbon of the South Downs Way, entering its homeward straight. Plus a premier kite-flying opportunity, of course, and a lonely ice-cream van in the car park that does a roaring summer trade.

For sustenance, head instead to the 200-year-old **Half Moon** (Ditchling Road, 01273 890253, www.halfmoonplumpton.com) in nearby Plumpton, and grab a picnic table or a chair by the flint fireplace, depending on the season. Ramblers' favourites include sausage and mash made with Harvey's ale, and game

dishes with meat from local shoots are a speciality.

The Half Moon is ten minutes drive from the ancient and rather arty village of Ditchling, famously once home to two major British 20th century artists, Eric Gill and David Jones. Both are represented at the **Ditchling Museum of Art and Craft** (01273 844744, www.ditchling museumartcraft.org.uk) next to the village green, which reopened in 2013 after major refurbishment.

Devil's Dyke

The Victorians, like many modern-day visitors, loved the drama of Devil's Dyke, a five-mile walk along the South Downs Way from Ditchling Beacon (or take the 77 bus from Brighton train station). This vertiginous gulf was carved out of the chalk strata as the Ice Age snowfields retreated. Local folklore has it rather differently: according to most variations, it was dug by the Devil in a failed attempt to let in the sea and drown the pious parishioners of the Weald. In its tourist heyday at the end of the 19th century, day-trippers flocked to peer into the abyss – there was even a cable car, perilously strung across the valley. Today, it's popular with walkers, picnickers and hang-gliders.

Once at the top, admire the panorama across the Weald below. According to John Constable, the view is 'perhaps the most grand & affecting natural landscape in the world – and consequently, a scene most unfit for a picture'.

There's a large pub at the top of Devil's Dyke, but it's best to head down into the Weald, to the **Shepherd & Dog** (the Street, 01273 857382, www.shepherdanddogpub. co.uk) in Fulking. This 17th-century inn at the foot of the Downs has low, beamed ceilings, an inglenook fireplace and a glorious beer garden crossed by a babbling brook.

Essentials

A Room With a View
p181

Hotels

Brighton's hotels are doing an increasingly good job of being all things to all people. There are romantic retreats and saucy play-dens, comfy family suites and clubbers' crash pads, smart business accommodation and backpacking hostels, and design showrooms in which you just happen to be able to sleep. Gone, for the most part, are the seedy boarding houses with which the city was once synonymous.

The newest breed of Brighton landlady and landlord is likely to be an artist, gallery owner or salvage stylist with an eye for a unique property. Recent North Laine addition the **Chapel Townhouse**, for instance, is a one-room hotel with its own stained glass window and a gallery downstairs. Other enticing converted spaces now cater for larger groups (see box p180).

Kemp Town is where you'll find most of the guesthouses. Many are either gay-run, or at least notably gay-friendly – though sexual orientation isn't going to be an issue anywhere. Owners often make up for the lack of space by cramming in services: organic breakfasts in your room, luxurious toiletries or DVD libraries.

Among Brighton's art-loving hotels is **Fab Guest**, where wall art and items of furniture have been specially commissioned from local artists. The trend for letting artists run creatively amok was started in earnest by **Artist Residence**. Also on Regency Square, **Hotel Pelirocco** is renowned for its quirky collaborations. The **Oriental** and **Nineteen** also exhibit work by local artists.

The success of the Pelirocco has spawned a craze for themed rooms, though take this with a pinch of salt: 'theme' may simply indicate a leopard print bedspread or a stencil of Elvis on your pillow. For individuality with guaranteed class, **Hotel du Vin** and **Drakes** (which

ESSENTIALS

both have their own acclaimed restaurants) are still hard to beat.

Some of the big seafront chains have been pulling their socks up lately too. The **Holiday Inn** and **Hilton Brighton Metropole** have undergone extensive renovations in 2015.

But the biggest wow factor comes courtesy of the new **YHA** in the old Royal York Hotel – a youth hostel with Grade II-listed glamour.

We have highlighted seafront hotels in our listings, but bear in mind that some others may have rooms with sea views.

Price wise

As Brighton is a popular weekend destination, all good hotels book up in advance on Friday, Saturday and occasionally Sunday nights. Also be warned that some only accept a minimum two-night stay. This does mean, however, that there are some excellent bargains to be had midweek.

As a very rough guide, standard prices for expensive hotels (**£££**) tend to be over £200 for a weekend stay in a standard double with prices dipping during the week; moderate-priced (**££**) properties are around £100-£200, sometimes a little less during the week; budget rooms (**£**) are generally under £100.

Needless to say, the summer is significantly busier, and weekends with festivals get particularly booked up, so check what is on first. For the month-long Brighton Festival in May, Pride weekend in August and for any political party conference in September, hotels fill up fast.

The Visitor Information Point at the Brighton Centre Box Office can make same-day bookings for serviced accommodation. This service is available 10am-4pm Mon-Sat, subject to a 10 per cent deposit and a booking fee of £1.50 per adult.

SHORTLIST

Best for romance
- Chapel Townhouse (p178)
- Drakes (p179)
- Hotel Du Vin (p176)

Arty stays
- Artist House (p180)
- Artist Residence (p175)
- Fab Guest (p179)
- Nineteen (p181)

For design buffs
- Fab Guest (p179)
- Vine Street Studio (p180)

Best for foodies
- Artist Residence (p175)
- Drakes (p179)

Best breakfast
- A Room With A View (p181)
- Five Brighton (p181)
- Paskins Town House (p181)

Best bar
- Blanch House (p179)
- Drakes (p179)
- Hotel Una (p175)
- Myhotel (p178)

Best for views
- A Room With A View (p181)
- Alias Hotel Seattle (p182)
- Drakes (p179)

Chic on the cheap
- Neo Hotel (p176)
- Snooze Guest House (p182)
- Umi Brighton (p178)
- YHA (p178)

Friendliest welcome
- Guest & the City (p181)
- Sea Spray (p182)
- Twenty One (p182)

Notably gay-friendly
- Amsterdam (p178)
- Legends (p181)

ESSENTIALS

JEREMY HOYE

Inspiring contemporary jewellery

City Centre

Artist Residence

33 Regency Square, BN1 2GG (01273 324302, www.artistresidence.co.uk). **££**.
Set in a Regency Square townhouse, the Brighton branch of this three-strong mini-chain originally offered free accommodation to artists such as local graffer Pinky. Now, staff grow herbs for no-waste restaurant Silo (p79) in the garden; there's a new restaurant, the Set (p67), plus a new café and ping-pong room. The place has also expanded next door with the Cocktail Shack (p61). Designer Hannah Stacey put together the latest 'artist room', and three more new rooms feature cast-iron baths.

Grand

99 Kings Road, BN1 2FW (0871 2224 684, www.grandbrighton.co.uk). **Seafront. £££**.
The Grand is an opulent Victorian masterpiece built in the 1860s. Marble, mirrors and chandeliers gleam in the high entrance hall, curving round to the lounge bar and GB1 Seafood Restaurant (p62). The 201 spotless rooms are well-appointed, comfortable, and decorated in pastel shades. All have complimentary Wi-Fi. There's also an eight-room spa, plus gym.

Granville

124 Kings Road, BN1 2FY (01273 326302, www.granvillehotel.co.uk). **Seafront. £**.
This boutique seafront hotel has two dozen themed rooms, ranging from the Brighton Rock (with a king-sized four-poster and jacuzzi) to the Noel Coward (art deco mirrors and gowns provided). You can breakfast on a burrito from Smokey's, the American-style in-house restaurant. This is one of several seafront hotels that has benefited from having views of the derelict West Pier. Staff are confident the i360 (p55) will prove just as enticing.

Hilton Brighton Metropole

Kings Road, BN1 2FU (01273 775432, www.hilton.co.uk). **Seafront. £££**.
Brighton's largest hotel emerged from a £3.75-million renovation at the start of 2015, marking its 125th birthday by refurbishing 185 of its 340 guest rooms, launching the Salt Room (p67), and overhauling its spa as Schmoo by the Sea. The red brick Metropole was controversial when it first appeared on the white stuccoed seafront. Today, it's an elegant if slightly bland affair.

Holiday Inn

137 Kings Road, BN1 2JF (01273 828250, www.hibrighton.com). **Seafront. ££**.
There's no getting away from the ugly exterior of this branch of the international chain, but once through the doors you'll benefit from the full refurbishment undertaken in 2015. There are clear sea views from the front rooms, especially on the fourth and fifth storeys.

Hotel Pelirocco

10 Regency Square, BN1 2FG (01273 327055, www.hotelpelirocco.co.uk). **££**.
'England's most rock 'n' roll hotel' has been recommended so often it's in danger of becoming too mainstream for its own good. But then they go and restyle the most popular suite (the one with the mirrored ceiling) as the Kraken's Lair – tentacles, plunge pool, black rubber curtains and all. The Pelirocco remains Brighton's best and most genuinely bonkers alternative hotel, which is why the likes of Primal Scream's Bobby Gillespie (who designed a room) keep coming back. If you're travelling solo, we recommend the Rough Trade Rough Nite, complete with decks, headphones and a stack of promos. The bar also has weekly DJ nights.

Hotel Una

55-56 Regency Square, BN1 2FF (01273 820464, www.hotel-una.co.uk). **££**.
One of Brighton's fancier boutique hotels, with a great in-house cocktail

bar. Owned by architect Zoran Maricevic, Hotel Una has 19 rooms in which the decor rarely stands still. Most popular is the Danube, with a free-standing roll-top bath beneath the window; most recently refurbished is Flores, which has a mezzanine and new jacuzzi.

Ibis

88-92 Queens Road, BN1 3XE (01273 201000, www.ibis.com). **££**.
Extremely handy for the train station, this 140-room modern chain hotel is clean and comfortable, with boxy, functional rooms, a smart bar and restaurant, and an all-you-can eat hot and continental breakfast buffet.

Mercure Brighton

149 King's Road, BN1 2PP (0844 815 9061, www.mercurebrighton.co.uk). **Seafront. ££**.
This Grade II-listed grand Victorian hotel was built in 1864 and has retained many of its original features, including the mirrors, chandeliers and huge sweeping staircase. The rooms, however, are thoroughly modern identikit affairs in dark mahogany and cream.

Neo Hotel

19 Oriental Place, BN1 2LL (01273 711104, www.neohotel.com). **££**.
Squeezing elegant style into a Grade II-listed townhouse (with the help of numerous varieties of vintage wallpaper), this nine-room hotel is on the corner of Oriental Place. Each room has waffle-textured kimonos, superior toiletries, and access to a good DVD library.

Oriental

9 Oriental Place, BN1 2LJ (01273 205050, www.orientalbrighton.co.uk). **££**.
Only 30 seconds from the sea and two minutes from Western Road, the Oriental is a typical Brighton Regency townhouse with nine modern rooms over five floors, all en-suite. There's a cocktail bar, and public areas are used as exhibition spaces. Excellent breakfasts are made from organic local produce.

Hotel du Vin

2 Ship Street, BN1 1AD (0844 736 4251, www.hotelduvin.com). **£££**.
One of half-a-dozen venues in this classy mini chain, the Brighton Hotel du Vin is set in an olive-green jumble of mock Tudor and Gothic revival buildings. High-quality bistro food brings many non-guests to the restaurant, and there's a walk-in cigar humidor in the bar. The 49 rooms verge on the masculine, but each is slightly different. The nine suites are huge, and have roll-top baths and monsoon showers.

Old Ship Hotel

31-38 Kings Road, BN1 1NR (01273 329001, www.thehotelcollection.co.uk). **Seafront. ££**.
The oldest hotel in Brighton (it accommodated the likes of Charles II and Paganini) was established before 1600, but the current building dates from 1794, with a sensitive refurbishment in the 1960s. The assembly room and ballroom, dating from 1761, are spectacular, and the hotel now uses the 400-year-old cellars for special events. There are 154 traditional but crisply decorated rooms, some with sea views. The resident Steak On Sea Restaurant offers alfresco dining in the summer.

Premier Inn

144 North Street, BN1 1RE. (0871 527 8150, www.premierinn.com). **£**.
You can't get more central than this branch of the well-known budget chain: slap bang between the North Laine and the Lanes, Western Road and the Old Steine. It's a three-storey stretch of concrete above a Subway and Poundland. But if you're staying in it, then you're not looking at it.

Queens Hotel

1 Kings Road, BN1 1NS (01273 321222, www.queenshotelbrighton.com). **Seafront. ££**.

Cheap stays

Good looks, budget prices.

YHA

Brighton's backpacker-friendly accommodation is increasingly combining budget appeal with the cool, urban style of a boutique hotel. You may still have to sleep in a room with snoring strangers, but the rest of the time you can lounge in the bar on retro space-age chairs. The new **YHA** (p178) even offers double rooms with roll-top baths.

There are two **Grapevine** hostels, one by the seafront and the other in North Laine. The seafront branch (75-76 Middle Street, BN1 1AL, 01273 777717, www.grapevine website.co.uk) is smartly appointed. The location in the North Laine (29-30 North Road, same contact details) has larger dorm rooms.

Seadragon (36 Waterloo Street, BN3 1AY, 01273 711854, www. seadragonbackpackers.co.uk) is one of the city's quieter hostels (well, it is in Hove), with two- or four-bed rooms. The latter have a seating area, and most have sash windows and bare floorboards.

Friendly **Kipps** (76 Grand Parade, BN2 9JA, 01273 604182, www. kipps-brighton.com), with views of the Royal Pavilion, organises regular Xbox, pizza and cocktail nights, while **Baggies Backpackers** (33 Oriental Place, BN1 2LL, 01273 733740, www.baggiesbackpackers. com), just up from the seafront, has a music room (complete with guitars and MP3 system) and a chill-out room with films and a projector. **HostelPoint** (10-12 Grand Junction Road, BN1 1NG, 01273 202036, www.hostel pointuk.com) has now replaced St Christopher's, and is updating the old building just opposite Brighton Pier.

The largest hostel is **Journeys** (33 Richmond Place, BN2 9NA, 01273 695866, www.visit journeys.com). It's slightly further from the seafront and the Lanes than its competitors, but there's an excellent curry place (Planet India, 4-5 Richmond Parade, 01273 818149) just round the corner, and pool and foosball tables.

ESSENTIALS

This large hotel is a popular choice for conference delegates, with 94 good-sized rooms (over half of which have sea views) decorated in a modern, inoffensive way. Amenities include a decent gym, 50sqm swimming pool and a bar and bistro with an extensive menu. The location is excellent, though the area can be noisy at night.

Thistle Brighton

King's Road, BN1 2GS (0871 376 9041, www.thistle.com). **Seafront. ££.**
This large seafront chain hotel is more impressive inside than out: it has a vast glass-ceilinged atrium bar complete with trees and a lamppost. There are 210 comfortable if corporate rooms, and good facilities make it popular for conferences. But website offers and a great central position make it worth checking out for leisure trips too. Local fragrance boutique Pecksniffs runs a Pamper Studio on the ground floor.

Umi Brighton

60-64 King's Road, BN1 1NA (01273 323221, www.umihotelbrighton.co.uk). **Seafront. ££.**
A stylish budget hotel. The 78 rooms are basic (inspirational wall stencils aside), but spotless and comfortable. The location couldn't be handier for the seafront nightlife – but it's on a busy junction on the corner of West Street, home of the biggest mainstream clubs and bars, so perhaps not the right choice for a romantic retreat.

YHA Brighton

Old Steine, BN1 1NH (0845 371 9176, www.yha.org.uk). **£.**
Youth hostels and Regency grandeur don't usually meet in the same sentence, but this branch of the YHA, in the former Royal York hotel, has retained many of the hotel's period features. The pillared entrance, chandeliers and fireplaces now play off against bold floral wallpapers and colourful modern prints. There's a self-catering kitchen, a funky café-bar, a movie and karaoke

room and a bike store, plus free Wi-Fi in the communal areas. All 51 rooms are en suite, including 18 doubles. If you want to secure a sea view (and a rolltop bath) book one of the 12 premium rooms.

North Laine

Chapel Townhouse

NEW *114 Church Street, BN1 1RL (01273 324432, www.chapeltownhouse. com).* **££.**
Fancy having a whole hotel to yourself? Run by the North Laine's No Walls art gallery and managed by Myhotel, the Chapel Townhouse is a one-bed accommodation in a former chapel dating to 1876, with a huge stained-glass window. You enter through a private door in Pavilion Gardens Mews, bang opposite Brighton Dome, and ascend a grand staircase. There's a roll-top bath, a mini bar, and a chandelier above the bed made from black Lego bricks.

Myhotel Brighton

17 Jubilee Street, BN1 1GE (01273 900300, www.myhotels.com). **££.**
This popular hotel just off Jubilee Square is built over its sleek public cocktail bar, the Merkaba. Stark white is the dominant theme, to which each curvaceous room adds a mandala artwork and colour-changing crystal light fixture. On the third floor are three studios with individual features – the Jade has a circular bed and freestanding bath that can be made private with a curtain. There's also a penthouse space, the Carousel, with a tiled steam room and (a real challenge to adventurous lovers, this one) a carousel horse.

Kemp Town

Amsterdam

11-12 Marine Parade, BN2 1TL (01273 688825, www.amsterdam.uk.com). Bus 12, 13, 14, 27, 37, 47. **Seafront. ££.**
A large gay-friendly venture with a hotel, bar, restaurant and sauna. You can also order massage treatments. The

late-opening A Bar hosts live entertainment on Wednesday and Friday nights. There's a good variety of rooms, all redecorated and given new beds in 2015, ranging from singles to the penthouse.

Avalon

7 Upper Rock Gardens, BN2 1QE (01732 692344, www.avalonbrighton.co.uk). Bus 1, 2, 7, 16, 18, 21, 37, 38. **£.**
This traditional B&B has a very loyal set of regulars (and their dogs), who return as much for friendly hosts Brian, Tom and George as for the seven well-appointed and cosily furnished rooms. They're a good source of information and will loan out maps for walkers.

Blanch House

17 Atlingworth Street, BN2 1PL (01273 603504, www.blanchhouse.co.uk). Bus 12, 13, 14, 27, 37, 47. **££.**
The 12 individually furnished rooms here have a more restrained take on theming than some – the Perrier Jouët, for instance, takes its colour scheme from the champagne. This hotel, with its bijou cocktail bar and acclaimed restaurant, was once a favourite late-night drinking den among Brighton celebrities. The new owners have brought the focus back on to the guests, winning plaudits for their attentiveness if sacrificing some of that 'hang out' vibe.

Brighton Wave

10 Madeira Place, BN2 1TN (01273 676794, www.brightonwave.co.uk). Bus 12, 13, 14, 27, 37, 47. **£.**
This warmly welcoming B&B has eight en-suite double rooms decorated with solid furnishings, muted colours and splashes of modern art. The communal areas exhibit work by local artists. With late checkout and late breakfast options, the emphasis is on chilling. The basement room has a whirlpool and walled patio garden, and another has a balcony.

Drakes

43-44 Marine Parade, BN2 1PL (01273 696934, www.drakesofbrighton.com). Bus 12, 13, 14, 27, 37, 47. **Seafront. £££.**
This high-end designer hotel is still a top booking. Snag a room with a view of Brighton Pier and sink into the free-standing bath to enjoy it. All 20 rooms are individually decorated, with free Wi-Fi. The in-house restaurant is a name to drop in its own right, and the cocktail lounge is one of the city's favourite spots for a classy evening drink. Drakes also offers a full concierge service.

Fab Guest

NEW *9 Charlotte Street, BN2 1AG (01273 625505, www.fabguest.co.uk/ brighton). Bus 12, 13, 14, 27, 37, 47.* **££.**

Fab Guest

ESSENTIALS

clean white walls and warm wood fittings. The Roof Terrace Room has a staircase leading up to a private terrace. Smoked salmon and blueberry pancakes are on the breakfast menu.

Sea Spray

25 New Steine, BN2 1PD (01273 680332, www.seaspraybrighton.co.uk). Bus 12, 13, 14, 27, 37, 47. **££**.
There are 15 themed rooms to choose from at this affordable, fun and family-run take on the boutique hotel. The latest addition is the Eden Suite, which has a hot tub in its own little walled garden. Sea Spray also has a small massage and sauna room.

Snooze Guest House

25 St George's Terrace, BN2 1JJ (01273 605797, www.snoozebrighton.com). Bus 37, 47. **£**.
Recently refurbished, this good-value guesthouse in the quieter reaches of Kemp Town has six 'super snooze' rooms, and four 'snooze light' options for those on a budget. Room 1 has red leather armchairs and a jumble of mirrors, Room 6 comes with swirling wallpaper and 1960s loungers. The two '70s-themed top-floor suites have large TVs with DVD players, iPod docks and a breakfast in bed option.

Twenty One

21 Charlotte Street, BN2 1AG (01273 686450, www.thetwentyone.co.uk). Bus 12, 13, 14, 27, 37, 47. **££**.
Styling veers towards the old-fashioned (iron bedsteads, gold padded cushions) at this B&B, but Twenty One is far from stuffy. The owners are happy to bring you breakfast in bed, where you can listen to the digital radio or music through the iPod dock. There are eight rooms, two with sea views, all with generous hospitality trays.

White House

6 Bedford Street, BN2 1AN (01273 626266, www.whitehousebrighton.com). Bus 12, 13, 14, 27. **££**.

On a quiet Kemp Town street yet handy for the seafront and Concorde 2, this friendly B&B has ten rooms, two of which have private balconies, and a communal courtyard garden. Orla Kiely toiletries, iPod docks, and TVs with DVD players come as standard. There's an extensive and high-quality breakfast menu.

Hove

Claremont

13 Second Avenue, BN3 2LL (01273 735161, www.theclaremont.eu). Bus 1, 6, 49. **££**.
This upmarket guesthouse has 11 traditionally elegant rooms with huge beds, including a four-poster with billowing white curtains. Style-wise, it's one of the city's more traditional choices, but unbeatable for space.

New England Quarter

Jurys Inn

101 Stroudley Road, BN1 4DJ (01273 862121, www.brightonhotels.jurys inns.com). Bus 37, 38. **££**.
The first of several proposed hotels to be built in the ever-developing New England Quarter, just behind the station. Its 234 rooms are what you'd expect from a business chain – clean, comfortable, competitively priced and well-equipped. There is a bar and restaurant, and a Costa Coffee.

Brighton Marina

Alias Hotel Seattle

Merchants Quay, Brighton Marina, BN2 5WA (01273 679799, www.hotelseattle brighton.com). Bus 7, 21, 23. **££**.
There are 70 modern, spacious and largely light-filled rooms at Brighton Marina's only hotel. Over half face out over the bobbing boats. The feel is professional but relaxed, with minimal pale wood fittings and wicker recliners. The restaurant and bar are as good as the marina gets.

ESSENTIALS

Getting Around

Arriving by air

Gatwick Airport

25 miles north of Brighton, off the M23 (0844 892 0322, www. gatwickairport.com).

Brighton is, on average, a 30-minute train journey from Gatwick. Trains leave at least every 10 to 20 minutes, usually from platform 7. All are direct, although some will have more stops than others. The regular trains run from around 5am until 1am. There are sporadic trains overnight but they can take more than an hour.

From summer 2015 trains from Gatwick will be run by **Thameslink** (www.thameslinkrailway.com) and **Southern Railway** (www. southernrailway.com), a brand also operated by Thameslink. Peak-time **Gatwick Express** (www.gatwickexpress.com) trains also go to Brighton.

At the time of writing, a one-way ticket for any train costs £8.40. An off-peak day return costs £9.50; an anytime day return £10.50; and an open return (valid for 30 days) £20. Prices normally rise each new year.

By road, **National Express** (0871 781 8178, www.nationalexpress.com) runs a regular coach service for £8.50 each way (from £6 booked in advance). It takes 45 minutes. Taxis cost around £35-£45. **Brighton Airport Taxis** (01273 414144, www.brightonairportcabs.co.uk) charges £35 for up to four passengers. **Brighton Taxis** (01273 661998, www.brightontaxihire.co.uk) charges £40.

Other London airports

The other London airports are much less convenient for getting to Brighton, usually requiring a transfer in central London. Direct National Express coaches are available from **Heathrow Airport** for £28 (or from £14.90 if booked online) each way and take around 2 hours 30 minutes. First Capital Connect trains connect to the shuttle from **Luton Airport** and take a minimum of 2 hours; fares start at £33.40 (£33.50 return) for off-peak travel.

Arriving by coach

National Express (0871 781 8181, www.nationalexpress.com) operates coach services between Brighton and London (journey time around 2 hours 20 minutes), and other destinations in England, departing from **Pool Valley Coach Station**, located just off Old Steine.

Some of the services run by **Brighton & Hove Bus and Coach Company** (p184) to destinations in the south-east – including Arundel, Bognor Regis, Chichester and Littlehampton – also depart from here.

Arriving by train

Brighton's central station is served by one train operator with two brands. **Thameslink** (www.thameslink railway.com) has services to Bedford via London Bridge, Blackfriars, City Thameslink, Farringdon and St Pancras International (for direct high-speed Eurostar services to Paris and Brussels, as well as domestic connections to northern England and Scotland).

Southern Railway (www. southernrailway.com) operates on the main line to London (mostly to London Victoria, but some services go to London Bridge), and to other destinations along the south coast,

ESSENTIALS

including suburban stations in Brighton and Hove.

Fares from London vary by time of day and cost roughly £17.10-£25.30 single; £17.20-£48.80 return on weekdays. Weekend fares are cheaper: £10.40-£17.70 single and £10.50-£18.80 return. Cheaper advance fares, for as little as £5 single in off-peak hours, are available on the train companies' websites.

The information desk at Brighton station has timetables and details of discount travel, season tickets and international travel. **National Rail Enquiries** has details by phone on 08457 484950 (24 hours daily), or check www.nationalrail.co.uk. Brighton Station is also an official Visitor Information Point (p189).

Some services to London from coastal destinations to the west bypass Brighton station, but stop at Hove station instead.

Brighton Railway Station
Queens Road, BN1 3XP.
Hove Railway Station
Goldstone Villas, Hove, BN3 3RU.
Both *03451 272920, www. southernrailway.co.uk.*

Public transport

Buses

The city and its surrounding suburbs are very well served by a comprehensive (but difficult to decipher) bus network. **Brighton & Hove Bus and Coach Company** (01273 886200, www.buses.co.uk) runs the vast majority of bus services throughout Brighton & Hove.

Other operators are the **Big Lemon** (www.thebiglemon.com), which runs a service between the city centre, Lewes Road and the universities; and **Stagecoach** (www.stagecoach bus.com), whose Coastliner 700 route goes from the Old Steine to destinations along the coast as far west as Southsea.

Several parts of the city are served by a great number of buses. Below are the groupings for some of the most popular spots in Brighton used throughout this guide, together with a list of bus routes that serve the respective streets or areas. For full information on routes, timetables and maps see www.buses.co.uk.

There are a total of nine **night bus routes** in Brighton. Seven of these are Nightclub buses operating Thursday, Friday and Saturday nights (N1, N2, N5, N12, N14, N29 and N40). The N7 and N25 night buses run nightly around Brighton and into the suburbs.

Brighton City Centre 1, 1A, 2, 2A, 5, 5A, 5B, 6, 7, 12, 12A, 12C, 12X, 13X, 14, 14B, 14C, 17, 20X, 21B, 22, 22A, 24, 25, 26, 27, 27B, 28, 29, 29A, 29B, 29C, 37, 37B, 38A, 40, 40X, 46, 47, 49, 49A, 49E, 50, 52, 52A, 55, 56, 57, 59, 71, 73, 77, 78, 79, 81, 81A, 81B, 81C, 81E, 273, 700, N7, N25, N29, N69, N97, N98, N99.

Brighton Marina 7, 14B, 21, 21B, 23, 27, 47, 52, 57, N7, N99.

Brighton Pier 12, 12A, 12C, 12X, 13X, 14, 14B, 14C, 37, 37B, 38A, 47, 49, 57, 59, 77, 78, 79, N12 and N14.

Brighton Train Station 6, 7, 12, 12A, 12C, 12X, 13X, 14, 14B, 14C, 18, 21, 22, 27, 27B, 37, 37B, 38A, 47, 48, 49E, 50, 52, 52A, 57, 59, 77, 78, 79, 81A, N7.

Hove Town Centre 1, 1A, 2A, 5, 5A, 5B, 6, 7, 11X, 20X, 25, 46, 49, 49A, 71, 81, 81C, 93, 95, 95A, 700, N7, N25, N98.

London Road Shops 5, 5A, 5B, 17, 21, 21B, 22, 22A, 24, 26, 37, 37B, 38, 38A, 40, 40X, 46, 49, 49A, 49E, 50, 55, 56, 78, 79, 81, 81B, 81E, 273, N69.

North Street 1, 2, 5, 7, 12, 13, 14, 18, 21, 22, 24, 25, 26, 27, 28, 29, 37, 46, 47, 48, 49, 50, 52, 56, N1, N5, N7, N12, N14, N25, N29.

Western Road 1, 1A, 2, 5, 5A, 5B, 6, 18, 21, 21A, 25, 46, 49, 60, 77, 700. N1, N5, N7, N12, N14, N25, N29.

There is no longer a daily bus route along the seafront – Western Road buses run closest. However the 77 Saturday and Sunday bus to Devil's Dyke includes a stretch of seafront from the bottom of Preston Street to Brighton Pier. From 2015, during high summer season, an enhanced 77 service will run daily, with an hourly to half-hourly open-top bus running between Brighton Station, the seafront and hotels.

Fares

There is a flat fare for most journeys in Brighton of £2.40, with a Centre Fare of £2 that will take you from Hove Town Hall to Brighton station, for instance. Under-5s travel free, up to a maximum of three children per adult passenger. For children ages 5-13, the fare is half the adult fare. Ages 14 and up pay the full adult fare. A single journey on the city's night buses N7 and N25 costs £4. The Nightclub buses are also £4. Exact change is required for all single fares.

Visitor tickets & passes

Visitors may want to make the most of the **Short Hop** fares, which are available across the city for £1.80. Popular journeys include Hove Station to Hove Town Hall, Downs Park to Portslade and Fiveways to London Road. There is also a tourist fare between Brighton Station and Churchill Square, Brighton Pier or the Royal Pavilion for just £1.80.

If you're planning on making several journeys during one day, it may be worth buying a **Saver** ticket, which allows for unlimited travel on the Brighton & Hove bus network (excluding night buses and Nightclub buses).

A one-day Saver ticket is available from bus drivers for £4.70, from the website (£4.10) or newsagents (£4.60). A seven-day Saver ticket costs £22.50 if bought at the One Stop Travel shop (26 North Street), or £18 if bought in advance from the website or smart phone app. For more information, see www.buses.co.uk/tickets/saver.

Trains

The city has a few suburban rail stations, including London Road, Moulsecoomb and Falmer (for the Stadium and the University of Sussex) to the north-east, and Hove (a five-minute walk from pedestrianised George Street), Aldrington and Portslade to the west. All can be accessed from Brighton station and are served by Southern Railway. Preston Park station, north on the main line to London, is served by both Southern and First Capital Connect trains. Single tickets for all are £2.60 from Brighton; return tickets vary depending on destination and time of day, and cost £2.90-£3.40.

Taxis

Taxis are a quick way to get around the city and are available 24 hours a day. There are plenty of taxi ranks throughout Brighton, with the main ranks situated in East Street, Queen's Square near the Clock Tower, and outside Hove Town Hall.

There are two types of licensed taxis: Hackney carriage vehicles, which are white and aqua and can be found on one of the ranks or hailed from the street; and private-hire vehicles, which can only be booked prior to the journey. Private-hire vehicles will not stop if you hail them. Many taxis are wheelchair accessible.

The minimum fare is £2.80 and it rises in 20p increments according to how far you travel. As a guide to what your journey may cost, the first mile will be £4.40 and each subsequent mile will be £2.20. For example, Churchill Square to Kemp Town will cost around £4.40. Vehicles carrying five to eight passengers are able to charge a higher fare (equivalent to

1.5 times the normal fare). There are additional charges at night, on Sundays, on public holidays, at Christmas and the New Year, and for telephone pre-bookings.
Brighton & Hove City Cabs *01273 205205.*
Brighton & Hove Radio Cabs *01273 204060, www.brightontaxis.com.*
Brighton & Hove Streamline Taxis *01273 202020, www.brighton-streamline.co.uk.*

Cycling

Cycling in Brighton is quick and easy (though the out-of-shape may find the hills challenging), with cycle lanes provided across the city, notably along the seafront. In 2014, a new shared cycle and pedestrian path was introduced on the route from Ditchling Road up to the South Downs.

For bike hire, try **Brighton Beach Bikes** at Brighton Sports Company next to Brighton Pier (07917 753794, www.brightonsports.co.uk/bike-hire), **Cyclelife Electric** at the Marina (01273 625060, www.cyclelife.com/brighton), or **Brighton Cycle Hire** under Brighton Station (01273 571555, www.brightoncyclehire.co.uk). More information on bike hire is available at Visitor Information Points (p189).

There is a multi-facility cycle hub at Brighton station, with smartcard-protected parking for up to 500 bikes.

Driving

Driving around Brighton is relatively easy but, as in most cities, roads can become congested during peak times. On-street parking can be difficult to find but there are plenty of car parks dotted around (below).

Vehicle hire

Most car rental firms insist that drivers are over 21 years old (at least), with a minimum of one year's driving experience and possess a current and full driving licence with no serious endorsements.
Avis *0844 544 6042, www.avis.co.uk.*
Enterprise Rent-A-Car *01273 688222, www.enterprise.co.uk.*
Europcar *0371 3843480, www.europcar.co.uk.*
Hertz *0843 309 3010, www.hertz.co.uk.*
National Car Rental *0871 384 3480, www.nationalcar.co.uk.*
Thrifty Car Hire *01273 738227, www.thrifty.co.uk.*

Car parks

All the car parks detailed below are open 24 hours a day. Rates are around £3.50 to £5 for two hours. For a full list (and map) of car parks, visit www.brighton-hove.gov.uk.

Brighton Lanes (Town Hall) Car Park *Black Lion Street (01273 294296).*
Church Street Car Park *0870 606 7050, www.ncp.co.uk.*
Churchill Square Car Park *01273 327428, www.churchillsquare.com.*
Regency Square Car Park *01273 294296, www.ncp.co.uk.*
Trafalgar Street Car Park *01273 294296, www.ncp.co.uk.*

Clamping & fines

Always carefully check street signs to find out the local parking regulations. Most on-street parking is pay-and-display. Each pay-and-display meter will state the hours when payment is required but for most areas it will be between 8am and 8pm daily. Payment should be made at the on-street pay-and-display ticket vending machines. There are lots of wardens, and they're notoriously ruthless, so it's unlikely you can get away with not paying.

The fine for parking illegally is £50 or £70 depending on the infraction, reduced to £25 or £35 if the ticket is paid within 14 days. Cars are no longer impounded.

Resources A-Z

Accident & emergency

In the event of a serious accident, fire or incident, call 999 and specify whether you require an ambulance, the fire service or the police.

Royal Sussex County Hospital *Eastern Road, Brighton, BN2 5BE (01273 696955). Bus 1, 1A, 7, 14B, 14C, 23, 37, 37B, 40X, 47, 52, 57, 71, 73, 90, 94A, N7, N99.*
The city's 24-hour casualty department.

Credit card loss

Report lost or stolen credit cards immediately, both to the police and the 24-hour phone lines listed below.

American Express *696933, www.americanexpress.com.*
Diners Club *0870 190 0011, www.dinersclub.co.uk.*
MasterCard *0800 964767, www.mastercard.com.*
Visa *0800 891725, www.visa.com.*

Customs

For customs allowances, check www.hmrc.gov.uk.

Dental emergency

If you need emergency dental care, call the dental helpline (0300 1000 899) and specify that you are in pain. They will give you an appointment at one of several local dental practices. Outside normal working hours, phone the emergency dental service in Brighton & Hove on 03000 242548. This service is available 5.30-9.30pm weekdays, and 9am-5.30pm Saturday, Sunday and bank holidays.

Disabled

For information about disabled access and accommodation in Brighton, see www.visitbrighton.com/plan-your-visit/accessibility. The majority of buses have easy access and priority seating for disabled people. For more information, visit www.buses.co.uk. For wheelchair-accessible taxis, try www.205205.com (01273 205205).

Electricity

The UK electricity supply is 220-240 volt, 50-cycle AC rather than the 110-120 volt, 60-cycle AC used in the US. Foreign visitors will need an adaptor or transformer to run appliances.

Embassies & consulates

For a list of consular offices, consult the Yellow Pages (118247, www.yell.com). All the embassies and consulates are in London. Most (the US is an exception) do not accept callers without an appointment.

American Embassy *24 Grosvenor Square, W1A 2LQ (7499 9000, http://london.usembassy.gov). Bond Street or Marble Arch tube.* **Open** 8.30am-5.30pm Mon-Fri.
Australian High Commission *Australia House, Strand, WC2B 4LA (7379 4334, www.uk.embassy.gov.au). Holborn or Temple tube.* **Open** 9am-5pm Mon-Fri.
Canadian High Commission *38 Grosvenor Street, W1K 4AA (7258 6600, www.canada.org.uk). Bond Street or Oxford Circus tube.* **Open** 8am-4pm Mon-Fri.
Embassy of Ireland *17 Grosvenor Place, SW1X 7HR (7235 2171, passports & visas, 7225 7700, www.embassyof ireland.co.uk). Hyde Park Corner tube.* **Open** 9.30am-5.30pm Mon-Fri.

New Zealand High Commission
*New Zealand House, 80 Haymarket,
SW1Y 4TQ (7930 8422, www.
nzembassy.com). Piccadilly Circus tube.*
Open 9am-5pm Mon-Fri.

Internet

Brighton is a 4G city, and public
internet access is abundant. Most
cafés, pubs and hotels offer free
wireless access, as do Churchill
Square Shopping Centre and the
Jubilee Library. Since April 2015, the
council has provided free public Wi-Fi
hotspots that can be accessed in town
halls, museums, leisure centres and
other buildings across the city.

If you're not toting a laptop or
smartphone, a handful of internet
cafés and shops have computers
available to rent, plus printing
and photocopying facilities. The
following are closest to the station
and city centre:

Bystander Café *1 Terminus Road, BN1
3PD (01273 823322).* **Open** 7am-10pm
Mon-Fri; 8am-10pm Sun.

Café Electronica *15 Trafalgar Street,
BN1 4EQ (01273 696695).* **Open**
10am-9pm Mon-Fri; 10am-6pm Sat.

Call Centre *7 Cranbourne Street, BN1
2RD (01273 771703).* **Open** 9am-7pm
Mon-Sat; 10am-6pm Sun.

Global Links *154 Western Road, BN1
2DA (01273 357687).* **Open** 10am-7pm
Mon-Wed, Fri, Sat; 10am-8pm Thur;
11am-6pm Sun.

Opening hours

High-street shops follow usual UK
opening hours of 9am to 5.30pm from
Monday to Saturday; the larger ones
also open on Sunday until 4pm. The
independent shops in Kemp Town,
North Laine and the Lanes may open
at 10am or as late as 11am, closing at
5.30 or 6pm. Nearly all open between
11am and 4pm on Sunday. Many cafés,
restaurants and shops along the
seafront adjust their hours seasonally,

and according to the weather – where
this is the case we have tried to list the
minimum opening hours. Don't be
surprised to find late openings in high
summer, and the run up to Christmas.
Officially, closing time for pubs is
11pm, but most have licences to sell
alcohol until 1am. Many owners will
stay open at their discretion. Several
establishments now operate 24 hour
licenses, the Bulldog bar (p125) and
Buddies (50 King's Rd, 01273 220313,
www.buddies24hour.net) being the
best known.

Pharmacies

There are pharmacies on most high
streets; the branch of Boots at 129
North Street (01273 207461, www.
boots.com, 8am-7pm Mon-Sat,
11am-5pm Sun) has an after-hours
pharmacy open until midnight
(Mon-Sat).

Police

If you've been the victim of a crime,
call 101, or 999 for an emergency.

Brighton Central Police Station *John
Street, BN2 0LA (0845 607 0999, www.
sussex.police.uk).* **Open** 24 hours daily.

Hove Police Station *Norton Road, BN3
4HA (0845 60 70 999,
www.sussex.police.uk).* **Open** 8.45am-
5pm Mon-Fri. Closed bank holidays.

Post

Post offices are usually open
9am-5.30pm during the week and
9am-noon on Saturdays. For the
nearest branch, call the Royal Mail
on 08457 223344 or check www.royal
mail.com. The main post office is
located in WHSmith in the Churchill
Square Shopping Centre (p54).

Smoking

Smoking has been banned in enclosed
public spaces across England, including

all pubs and restaurants, since 2007. Until government regulation of e-cigarettes is in place, most cafés and bars continue to allow them.

Telephones

The area code for Brighton is 01273 and must now be included on all calls, even local ones. International codes are as follows: Australia 61; Canada 1; France 33; Germany 49; Ireland 353; Italy 39; Japan 81; Netherlands 31; New Zealand 64; Spain 34; USA 1.

Tickets

Most venues sell tickets through their own website or **Ticketmaster** (www.ticketmaster.co.uk, 0870 5344 4444). The **Brighton Dome** (p86) sells tickets for its own and other venues at www.brightonticketshop.com. For gig tickets, try record shop **Resident** (28 Kensington Gardens, 01273 606312, www.resident-music.com).

Time

Brighton operates on Greenwich Mean Time (GMT). Clocks go forward to run on British Summer Time (BST) on the last Saturday in March, and return to GMT on the last Saturday in October.

Tipping

Tipping 10-15 per cent in taxis, restaurants, hairdressers and some bars (but not pubs) is normal. Some restaurants and bars add service automatically to all bills; always check to avoid paying twice.

Tourist information

There are 14 Visitor Information Points across the city, including the following:
Brighton Centre Box Office *King's Road, BN1 2GR.*

Brighton Pier *Madeira Drive, BN2 1TW.*
Brighton Station Travel Centre *Queens Road, BN1 3XP.*
Brighton Toy & Model Museum *Trafalgar Street, BN1 4EB.*
Churchill Square *Western Road, BN1 2RG.*
Jubilee Library *Jubilee Street, BN1 1GE.*
The Old Market *Upper Market Street, Hove, BN3 1AS.*
St Paul's Church *West Street, BN1 2RE.*

The Brighton Centre Box Office (open 10am-4pm Mon-Sat), offers the widest range of services including accommodation, train and coach ticket bookings.

Visas

EU citizens do not require a visa to visit the UK; citizens of the USA, Canada, Australia, South Africa and New Zealand can also enter with only a passport for tourist visits of up to six months, as long as they can show they can support themselves during their visit and plan to return home. Use www.ukvisas.gov.uk to check your visa status well before you travel, or contact the British embassy, consulate or high commission in your own country. You can arrange visas online at www.fco.gov.uk.

What's on

Brighton & Hove has a number of free monthly listings and what's on publications including *BN1 Magazine* (www.bn1magazine.co.uk), the more music-oriented *XYZ* (www.xyz magazine.co.uk), and the excellent *Viva Brighton* (www.vivabrighton. com). For gay listings, look out for the free magazine *Gscene* (www.gscene.com). They're all widely available from pubs, cafes and shops around the city.

ESSENTIALS

Index

Sights & Areas

Eating & drinking

ESSENTIALS

Go Beyond The Usual.

TUACA
LIQUORE ORIGINALE

PREMIUM VANILLA LIQUEUR
WITH CITRUS ESSENCES

TUACA
LIQUORE ORIGINALE

 Find Tuaca at
facebook.com/tuacaliqueur

START CHILLED.
FINISH RESPONSIBLY.

for the facts **drinkaware.co.uk**